YES YES Y'ALL

BOOK 2

A Novel by

Latif Mercado

YES YES Y'ALL Book 2

Printed in the United States of America

First Printing, 2020

ISBN 978-0-9993189-4-2

Cover illustration by June ArcaMay

La' Entertainment

Monroe, NC 28110

www.LatifMercado.com

Dedication

Book Two of Yes Yes Y'all is dedicated to my daughter, Erica Skye Mercado. My second born, my only girl, I wrote this book when Erica was in her teens. She is currently in the United States Army, stationed in Germany.

Erica is the kid that I wish I could've been at that age. Clear mind, precise focus, though with the ability to change if that's where her heart takes her.

Erica, I dedicate this book to you. I love you, and God bless you.

Dad

Table of Contents

CHAPTER 1

First Date

I swore I was going to pass out, and fuckin' Jacq wasn't even trying to help.

"Push you sorry fuck!" He yelled directly into my ear, as I tried desperately to bench press the measly 90 pound barbell.

He then yanked the weights from my hands and placed them on the rack as if it were made from paper.

"Sit up!" He commanded.

I sat up and watched Jacq pace back and forth in front of me. With one hand on his hip, and the other on his chin, he stopped and turned to me, his chin finger about to point to me, but doesn't. He paced some more as I watched, just sitting there like a weakling, until he stopped again, and turned to me.

"You have absolutely no muscles!" He said, as if he couldn't believe it himself.

"Well, I have muscles. They're just not that strong."

"No, bullshit!" Jacq yelled at the top of his little lungs.

"You do not possess even an ounce of muscle anywhere in your body!" I wasn't about to argue with this man, because he would win. The fact that his English was bad, it was hard for me to decipher whether he meant what he was saying, or that he didn't know how to explain himself properly. For instance, he just said I don't have an ounce of muscle in my body, and it didn't sound like sarcasm, it sounded like he really believed that I have absolutely no muscles in my body.

Jacq picked up his clipboard and began reading it out loud.

"Poosh ups… Zedo! Seet ups… Zedo! Pooll ups… Forget that sheet! Curls twenty-five pound each hand… Zedo! Bench Press…Forget that sheet too!

Annoyed as hell, Jacq flung the clipboard across the room, and then stormed out.

I sat there, waiting for him to return, but he never did. I went out into the hall, but he was nowhere in sight. *Did this mother fucker actually quit?*

"Hey!" Said Roller Girl as she rolled out as usual from nowhere, scaring the shit out of me. "I'm sorry!" She said with a giggle.

"Have you seen Jacq?" I asked. "No. What happened?'

"I don't know, I was in there pumping iron, and he just got up and left. That guy's a serious weirdo.

"You want me to go look for him?' She asked.

"Nah, but give me a second." I told her and then went back into the gym and grabbed my things. I invited her to have a little breakfast with me over at Craft Services before my actual day got crazy.

The Cafeteria was the only room where you truly get to realize just how many people work at the Funky Junky. Everyone turned to us as we entered. Most nodded, others just smiled. It was hard to tell if they were like that with everyone, or just me.

The room was huge, with round tables that sat six, scattered about. Against the wall was a long clothed table with an incredible spread. You name it, they had it. Hot or cold didn't matter. Lunch and dinners were also laid out at the appropriate times. Mr. D did whatever it took to keep people in the office for as long as he could.

There was even a room for power naps, available to anyone who felt they needed one. A small carpeted room, with dimmed lights and soft music, enclosed an incredibly comfortable looking lounge chair that sat in the middle of the room suggesting that although naps were available, they were intended for just one person at a time.

A staff of four ran all three meals. A small kitchen sat inside another room, with two cooks. The other two staff members cleaned up, and set tables. The food here was great of course, that's the only way Mr. D would have it.

I grabbed some pancakes, home fries a couple of strips of bacon, and a container of orange juice. Roller Girl poured herself a cup of coffee and grabbed a Danish. We found the only unoccupied table in the center of the room and sat there.

"That's all you're gonna have?"

"Hey, I'm a white girl with a fat ass. Trust me, this is all I need!" Roller Girl replied. We both laughed, and though I found nothing wrong with her fat ass, I decided to keep *that* to myself!"

"So, how do you like it here?" She asked. I looked at her and then stared into the air to find the right words.

"It's like walking on a treadmill."

Roller Girl looked at me with a tilted head.

"Seems like I keep walking but never really getting anywhere."

"I wouldn't doubt it." She replied. "If that was just a characteristic of a successful person, which is probably why success, is only for certain people."

"Certain people?"

"Yeah, like people who would actually walk that treadmill until they finally got somewhere."

"But it's a treadmill. You don't actually get anywhere."

"But successful people don't think like that. They stay on it, until it either gets them to where they want to go, or something else presents itself."

"Like what?" I asked.

"Like they die!"

I stared at Roller Girl for a long moment, and though I wasn't quite sure about her analogy, I was in fact fascinated by her unexpected wisdom, or maybe I was just turned on?

"Yes, I'm a natural blonde!" She said out of nowhere, and we both started laughing.

"So, currently, this has been my life." I said, gesturing out to my surroundings, "but what about you? What's your story?"

Roller Girl took a bite of her Danish and a sip of her coffee. She stared at me for a long moment. Buying time while she decides whether or not I was worthy of her story. I didn't say anything, just looked at her, assuming that there was a lot more to her than what she had us all believing.

"It's sort of a long story."

"Well we can break it up into a series of dates, starting with this one."

"I didn't realize this was a date." She said with a smile.

"That's because it's going so smooth."

Roller Girl laughed half-heartedly because it seemed to me like whatever she was contemplating on telling me, she had never told another. I remained quiet, giving her my undivided attention. She stared into my eyes one last time while she took a deep breath, and just as she was about to begin, Mr. D walked into the room. Everyone turned toward the door, including Roller Girl. The entire vibe was broken, but it was probably for the better. It seemed like whatever she had to tell me was some serious shit, and I don't think that was the place for it.

"King!" Mr. D called out from the door. I looked his way and he waved me over, but before I excused myself I asked her,

"can we do this again?" She smiled and nodded. I got up, dumped my tray and headed out.

CHAPTER 2

The Card

"So Jacq came to me saying that you have no muscles?" Mr. D asked, as we walked up Stairs.

"I told you that I wasn't really an athletic guy."

"Yeah, not being athletic is one thing, but Jacq said you can't even do pushups!" "Well, I've never done them before."

"You never did pushups?"

"Never!" I replied, shaking my head.

"What about in school?"

"My Grandmother would just write me a note, telling them I had asthma."

"You have asthma?" Mr. D asked, stopping mid step.

"Nah. She just told them that."

Mr. D looked relieved, and continued walking.

"And they just took her word for it?"

"Sure. I mean, what parent would lie about something like that?" Mr. D didn't comment.

"You gotta understand. My Grandmother always felt sorry for me. She felt I was dealt a bad hand, so whatever she had to do to make my life a little happier, she did."

Mr. D, seemed to have understood. We quieted down as a couple of his employees passed us in the hall.

"Good morning Mr. D, King!" We both said good morning and continued.

"Well, look, I need your help, King."

"Sure. What's up?"

"I need you to somehow convince Jacq that you really *do* have muscles."

"I do. They're just not developed."

"Yeah, I'm not going there with him again. That's your job." We got to his office and stopped just outside the door. "Please King I don't want to lose him."

"Okay, don't worry I'll take care of it." Mr. D smiled and patted me on the back. "Oh, and that wasn't the reason why I interrupted your breakfast." He continued.

Then reached into his back pocket and pulled out an envelope and handed it to me. "What's this?" I asked,

"It's for you."

I opened the envelope and pulled out a credit card with my name, and the Funky Junky logo on it.

"There's a thousand dollars on it right now, and a thousand will be added by the first of each month."

"Are you serious? I mean, this really isn't necessary, Mr. D!"

"King, Listen to me, and let's be clear about it. Unless you're a non-profit organization that's geared to helping children, I don't give charity. This is for you. For all the hard work you've been putting in."

I looked down at the card in disbelief. I've never even seen one of these up close, let alone one with my name on it.

"Our next step is going to be the video."

"Yeah, I know."

"You think you're ready?"

"I think so! But of course, Princess will have the final say.

"Well, if you feel like you're ready, that's enough for me to assume that, so will Princess."

Had Mr. D asked me that before giving me this card, I might've spoke different, because in all honesty, my confidence was in the trash!

I didn't think I was ready. In fact, I didn't think I'd ever be ready, but shit if I said that now Mr. D might just take back his card.

CHAPTER 3

The Most Beautiful Woman In The World

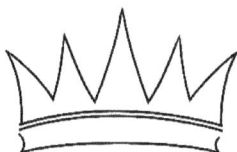

Of course Grams couldn't believe that Mr. D just gave me a credit card with a thousand dollars on it, with the promise of adding more every month.

No matter what I said, she questioned it, and thought the absolute worst, until I took her by the shoulders and looked her straight in the eyes, and said.

"Who raised me?" Grams didn't reply, she just looked at me.

"You always said, you didn't raise a dummy."

"But…" She tried to speak. I didn't let her.

"I need you to believe me, and trust me."

"I trust you Mijo. I just don't trust anyone else."

"I understand that. But in this case, I don't need you to trust anyone *but* me."

Grams looked to the floor and thought hard, before looking back up at me. She smiled, and gave me a big hug. I could feel her teary eyes on my neck, and I heard a sniffle, so I didn't rush it, I just held her.

"So I'm taking you out tonight." I whispered in her ear. "We're going on a date, me and you, like *you* use to take me when I was little." She laughed into my neck.

"A movie and Pizza, that was all I could afford."

"But they were the best movies and pizzas I ever had."

She looked at me, this time her eyes were soft and glossy.

"Not tonight, Mijo, I have all my nice clothes packed away. I don't even know what fits me anymore.

"Hold that note!" I told her and then dashed into my room, returning with two Macy's shopping bags. Upon seeing this, Grams immediately broke down again. Macy's was always her favorite department store.

"I picked you up a few things." I said placing them all on the sofa.

She looked at me and then stepped toward the bags. She put her hands behind her back and leaned forward to peek in.

"Come on, open them!" I told her. She looked at me, and with tears continuing down her face, she gently opened the first bag, and pulled out a beautiful dress that I had picked out especially for her. It was Kelly Green, her favorite color, and came just past her knee, thank God for the saleswoman who helped me out.

"This is so beautiful." She said, in her crying voice. I smiled as I watched her place it against her body.

"You're not done yet." I said gesturing back to the bags. Grams acted as if I did this wonderful thing for her, but no matter what, I'll live a thousand lives before I'll ever come close to repaying her for what she's given me, and that doesn't even include the material things.

We had so little when I was growing up. But I would only realize this once I was grown. 'Cause as a kid, I seriously thought we were rich!

She continued removing her gifts from the bags, which included of course a huge bottle of Chanel No. 5, her favorite! Lately, the closest she's been able to get to one, was the ninety-nine cent knock off, *Shanel # 9.*

Every item she pulled out made her cry. I knew my Grandmother very well, I remember how she used to dress and even more so… How she smelled.

I even remember the makeup she wore, not much. Just a little lipstick, as her beautiful dark complexion never needed much help, and amazingly… still doesn't!

Shoes, a sweater, costume Jewelry, perfume. I even bought her some new…

"Underwear?" She said holding them up, her tears now turning to laughter.

"You always bought me mine!"

"I still do!" She replied, and wasn't lying.

"Sal's picking us up at 5:00 p.m. We have an hour, so go get ready."

"But wait, where are we going?"

"It's a surprise!"

I let Grams take her bath first, and then took mine while she got dressed and did her make up. I knew I didn't have to worry about her hair and nails, because no matter what,

Grams always made sure, those were on point by doing them herself.

I wasn't much of a suit guy, but for this occasion, I felt at least a tie was appropriate. Too bad I had to buy one of those clip-ons, because I never learned how to tie a real one, and I wasn't sure if Grams did.

My outfit was black slacks, shoes, a white shirt, and my Burgundy tie. I always wanted a Members Only jacket, so I treated myself to a black one. I looked pretty sharp, even though I wasn't used to dressing this way. Even my hair style was growing on me.

I loved Princesses' Polaroid camera, and so I decided to invest in one. I waited for Grams in the living room, and just as she entered, I snapped a picture.

I looked at her, and now it was *my* eyes that were beginning to water. This was the grandmother I remember growing up. The strong one, the confident one, the one who tackled everything thrown at her, and still came out victorious!

There she was. It was like she was gone all these years and now she was back. I watched as she danced and hummed to some old song that I couldn't make out. She grabbed me and made me dance with her. We laughed because I had no idea what the hell I was doing.

"You look beautiful." I told her, and could tell she felt beautiful too.

"And look at you, my handsome boy! Correction... My handsome man!"

"Ready to go?" Grams nodded a tight smile, trying

desperately not to cry. I held open the door, and watched as the most beautiful woman in the world stepped out.

CHAPTER 4

Cheers

The host sat us at a table next to a window with the most incredible view of New York City.

"Your waiter will be with you in just a moment." He said as he handed us our menus,

"Thank you." I replied, as Grams smiled and nodded.

After glancing at the menu, Grams leaned toward me and whispered.

"There's no prices!"

"Don't worry about that, anything you want, you order."

"Mijo, I would've been okay with some White Castles."

"Will you stop it!" I said in a loud whisper, unable to stop laughing.

"Hello, my name is Sergio, I will be your server this evening." The waiter said as he stood beside our table, his hands clasped in front of him. "May I start you off with a bottle of wine?" Grams had already begun shaking her head.

"Yes please, what do you recommend?"

The waiter proceeded to recommend two bottles, one red, one white. Grams chose the red.

I was hoping that the wine would hurry up and come because Grams needed to relax.

She was so worried about something going wrong, though she had no reason to be, and I hated that she felt so out of place, as if she didn't deserve to be here.

Sergio returned with our bottle of wine, and poured our glasses. I took mine, and stood up. Grams looked up at me with a smile I hadn't seen in years.

"To the most beautiful and amazing woman on the face of the earth!" and at that very moment, every glass in the house was raised.

"To you, Grams," I said as everyone followed with *Cheers!*

"Oh my God, I'm going to look like a raccoon by the time this night is over," she said, patting her eyes dry with her napkin.

We were having such a wonderful time, laughing and joking. She was telling me all these stories. Many I heard before, a few I didn't. Stories about me, about her, our family, and in particular…my parents!

She said she never knew who my father was because my mother's personal life was kept a secret.

"Mijo, whoever your father was, he must've been a good man, because look how you turned out."

"I didn't turn out like this because of my father. I turned out like this because of you!"

"I just wanted you to be happy, to have a good life."

"And you did that."

"But I couldn't give you your parents."

"If I had to do this all over again, I wouldn't change a thing. I can't even imagine my life without you. You are the most important person in my universe." Grams began to sob. I reached over and took both her hands.

"You ready for your next surprise?" I said with a burst, hoping to lighten the subject.

"There's more!"

Grams carefully wiped her eyes with a tissue as she nodded. I raised my hand, gesturing for the waiter to bring the check. When he did, I took a quick glance at it. Grams must've noticed my eyebrows arch, because she quickly said to me.

"I have fifty dollars on me." She whispered, little did she know that would barely cover the tip.

I pulled out my Funky Junky credit card and placed it into the little leather bill folder left on our table. I became quiet as I began to do the math in my head, adding up everything I bought today, a bit nervous myself whether or not the card would cover it. Grams was staring at me, as if she could read my mind. She didn't say anything, but I could tell, she was praying. The waiter came by and grabbed the card.

"I'll be right back," he said, as Grams and I watched him disappear through the double swinging doors in the back.

We tried to engage in small talk, but it was obvious, we were both a bit nervous. Her lips moved uncontrollably as she prayed under her breath. I caught myself doing the same.

I glanced back toward the doors where the waiter had gone, and noticed that he and another gentleman were peeking out at us. A moment later, the gentleman came out from the back and headed our way holding in his hand my credit card.

"Mr. Rosario?" the man said as he approached our table.

"Yes?"

"Good evening, sir, my name is Olivio, I am the manager."

"Oh no," Grams interrupted, a little louder than she probably should've.

"Is something wrong?" I asked.

"Well, actually there is," he said. I could feel the entire restaurant staring in our direction.

"It's your card sir," he began, handing it back to me. Grams was already in her pocketbook, pulling from it whatever money she could find on top of the fifty she had already placed on the table.

"Wow, I just got this card, but I'm sure whatever it is, will be taken care of," Grams had practically emptied out her entire purse by now, topping off the bills with a mixture of pennies and butterscotch candies.

"No, please sir, ma'am my apologies. Your card is fine! It just all associates of The Funky Junky, are welcomed to dine with us at absolutely no charge."

"No charge?"

"No sir, and we really hope that you and your mother enjoyed your dinner, and hope that you will come back to see us again soon!"

Grams looked around and smiled at the surrounding tables, placing everything back into her pocketbook.

"Oh wow, well, um thank you, can I at least like leave a tip? Sergio did a wonderful job."

"Gratuity as well has been taken care of sir," the manager said with a smile and a slight bow. "Enjoy the rest of your evening," he said smiling as he walked off.

"I think we should hurry out of here, before they realize they made a mistake." Grams said, and I agreed.

The two of us laughed hysterically as we hurried down the street. Once we were far enough from the restaurant, we slowed down, still laughing like a couple of school kids up to no good.

The lights on Broadway were magical, and I could tell Grams was really enjoying herself. Sal wanted to drive us around the city, but it was such a perfect night that we wanted to walk, and so we set up a time and place to meet up with him at the end of the night.

"When was the last time you been out here?" I asked, as she grabbed on to my arm. Grams just smiled and shook her head.

"That long, huh?" I asked.

"It was before you were born," she said. "I got a call from a friend of mine one evening, telling me that she saw your mommy hanging out in the park with some other kids, so I went looking for her."

"Central Park at night? You weren't scared?"

"Not if it's your child, I would've gone into a lion's cage if that's where I knew she was."

"Did you find her?"

"I walked for hours, covered the entire park, and just when I was about to go back home, I saw a bunch of kids hanging out by the rocks. It was starting to get light out, and everyone was kind of shadowy, but I knew my daughter anywhere. When I got closer, I called her name. Everyone turned and looked at me. I heard one girl ask her, who is that, and at that very moment they all took off running."

"I'm sorry, Grams. I didn't mean to…"

"No. No, it was actually a good thing, you see I hadn't heard from her in a couple of months. The police said they were looking, but they weren't. I thought the worst, picturing her lying dead in the gutter somewhere, it was horrible, so seeing her, and seeing her happy, even though she was probably up to no good, gave me some piece of mind, not to mention… Hope!"

Grams smiled up at me, and squeezed my arm, placing her head up against it as we continued walking.

"But now I'm here with you, and from here on, the city will once again be my happy place. Thank you, Mijo.

"I do have a question for you though?" Grams asked.

"Sure, what is it?"

"At the restaurant, I mean, how did you know about any of that?"

"What do you mean?"

"I mean, you knew what restaurant to pick, how to order, the whole the wine thing, like… how?"

"Okay, okay, I confess… It was Sal!"

"Sal?"

"Yeah, he set up everything for me. The reservation, told me what to order, how to pick the wine. You caught me, Grams… I'm a phony!"

She looked at me with a smile that said I was the cutest thing ever just as we came upon a huge crowd of people.

"Oh my God, look Rey, this is where they're playing CATS!" The hit Broadway Musical, had people blocking the entire sidewalk.

"I heard it's sold out for the next two years." Grams said, looking at all the lucky people.

"That's why I made sure to grab the last two tickets!" I said holding them up. Grams let out a scream I had never before heard. Everyone turned and looked at us, and once they figured out what was happening, they all started laughing along. I got a little scared for a minute there, as she seemed to be hyperventilating.

"Grams, you okay?" I asked placing my arm around her. Come to find out, she was just trying to not cry around all these people. You see, I knew how badly Grams wanted to see this play, but she wrote it off as something that would just never happen. It was the only commercial that she would actually sit through when watching TV.

There weren't too many seats better than the fifth row

center that we were able to get, giving Grams an absolute perfect view. As she sat there, completely memorized by their spectacular performance, I sat there completely mesmerized by her, and so grateful that I was able to do this. On our way out, this older woman walked up to us and cupped my hand with the two of hers.

"Pardon my intrusion," said the woman in a soft and gentle tone, but what a wonderful thing for your mother," turning to Grams, she continued, "you are so very blessed."

"Yes I am, thank you."

The woman smiled then turned and walked away. We remained quiet as we walked up the block, letting the night's experience marinate, not to mention, what the old woman had told us. I know grams wondered why I didn't correct her when she called her my mother, but it's because she wasn't wrong. You see, a mother sits closest to God, and that seat definitely belongs to my grandmother.

CHAPTER 5

Crackheads and Hoes

"She seemed to have really enjoyed herself last night." Sal said as we pulled out from in front of my building

"Yeah, she really did, thanks again, man."

"I'm glad I was able to help, but it was all you, King."

Sal and I continued with small talk when suddenly he yelled "Sonofabitch!"

I looked out the window and noticed that the road we normally took was detoured.

He pounded the wheel before making a screeching U-Turn.

"I hate going this way," he growled. "Nothing but fucking crackheads and hoes!" and he was right, because no sooner than he said that, they were everywhere, and it was still early in the morning.

"I've never been through here, before" I said as I looked through my window. Johns were already rolling up, and parked cars already bouncing.

"Must be last night's leftovers," I said.

"No such thing," Sal clarified. "These people go twenty-four seven.

Suddenly, like out of nowhere, some bum-ass dude jumped in front of the car with a squeegee.

"No no, buddy, that's okay, we're good!" Sal pleaded, but it was too late! He placed his dirty squeegee onto Sal's spotless windshield and gave it a wipe that left a thick greasy streak.

"Mother fucker!" Sal yelled, as he jumped out the car and pushed Squeegee Man off his windshield. While standing there scolding him, out from behind an abandoned car, came another guy who grabbed Sal from around the neck. I heard a sound beside me and noticed it was Squeegee Man trying to open my door, but it was locked, in fact, they were all locked.

I quickly climbed over the front seat to figure out how to open the doors. I wanted to get out before he got in, but I couldn't. I looked back over at Sal just as he Judo flipped the guy over his shoulder, sending him face first onto the glass shattered street.

Squeegee Man appeared in front of the car, a brick held high in his hand as he was about to toss it through the windshield. I dropped to the floor and awaited the crash, but it never came. Instead, the driver's side door opened.

"Oh shit!" I yelled, when I realized, it was Sal!

I sat up on my seat and looked out the window when I spotted Squeegee Man on the ground, his squeegee sticking out the side of his neck.

"Oh God!" I gasped. "What we gonna do?" I asked, but Sal paid me no mind as he made a wide U Turn, which is when I noticed the second guy, just lying there.

"Oh damn!" I turned to Sal. "We gotta get them some help."

"Sit back and don't say shit."

As we drove for a couple of blocks, Sal pulled up alongside a police car parked at the corner. He slid down his window and said,

"Morning, Officers!" His tone, cool and calm, as if nothing had ever happened.

"You mind telling me how do I get back on the main road?" he asked.

"You're going the right way, one of them finally said. "Just keep going straight."

Sal thanked them, as one nodded, and the other raised his cup of coffee!

"Was that a good idea?" I asked Sal as we headed in the direction they told us.

"How else would we get the fuck out of here?"

"So, you think they'll be okay?"

"Who?" he asked.

"Those two guys?"

He never answered me.

Sal seemed to not wanna talk, so I just sat back and stared out the window, thinking about what I just saw, and wondering, was this also a dream?

We pulled up in front of the Funky Junky. I got out and waited for Sal. The passenger window went down and he leaned over.

"You go on up, I have to take care of something."

This wasn't at all typical. Sal always brought me up. I just hoped that he was okay.

"You know I tried to get out the car." I said.

"Well, next time don't try. Just stay put till I get back."

The window slid up, and off he went.

CHAPTER 6

Sheltered

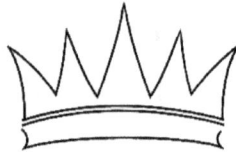

"Poosh! Phoosh!" Yelled Jacq, standing over me guiding the barbell to and from my chest. I thought he was bit too close though, as his balls were practically on my forehead. I pushed so hard that my eyes felt as if the blood vessels were about to burst. He had lowered the weight from the original one hundred pounds that he thought I should've started with, down to just eighty. I really wanted to start with forty, but he didn't go for it.

The Barbell hovered just inches from my throat and I couldn't help but think about the severe damage it would do, had it dropped. My arms shook, and my knuckles were whitened by the tight grasp in which most of my energy had gone.

"Keep your feet down!" Jacq yelled again, as my legs seemed to be climbing some invisible wall as I struggled with that final press. Jacq grabbed the barbell from my hands, and slammed it back on the rack, really annoyed.

I sat up stared at the sorry-ass reflection that stared back at me through the mirror.

I could see Jacq pacing back and forth behind me. Either this guy had zero patience to train anyone, or I was just that bad. I could've blamed it on the really fucked up morning I had, but I was like this yesterday as well.

I watched as Jacq grabbed a chair and carried it over to where I was sitting. At first I honestly thought he was going to throw it at me, because I've seen him throw these shits around before, but instead he placed it in front of me and sat.

"Why you don't like me?" Jacq asked as he crossed his legs and wrapped his hands over his knee.

"What do you mean?" I asked, no idea what he was talking about.

"Nothing I ask for you to do, you do, how come?"

I looked at Jacq, allowing what he just told me to sink in.

"Has nothing to do with you, Jacq, just that weights were never my thing."

"You help your mama with the grocery bags, no?"

"Well, yeah, my Grandmother."

"Do you have trouble carrying them?"

"It's only the two of us, so there's never really a lot of bags." Jacq gave me a look, like he wanted to punch me in my fucking face.

"In your whole life, King, have you ever lifted anything heavy?" Normally I would think he was being sarcastic, but in my case, it seemed to be a legitimate question.

"Well, no... not really, not that I could remember."

Jacq quickly stood up and knocked the chair over. He began pacing again, this time in front of me.

"Can I make a suggestion?" I asked. Jacq stopped in his tracks and looked at me.

"A suggestion?"

"Yeah, on how we could maybe pull through this?"

"There is no we. I can lift everything in this room!" Jacq yelled out as he rushed toward me. I got up from the bench and stepped to the side as he laid down and grabbed the barbell that I had been struggling with, and pressed it as if it was made of nothing but feathers.

"Look at me!" He yelled as he pumped away. "You are much bigger than I am, much taller, why can I do this and you cannot?"

I didn't have an answer, and watched as Jacq was now showing off by tossing each press into the air and then catching it.

"Look at this, no struggle, eighty pounds, easy for me!" He explained as he did about twenty reps and then tossed them back on the rack before heading over to the leg press. "Looky here, over five hundred pounds, like nothing!" Another fifteen reps, Jacq finished and then stood in front of me. "This is to prove to you that I am not asking you to do something that not even I can do. This is all possible, and easy. I feel that you are convinced in your head that you cannot lift anything and therefore you do not.

The first muscle you must condition is this one!" he said, tapping his rock hard finger on my forehead, which I was sure left a mark.

"And the second muscle is what?" He asked. I looked at him, and instead of letting him tell me, my dumb ass tried to guess.

"Um, arms?" I asked.

"No! you stoopid! "Yo heart!" He said as he tapped now on my chest, leaving I'm sure another mark from his little stone-like fingers.

I was going to suggest to Jacq that I start with lighter weights, but now I'm thinking, maybe he's right. Maybe it isn't my muscles, but rather my mind, and my heart. Grams had me pretty sheltered. The only time I even got into fights were in school, other than that I was home, inside my house. The few friends I had on the block were the few that I walked to school with, and way up until High School, Grams walked me herself. I never even realized how stupid I looked until someone actually told me.

Yes, I was a sheltered child, made afraid to even go outside because she always told me that there were people out there that stole little kids, and now, I'm a grown man, having never gone through my own rites of passage.

I don't blame Grams at all, her intentions were understandable. I was all she had in this world, and she was going to protect me any way she could. I looked at Jacq who stood there waiting on my suggestion, but it had vanished.

"I want to try this again," I told him as I laid back down on the bench. Jacq looked at me, hesitant to even go along with it, but he did. He positioned himself over me once again, his balls mere inches from my forehead. I looked up at him, he down at me. I took a deep breath, and at Jacq's count of three I lifted the barbell straight over my chest.

"Don't fucking look at me, he yelled. "Look at the bar!" and so I did.

"Ready… down!" He ordered. I brought the barbell to my chest. "Now, blow out and poosh!" I did exactly as he said, and watched as the barbell rose back to its starting position.

CHAPTER 7

Second Place Trophies

"Come on Sunshine, keep up!" Princess yelled out as we went through the rehearsal for the umpteenth time. "Stop!" he ordered as he waved the music off and shook his head. He walked up to me, and in a calm tone asked.

"What's going on?"

"Just getting tired," I replied.

Princess looked around and asked if anyone else was tired, everyone shook their head.

"Nobody else is tired," he said.

"I'm not just doing the routine, I'm also rapping."

"But that's what you are, aren't you, a Rapper?"

"Well, yeah, but Rappers don't usually do all this extra stuff."

"Extra stuff?"

"Yeah, you know, like dance."

"So what do Rappers usually do?"

I could see everyone watching me through the mirror.

"They just sort of move around, and you know… Rap!"

"Really?"

I nodded.

"So, would you mind showing us?"

Why didn't I see that coming? I tried to apologize because I could see the rest of the group was getting a bit annoyed.

"No, please, I insist. You might have something good that I can incorporate into the routine. I want to keep it as real as possible."

It was hard to tell whether Princess was serious or just be sarcastic.

"Everyone, take a seat. He said, and then pressed play on the stereo. Immediately the music began. I started walking back and forth, adding a little bop to each of my steps. I faced forward, yet my eyes were sidelining my classmates, spread out on the floor.

I started rapping, unable to make eye contact with anyone, except Princess. I couldn't help but catch his, as it seemed to be burning a hole in the side of my head.

The question as to whether or not he was being sarcastic was now answered by the way he stood there staring at me.

I'll admit it. A few of the moves I got from Nemesis, watching him once on the Tonight Show. I thought they were pretty cool… I just made them cooler!

Like the one where he spun around and then pointed to a girl. I should've practiced though, because not only did I spin too many times, I accidentally pointed at Emerald, sending the entire room into an uproar.

"Okay, stop! That's it, no more!" Princes commanded after turning off the music. All was still and silent, as I stood there, font center. Suddenly, and totally unexpected, Vanessa stood up and began to applaud and cheer. I waited for the others to follow, but they never did, and even though Princess was giving her the look of death, she paid him no mind.

She knew what Princess was doing, and she didn't like it. I on the other hand had no idea and just went along with it. I honestly believed that there was a certain element that had to be incorporated into my show. That the representation of what rap stood for has to be correct, or else I would come across as a phony.

"Okay, Vanessa, you made your point. You can sit your ass down now." But she continued to ignore him, and just kept clapping, and yelling out words of encouragement.

"Vanessa, I said that's it!" He yelled out, and finally she stopped. The two looked at each other for a quick moment when all of a suddenly, she let him have it.

"I'm tired of you making fun of him, picking on him. Give him a chance, a word or two of encouragement. We do it, but that doesn't matter. He needs to hear it from you once in a while. We all do! You're nothing but a fucking bully!"

"What's the matter, you're getting jealous, 'cause nobody's paying attention to *you*?" "You're a real dick, Princess!" She yelled back and then headed to the locker room to gather her things.

"Oh, no no no… Hold up, please." I chased after Vanessa

and caught her shoving her things into her bag. "Don't do this Vee, please."

"He's a fucking miserable asshole, I'm tired of him!"

"But I can handle it, Vee."

"Look Rey, you have a future here, I don't. What I'm doing here I can pretty much do anywhere. I'm a background dancer, that's all."

Vanessa grabbed her bag and then gave me a kiss, before storming out of the dressing room across the huge studio. I stood just outside the dressing room and watched.

"There she goes another frustrated lesbian." Princess called out from the front of the room as she walked across the back. She just looked his way and gave him the finger, before exiting the studio.

The place was silent. So silent in fact, that I swore I heard a cricket.

"Okay ladies and gentlemen, I hope you enjoyed today's episode of One Life To Lick. Join us next week as Vanessa gets evicted from her apartment because her old fat ass will never find another job."

Princess gave his hands a double clap dismissing the class. The dressing room was pretty quiet as everyone changed. Vee, was well liked and helped out a lot of people, and everyone felt bad about not standing up for her, but I felt the worst.

I was the last one to change and when everyone was gone, I stepped into Princess' office. He was doing some paperwork, as I just stood there at his door waiting for his attention.

"She's the one that left." Princess said not once looking up from what he was doing.

"If I wasn't convinced that she was a stone cold lesbian, I'd swear y'all were fucking!"

"She needs to come back." I told him. Princess stopped writing and looked up at me.

"Vanessa has been doing this since she was a little girl. If anyone here knows what it takes to even get noticed, let alone be successful… it's her!

So when I have to cram fifteen years of work into two months, and make that shit look good, then there is no taking it easy, no being nice, and absolutely no time for screw ups or the fucking excuses that come with it!

This is not a fucking talent show we're working towards. There are no second place trophies or Plan B's, We have to win, there is no other choice, and it's my responsibility to make sure that's what we do.

But I can't do it the way you want me to do it, or the way Vanessa wants me to do it. I have to do it my way, because, that is the only way this shit will ever work!

CHAPTER 8

Chinese or Pizza

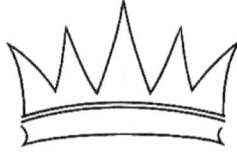

Vanessa opened the door and didn't look a bit surprised when she saw me standing there. She turned around and walked back into her apartment leaving the door open for me to enter. She sat in the corner of her couch, legs crossed, and picked up her sketch pad to continue with whatever it was she was doing before I got there.

"I've been calling you all day. Left you a bunch of messages" I said, standing in the middle of her studio apartment. Vee, didn't look up, just kept drawing.

"I've been here all day." She said shaking her head as if she had no idea I'd been calling, when suddenly the phone rang. Her pencil stopped moving but she maintained her position.

"*Vanessa, it's me, pick up. I just want to see what time I can stop by to pick up the rest of my things. Pick up, I know you're there.*" I watched as a teardrop fell onto her pad, as we both listened to a second girl in the background goofing around with Julie while she was on the phone.

"Stop!" Julie whispered, and then laughed and hung up.

"Oh God, I'm sorry." I told her. Vee, reached over and grabbed a tissue from the box on the end table and patted her eyes.

"I'm so ready to give boys another shot." She said, and though it came across like a joke, I sensed a hint of seriousness.

"They could be assholes too." I assured her. "And they ain't even pretty." A short burst of laughter shot out of Vanessa as she quickly grabbed a tissue and blew her nose, only to break down once again.

I did the only thing I could think of at the moment and slid over to her side and held her. I wasn't sure if I was breaking any lesbian rules, as I never really knew any. At least I didn't think I did. Vanessa welcomed my embrace and laid her head on my shoulder. A bit hesitant at first, I subtly rubbed her back and did my best to try and comfort her.

I liked Vanessa. She was genuine, down to earth, and very sweet. I was sort of glad she was a lesbian though, 'cause I could've seen myself falling for her, and I wouldn't want to mess up what we had.

"Did you eat?" I asked. She shook her head, "Chinese or Pizza?" She expressed not being hungry, but I talked her into it, and Chinese it was!

The food was delivered and we sat on the floor around the coffee table talking and eating. Sal had dropped me off and would be picking me up in about an hour.

"I like this place." Trying to change the conversation we

were having about relationships.

"It was my granny's. She bought it in the 50s, and kept it in the family. I only pay two hundred a month for maintenance and utilities."

"Wow, my Grandmother rents, has been in the same apartment since before I was born.

She pays about three. It's stabilized.

"I hear of so many people renting, and paying well over a thousand dollars a month for a bullshit studio. I'm blessed not to be in that position.

"You ever thought of selling, maybe buying a house somewhere?"

"Yeah, but not yet, maybe once I'm settled.

"Settled?"

"Yeah, I'd like to have a family someday."

"Kids?"

"Oh yeah, a bunch, I love kids." I watched as Vanessa gave space a quick stare, and then changed the subject

"Thank you Rey," she said as I took a bite into my Egg roll.

"For what?"

"For everything! for checking up on me, consoling me, hanging out with me, feeding me. I swear, you're like the perfect Gay boyfriend!"

"Do I take that as a compliment?"

"Absolutely!"

"Well, thank you… I guess!" We laughed some more and

then became quiet for moment.

"Tomorrow we start shooting." I told her.

"Yeah, I know."

"You want me to pick you up?"

"No, that's not a good idea, I caused a scene, and Princess can be a pretty stiff dick!"

"I'll handle the dick," I told her, then we realized that didn't come out right, and started laughing."

"You don't know him, Rey. Growing up, Princess was one of those kids who were bullied every day. It was so bad that he actually tried to kill himself!"

"Damn," was all I could say.

"Sometimes after living their whole life like that, they can't help but be assholes."

"So you're justifying his dickness?" Vanessa gave it some thought, and then nodded. "Look, I know for a fact that this is probably the last important job Princess will ever have. He's old, won't nobody ever hire him again, at least not for something like this."

I could tell Vanessa really cared for Princess. He's been good to her, she just didn't like how he was with me, but I could handle him.

"We're meeting in front of the Funky Junky at 6:00 am."

"Rey…!" She began to say, but I cut her off. You want me to pick you up?"

She looked at me and then smiled. "No, I'll be there."

"You promise?"

Vee nodded, and I smiled back, and then looked up at the clock.

"Sal should be down stairs any minute." I said, as I got up and gave myself a stretch. I was about to grab my plate and the empty containers when Vanessa gestured for me to leave it all there.

"I got that, don't worry."

"You sure?"

She nodded, and I grabbed my jacket. Vanessa opened the door to let me out and we both stood there, looking at each other. There was something so special about Vanessa, and I was so blessed to have met her.

Her eyes were soft and sincere, and for a moment I thought, why'd she have to be gay? Then suddenly, she moved in close and I couldn't believe what was about to go down, but thank God I didn't react, because all she did was give me a great big brotherly hug.

CHAPTER 9

Six on the Dot

It was six on the dot, when Sal pulled up to the Funky Junky. Three busses parked in front, engines running. I watched as the people loaded. Many I knew, others I had never seen before.

"What the hell's all this?" I asked Sal.

"Your video shoot!"

"Who are they?" I said, pointing to a huge group of people boarding.

"Those are Extras"

"Extra what?" I asked, before getting out of the car.

"Don't wander off, King, we're just waiting on Mr. D."

I walked to the first bus which I noticed had all of the dancers. I looked inside and greeted everyone."

"Anyone seen Vanessa?" Everyone shook their head

"I don't think she's coming, Sunshine!" Lily said. I looked at her, and disappointedly nodded. As I stepped off the bus, I noticed Princess and Antonio carrying a few boxes, most likely, costumes. I walked up beside Princess and asked.

"Have you seen Vanessa?"

"Last time I saw Vanessa she disrupted my class, insulted me, and then stormed off while giving me the finger." I stopped in my tracks and watched as he and Antonio tossed the boxes in the compartment beneath the bus.

"Okay, everyone, find a seat and settle down, we have a bit of a drive," yelled out the production assistant who I at first had no idea who he was. He looked at me.

"Come on, buddy, let's move it, which bus?" He asked. I wasn't sure until Mr. D. Walked up beside me and placed his arm around me.

"He's riding with me."

"Oh shit, I'm really sorry, Mr. King." The P.A. said after realizing who I was.

"Oh, don't worry about, it's cool," I said shaking his hand.

"Is there anything I can do for either of you?" He asked.

"No, we're good, thanks..." Said Mr. D, leaning forward and reading the P.A.'s name tag.

"Um... Chris!" He then gave Chris a quick smiled, and then turned and guided me to a stretched Limo.

"Wow! We're riding in this?

"Get used to it," he replied.

"Oh, Mr. D," I started to explain. "Before we go, I wanna let you know, that there was a slight problem yesterday with..."

"… With her?" He suddenly interrupted, pointing over to where Princess and Vanessa were hugging.

"What the hell happened?" I asked.

"Ah, those two are like husband and wife, except I can never tell who's who."

" I didn't know what to say, but what I did know was, it was a great way to start my day.

"You guy's ready?" Sal asked as he walked up and opened the car door.

CHAPTER 10

Domingo

"Whoa!" I said, startled when I noticed a man already sitting inside.

"King meet your Director, Domingo." Mr. D said as I entered the limo. Domingo made his way over to me and shook my hand.

"Nice to meet you," I told him. "Mr. D said some great things about you."

Domingo was a short pudgy man, who looked like he hadn't brushed his hair in years. He was mid- fifties, with this thick mustache trimmed just above the lip.

"Domingo's from Mexico." Mr. D continued, He did me a huge favor by agreeing to direct your first video."

"Thank you." I said.

"You're welcome." He replied, another one with a thick accent. "I love your song, it's going to be a big hit!"

I glanced over at Mr. D and he smiled.

"Sal got behind the wheel and just as he was pulling out, I

noticed Chris the P.A. standing on the sidewalk talking to a woman. He didn't look too happy, and when she yanked the name tag off his jacket, I knew why.

"Oh no!" I sighed, turning to Mr. D. When he realized what I was looking at, he shrugged his shoulders and said.

"We can't afford lose apples," and though at the moment I didn't quite understand what he meant, eventually, got it!

"King!" Mr. D said, snapping me out of my thoughts. I looked as if to say, what!"

"I asked you a question."

"I'm sorry Mr. D, I was just thinking about something.

"I was just wondering if you were excited?"

"Oh yeah, of course, this is all so just so amazing, thank you, But..." Mr. D looked at me, as did Domingo.

"But what?" he asked.

I just wish I had a little more information about the video."

"And which is why I asked Domingo to ride with us."

Domingo opened up his briefcase and handed both Mr. D and I a stack of sheets fastened along the edge with these brass rings. I looked at the cover and it read *I am King!*"

I flipped open to the first page and began reading to myself, the synopsis of what the video would be about.

It was to take place in the 1300's, the story was about a man who was fighting his way to be King. I flipped to the next page where the drawings began. It was professionally drawn and detailed. I looked at Mr. D and he smiled back at me.

"What do you think?" He asked.

"Looks cool, but what is this supposed to be?"

"It's called a Storyboard." Domingo explained. "Each of those little squares are called frames, each frame represents a scene. By following each of the frames, we know whether it takes place indoors or out. What character is being filmed, and from what angle, as well as a bunch of other information to help us make the best video possible.

"Did you read this?"

"Of course. Genius huh?"

"Overwhelming if anything, this is insane, how am I supposed to learn this in three hours?"

"The song and the choreography are the key ingredients and you know them both, no?" Domingo asked.

"Yeah," I replied.

"King, this entire production has been planned out, rehearsed, etc."

"But why wasn't I included?"

"Because we didn't need you for this, we needed you to do what you were doing. Princess is very familiar with this storyboard, and all choreography you've been learning was created to work with the video. You just do what is asked of you without question, and I promise you, you will be very happy with the finished product. Not to mention, Domingo here is the best in the world! He's going to pull from you shit you didn't even know you had. All you have to do, is let him direct."

"Okay," Domingo began. "let's start from page one."

Together we read the script, and discussed the vision. It was a good idea after all to have the three of us ride together, because we all had to be on the same page, at least somewhat, to get this done.

By the time we got to the location I understood the entire concept, and was clear of what I had to do. Mr. D did it again, because Domingo was in fact…extraordinary!

CHAPTER 11

Sharks and Whales

They acted as though it was just a coincidence, however, I found many symbolic, and hidden meanings. Apparently I was the White Knight, who had come to challenge the Black Knight who was also the king. Our microphones were like our swords and I was battling him, not just for his crown, but also for his village, and ultimately, his Queen.

This video shoot was nothing that I would have ever imagined. It was top notch, a huge cast and crew, armored suites, jeweled crowns, and these beautiful horses that I learned were called, destriers.

"Cut!" Domingo yelled out, "and print!" He added, and immediately the cast and crew began preparing for the next scene. Domingo walked up to me and placed his hand on my shoulder.

"King, you are doing a fantastic job."

"Thank you." I replied.

"You are a natural, you might want to reconsider your career."

"What, to acting?"

"You will maintain employment well into your twilight years."

"Nah, that's okay, I love music it's truly where my heart is."

At that moment Mr. D walked up on us and placed his hands on both of our shoulders.

"So what do you think?" He asked, Domingo.

"I was just telling him, he's a natural!"

Mr. D gave my shoulder a slight squeeze and smiled.

"Okay, King," Domingo continued, "so in this scene, you meet for the first time, the Court Jester."

"Court Jester?"

"Yes, you see in those days, the Court Jester was hired by the King for entertainment. This job was an important one, so important in fact, that if the Court Jester didn't do his job correctly, he was executed, usually at the guillotine."

"What exactly was his job?" I asked.

"To make the King laugh!" replied Domingo.

"That's it?"

"That's it? The king was the toughest audience. Anyhow, in this scene you will watch as the Court Jester tries desperately to make the king laugh, but he can't. In fact the only one who starts to laugh is you, which infuriates the king even more and immediately the Court Jester is tossed into a cell until his execution. You feel guilty, not to mention you really felt that he was funny, so you save him, and because of that, you gain his trust as well as his knowledge of the castle which he shares with you"

This video seemed more like a movie than a music video, and I was curious to know how he planned to cut it down to five minutes.

Mr. D was excited the whole time, nodding and smiling at every direction given by Domingo. I asked who would be playing the Court Jester, and at that moment, out stepped this little clown-like dude.

I couldn't recall what a Court Jester looked like, until I saw him walking toward me. They kept saying, like on the playing cards, but I had never played cards.

The costume was definitely on point, a mixture of bright vibrant colors, with these gold ankle-high boots so pointy that they curled up at the toe. The hat was just as crazy, with these three points that hung down by the weight of these big round bells that jingled with every step.

He was a little guy, with his face plastered in white make-up, and when I stepped forward to introduce myself, all I heard was...

"Damn, nigga! You can't tell it's me?"

I jumped back, nearly knocking over one of the production guys carrying a light.

"Quenepa?"

I asked, as my brain tried to make the connection between the voice and that crazy looking face.

"You know each other?" Domingo asked.

"Well, um..." I began until Quenepa cut in.

"Hell the fuck yeah, we boys!" He proudly announced, shadow boxing against my stomach.

"Okay, this is good!" Domingo replied. "The chemistry is already there." I looked over at Mr. D who just stood there quietly watching everything go down.

"Watch this." Domingo said to both Mr. D and I.

"Quenepa, go ahead and do the walk!"

We all watched as Quenepa began to do a walk, that even though I had never seen how a Court Jester walked, I was sure that was it.

Each step had a bounce that made him look like he was walking faster than he actually was. With each step, rang his bells, and he had this uncanny ability to make the absolute perfect smile. We couldn't help ourselves and we all started to laugh. If they would've told me that he came from a long line of Court Jesters, I would've believed it.

"Okay guys, wait here, I will be right back, so we can start the next scene." Domingo walked off, and Mr. D came over to us.

"Surprised?" Quenepa asked me.

"The Court mother fucking Jester!" I replied, shaking my head.

"Fresh and in the flesh!" he said with a spin. I was still laughing from before, but it was more so in disbelief that any of this was actually happening.

"I bet this was Sal's idea!?" I said, but Quenepa shook his head and gestured at Mr. D. "Quenepa and I go way back," Mr. D said

"Really?" I replied, even more surprised.

"Yeah, long story, I'll tell you about it one day. Actually I bet you didn't know that the crazy voice on your record is…"

"You?" I asked Quenepa.

Quenepa smiled and nodded, then gave me a sample of the lyric. I laughed even more, mainly to mask the fact that I wasn't happy about any of this.

"He's gonna be the perfect Sidekick." Domingo said as he walked back over to us. My laughter began to simmer, until finally it went silent.

"Sidekick?" I asked, my eyes glancing over at Mr. D, "For the

Video!"

"For everything," Mr. D replied. "Like Batman and Robin."

"Nah, fuck that!" Quenepa cut in, "Robin was a fag. More like The Green Hornet and Kato. I'm Kato!" He said, throwing a kick into the air, and making one of those Bruce Lee sounds, except his had bells.

"But you never mentioned this to me." I replied, trying my best to stay calm.

"Didn't think I had to," he replied.

"Wait, is there a problem?" Quenepa asked.

"Only that I'm always the last to find shit out. Mr. D, can I speak to you for a second?"

He looked at Domingo and Quenepa and asked to be excused. Him and I then turned and walked away.

"Don't fuck this up for me, yo!" Quenepa yelled out from the distance, but I acted like I didn't hear him.

"Man, I don't know if this is a good idea." I began.

"What's not a good idea?" Mr. D asked.

"Bringing him on, I mean, he could be a problem you know."

"I don't know what you know about him, King. But I've always known him as being a pretty good guy." I looked back at Quenepa, and then at Mr. D, wondering if we were we talking about the same guy?

"Give it some time, get to know him, I think you'll like him. Besides, he fits that costume perfectly."

Mr. D could tell, I was really upset about this.

"King, brother, listen to me man. You promised never to question my motives again."

"But this here is extreme!"

"This whole project is extreme. You're extreme, I'm extreme. That's what we do. We can't settle for some simple shit. We can't fish for guppies, we need sharks and whales! That's where the money's at."

"So in the video he plays my sidekick, okay cool, I can deal with that, but to go on tour, and be on stage? Come on Mr. D!"

"It's going to be great, King, I promise you!"

"I can't believe this is happening." I said as I looked at Domingo who was talking to Quenepa. However, Quenepa didn't seem to be paying him any mind, instead, he was staring at me!

CHAPTER 12

Grown Up Table

Shooting this video was beyond what I could have ever imagined. I expected a couple of kids running around with handheld cameras, but this was far from that. I'd never been on a actual movie set before, but if I had, I bet this is what it looked like.

At first I saw just this one sophisticated camera, but then I realized, it was just one of three, each with its own cameraman. One was on a dolly, and I was fascinated by how they laid the tracks, lots and lots of tracks. The cameraman would get up on the dolly while a couple of strong looking guys would either push or pull it. I learned that these guys were called Grips, or in this case, Dolly Grips. I found these guys to work the hardest, physically at least. I couldn't imagine them getting paid that much, and I wondered if this was ever their idea of what the movie business was like? I bet if they did, they would've sought another career, however, a few times during our breaks I caught myself mingling more with them than any of the so-called, *Important* people on the set.

I was amazed at how many of them really loved what they did, didn't matter the task, they just loved the whole vibe. Though each of them, I learned had dreams that were much bigger than what they were currently doing, as far as they were concerned, this was all part of the master plan.

Another camera was mounted on what to me looked like an actual crane that you would see on a construction site, and I was surprised to learn that that's what it was also called in the movie business… A Crane!

This thing had to extend at least a hundred feet in the air, and the cameraman would ride along with it, while another down at the base would control it. I couldn't really grasp how they were using it, and when I asked Domingo, he would only say, "You'll see!"

The third camera was handheld, and it must've been the most important one, because it ran constantly, whether alone, or in conjunction with one of the others. Finally I got to see the dailies. Watchable clips, that Domingo would get back every evening showing the day's work.

He would go over this footage to make sure it was something he could work with, if not, we'd have to shoot it again. He allowed me in on the first one, just to kill my curiosity. After that, I was not allowed.

I learned that the camera would shoot the same scene in many different angles, using various techniques, lighting. He would also give me an idea of how the edits will go, and from what my imagination was able to build, this shit was gonna look amazing!

I sure as hell developed a whole new level of respect for anyone who works on music videos, because the work that it takes to make at the very least, a decent one, was intense!

From the very first day, I ended up shooting quite a few scenes with Quenepa. Aside from our interactions on the set, we really didn't say much to one another. He remembered how I reacted when I found out he would be my sidekick, and I remembered too. One thing though, I have to give it up to Mr. D. He was right… Again!

Though he was an unusual character, Quenepa was in fact quite talented, and the way he carried himself on the set was nothing like how he carried himself on the street. I saw professionalism in him that I would've never thought even existed. It was like, who the fuck is this dude? Like day and night, Jekyll and Hyde.

We wrapped the first day with a round of applause for everyone involved just before midnight, and then went into the castle where a humongous buffet was set up for us.

We all sat around at scattered tables, talking and joking with one another. I of course ended up sitting at what felt like the grown up table, Mr. D, Domingo, Princess, and Antonio.

The entire time it was as if we hadn't stopped working. Domingo, even with his fat face full of food continued to give direction for the next day. I just wanted to eat, shower and hit the sack. I was beat!

While everyone at my table talked movie talk, dropped names, experiences, and stories, I just kept looking over at the Dancer's table. They all looked like they were having a ball. Quenepa sat with them, and I was jealous.

Vee noticed me watching, and gave me a smile. I smiled back, and when I turned around to try and pick up on what they were talking about, I noticed Mr. D had been watching me all along. I gave him a tight smile and a nod, he returned the gestured, and then sort of snapped his head in the direction of the dancer's table, as if to tell me… go join them!

I stood up, and immediately, Domingo stopped talking, as everyone looked at me. Maybe I should've at least waited till he finished his story?

"Sorry," I said, before grabbing my tray, and excusing myself.

"What's up everyone?" I said as I took a seat between Lily and Emerald. Across from us was Vanessa, Jini, and Quenepa who sat directly in front of me.

"Hey Sunshine!" Vanessa greeted with a high five over the table, everyone else followed, except Quenepa.

"Sunshine?" he asked with a laugh.

"I'll explain later." Vanessa told him.

"So, how you feeling?" Jini asked.

"Unreal." I replied.

"I've been on a lot of video sets." Emerald said. "But I have to admit, this one seriously tops them all!

"I didn't expect anything like this at all. I thought it was just gonna be some kid running around with a camcorder."

"I don't know about that." Lily said. "We're talking Mr. D here!" Everyone agreed.

As we all continued talking about the shoot, I glanced

over at Quenepa who still seemed pretty pissed at me.

"I'm sorry man." I said, beneath the conversation going on around us.

Quenepa looked at me and gave my apology some thought.

"You could've cost me this gig." He said.

"You're right, and again I'm sorry. It's just that so much is happening and so fast, that I find myself questioning just about everything that goes on.

"We're gonna take a little tour around the castle. Vanessa said. You guys coming?"

"Nah, my feet are done." I told her. She then looked at Quenepa.

"There's still food here I haven't even gotten to yet."

"You guys are wack!" She replied, waving us off as they walked away.

"You're actually pretty good at this." I said. "You've acted before?"

"I'm from the streets, yo. Acting is a survival mechanism."

I took a sip of my drink and glanced across the room, trying to think of something else to say.

"Look man." Quenepa began. "Let's be straight up. Looks like we're gonna be around each other probably more than either of us could care for."

"It's really not like that …" I said, trying to soften the situation up a bit, but Quenepa was right. We had to clear the air, so he continued.

"Can I be honest with you… King?"

"Absolutely, this is what we need." I replied.

"Okay, cool. Well. I think you're a fuckin' Corn Ball!" He blurted out.

"Hold up a minute." I began to say, But Quenepa raised his hand to stop me.

"You said we can be honest." He was right, so I sat back and let him continue.

"Look at you. Look at your hair. You're wearing a fucking dress man. Dude got you wearing a mother fucking dress!"

He was right, there was no arguing, no justifying it. I was wearing a mother fucking dress.

"Okay, cool." I replied. But check this out. Dude got you looking like a fuckin' clown!"

Quenepa remained quiet. I guess he didn't see that one coming.

"You got fucking bells on. You know why? Because he doesn't trust you! This way they always know where you are. Shit, you can't even scratch your ass without jingling!"

Quenepa's eyes opened wide, and he looked like he was trying to hold in his laughter.

"You know what I wanna see?" Quenepa asked. I looked at him as if to say what? "I wanna see the mother fuckers who are going to be buying your records!"

Now it was me trying not to laugh.

"Think about that shit!" You're making records for some

weird ass white folks, 'Cause ain't no black people gonna be buying this shit!" Suddenly he stood up and sang the hook. "I am the King!" and at that moment, I exploded. We both did. Everyone was looking at us.

I glanced back over at the grown-up table, and caught everyone there deep in conversation about, I will assume... business! Everyone except Mr. D. Mr. D was staring at us.

CHAPTER 13

Misunderstanding

"Who is it?" I called out, after hearing a knock on my hotel room door.

"Be ready to leave in fifteen!" One of the PAs replied before stepping over to the next room and repeating the process. I glanced at the clock beside the bed. It was 6:02 am.

Rooms had been reserved for all of us over at The Castle Inn, a small privately owned hotel just a couple of minutes down the road. After taking a quick shower and getting dressed I stepped outside and into the rush of cast and crew as they piled into the busses and headed back up to the set.

"Now this is the hard part!" Quenepa said.

"What is?"

"This early morning shit. I ain't use to it" I laughed as we both headed for one of the busses.

"King!" I heard someone call out. I looked and it was Domingo, about to get into the limo. He waved for me to come along.

"Go 'head!" I yelled back, Imma ride the bus!" Domingo looked at me with a distorted face, and then got into the limo. Sal closed the door behind him and then waved to me. I waved back. I looked at Quenepa who seemed pleased with what I had just done, patting me on the back as we boarded.

An entire spread was laid out for breakfast. We had twenty minutes to eat and have our coffee, and then over to hair and makeup. By 8:00 a.m. we had to be done and on set ready to shoot.

I got scared when they brought out a white horse for me to get up on.

"You ever ride a horse before?" Domingo asked. "No not really. I rode a pony at the zoo once!" Domingo looked at me and scratched his chin.

"So, you mean to tell me, that if I need you to ride this horse, at full speed to that tree and back, and then pull the horse back onto his hind legs, you wouldn't be able to do it?"

"Hell the fuck no!" I replied, looking at Domingo like he lost his damn mind. Domingo looked over at Mr. D, and said.

"And this is why we always use a stunt man." Domingo waved someone out of the small crowd that stood behind the camera. The person who stepped out was already dressed in the same exact costume as I, which removed the idea that mine was the only one in existence. But what threw me for an even bigger loop was the fact that the stunt man wasn't even a man. It was a woman!

I looked at Domingo, as if he was pulling some type of prank. But he wasn't even paying me any mind. He just stood there with a huge smile on his huge face as he watched the woman come our way. It didn't take much for me to realize what was going on here. From everyone who worked on this video, why did it have to be *my* stunt double that he was fucking?

I watched as he spoke softly to her, and then watched her get up on the horse. Yeah, she wore the kilt, except under hers, she wore panties, and I caught Domingo taking a peek.

Once she was on the horse, she took off doing exactly as Domingo had directed. "Isn't she great?" He said, as we watched her run through the scene a few times.

"You couldn't find a male stunt double for me?" both our eyes still on the girl.

"None with a pair of legs like that." He replied. I couldn't help looking down at mine.

During the day we shot all of the outside scenes, and at night we brought it into the castle.

It was another exciting day, I had called Grams from my room to check up on her and let her know how everything was going. I had two beds in my room, and I would've loved for her to have been here, but as much as she loved me, and everything I was doing. This would've been too much.

I was lying on the bed watching a little TV when someone knocked. I opened and it was Quenepa.

"What's up?" I asked. I stepped outside, because I really didn't want anyone in my room.

"So what you think about this Nemesis dude?" Quenepa asked, as he took a seat on the curb right outside my door.

"He's okay." I replied. And then took a seat beside him.

"Nothing special."

"Nigga getting paid, though!"

"Man, I don't know. Is he?

"What? Dude's everywhere, magazines, posters, TV, concerts. He even has his own Halloween mask! Now you know you done made it when you got your own Halloween mask!"

I didn't say anything. I just stared out at the cars parked across the lot.

"You think you better than him?"

"What?"

"You heard me. Do you think you're a better Rapper than that nigga, Nemesis?"

"Of course, that dude is wack!"

Quenepa started to laugh. I looked at him and asked.

"Why you asking?"

"Only because people are starting to talk?"

"Talk?"

"Yeah, comparing you to him."

"Man, ain't no one even hear me yet!"

"What are you talking about? Everyone's heard you!" I looked at him and realized he was referring to everyone here. We sat there in silence for a moment.

"I'm out." I said as I stood and stretched a bit.

"It's not even eleven O'clock!" Quenepa replied, looking up at me. "I was about to spark up this blunt." He said, sliding it under his nose.

"I don't smoke." I said slapping him five then walking to my room.

I went inside, and threw myself on the bed. I lay there for a while just staring up at the ceiling, thinking.

I was awaken by voices right outside my door, and when I sat up, I noticed flashing colored lights seeping in from the window.

I rushed over and peeked out from behind the curtain. I couldn't tell what was happening, but the cop cars parked in the middle of the lot told it must be serious.

I stepped outside to see if I can figure it out, when I spotted a cop placing Quenepa in the back seat.

"Oh shit!" I said as I rushed over just has he shut the door.

"What's going on?" I asked.

"Are you a relative?"

"No." I replied.

"Then it's none of your business!" He said before getting into the driver's seat and taking off.

"That sonofabitch stole my ring!" said the old clerk, walking up beside me. I turned to him, so he continued.

"That ring has been in my family since the 17th century, there isn't another one like it."

"He stole your ring?"

"He done come into my office demanding that I give it to him, right off my goddamn finger!"

"And you gave it to him?"

"Shit yeah, I don't know what that psycho sonofabitch would've done to me. He thinks he can just come into this town and help himself with whatever he wants? Bullshit!"

"You do know that we're out here filming a music video, right?"

"Of course I do, and so does the whole goddamn town, and believe me, nobody's happy about it. You need to hurry up with your business and then get your city asses up outta here!"

I watched as the old clerk headed back to his office, still talking shit.

I turned to go back to my room and noticed everyone standing in the doorway of theirs. I was about to ask if anyone knew what room Sal or Mr. D was in, but they were already going in. Mr. D and Sal were the only two who could possibly fix this, and they had to hurry.

The day nearly went perfect, but now, here we were, in the middle of shooting my music video, with Quenepa in practically every one of my scenes, and now he was headed to jail. I turned and spotted the clerk entering his office, and figured I'll go and find out Sal and Mr. D's room numbers to let them know what just happened.

But just as I was about to go, I saw Sal rush into the office right behind the clerk.

Something didn't seem right, so I crept up to the window and peaked inside. I was completely floored by what I was looking at. Sal had the clerk by the throat and pinned up against the wall. He was saying something to him, but I couldn't make it out through the glass.

It seemed as though whatever the clerk told him, he didn't like because suddenly he lifted the clerk a bit, his toes dangling just above the floor. I didn't know what t do.

Sal said something again to him, but whatever it was that the clerk told him, he didn't seem to like. In fact it seemed to have pissed Sal off even more, because he began to lift the clerk by the throat, completely off the floor.

The clerk began waving his arms and kicking his feet in panic. The only thing he could do, was yell for help.

It didn't look like Sal was going to ease off and I was about to run in and stop him, but then suddenly. The clerk must've told him whatever it was he wanted to hear, because he let him go! Allowing the clerk to drop to the floor like an old ragdoll, coughing and gagging, trying desperately to catch his breath. I exhaled a sigh of relief, until I watched Sal reach behind his back and pull out his gun. The clerk, already scared to death looked up and placed his hands in front of him in an attempt to shield himself.

Sal said something to him, and this time there was no hesitation… The clerk nodded. He then got up and went over to the phone and dialed. Sal stood there with the gun pressed up against the back of his head.

The clerk spoke to someone on the other line, and then hung up. But before he had a chance to turn around, Sal whacked him over the head, and knocked him the fuck out.

I watched Sal grab, what looked like a family photo off the wall and place it under his arm.

I got scared and backed up away from the window tripping over the small bushes that lined the walkway.

King! He said. "What are you doing?" He asked as he helped me up. I looked at the ground behind me, acting as though I tripped over something.

"Man, I was coming over here to find out your room number. They fuckin' took Q, said he stole a ring or some shit."

Sal placed his arm around me and together we walked back to my room.

"Don't worry about it, I just spoke to the clerk, apparently it was all a misunderstanding."

"Misunderstanding?"

"Yeah, he found the damn ring. Forgot he had left it on the sink when he was washing his hands. When we got to my room, I turned and asked him.

"So are they bringing him back?"

"No, I have to go get him."

"Can I go with you?"

"No, King, it's best you stay here and get some sleep. Tomorrow's going to be a crazy day, and you need to be at a hundred percent."

I unlocked my door and stepped inside.

"I'll let him know you were thinking of him... He'll appreciate that!"

CHAPTER 14

Gotta Be a Black Guy

I stepped out of my room and watched as some of the cast piled onto the buses to get to the set. Most of the crew was there already setting up. It was a cool clear morning, and the sun had yet to rise. This would be our last day on the set, and our last night in the hotel. The bulb in my lamp had gone out, and I wanted to let the clerk know so he can change it before I got back.

"Good morning, an old woman greeted me as I entered the front office "Good morning." I replied looking around for the regular night clerk. "Where's Jimmy?" I asked the old woman.

"Jimmy done got up and quit!" she huffed.

"Quit?"

"Yep, don't ask me why. He just called me around 2am and told me that he was leaving, and if I didn't want to leave the office empty, I'd best come over."

"So, *you* own this place?"

"For fifty four years! Now what can I help you with, son?"

I didn't catch her question right away as I was still registering what she had told me. The last time I saw Jimmy, he was laid out on the office floor, Sal standing over him.

"Um, the light bulb beside the bed blew out." I said. "Room 102."

"I'll be over there to change it in just a moment." she replied. I watched as she slowly got up from her chair behind the counter and waddled her ninety year old self a mere four foot to a shelf where she kept the light bulbs.

"Why don't you just give it to me, and I'll take care of it."

The old woman looked at me, at first hesitant, and then continued to grab one of the bulbs and handed it to me.

I stepped back out of my room after replacing the bulb just as Sal stepped out of his. "Good morning, King!" He said with a smile as he locked his door and I locked mine. I had no idea his room was right next to mine.

"So what's up with Quenepa?" I asked him.

"Come on, we'll talk in the car," he replied

We weren't going far so I sat up front.

"That knucklehead decided to go into the office and ask the clerk if he could borrow twenty dollars."

"Borrow twenty dollars?"

"Yeah I know I know. It's just them damn streets you can't get it out of him. Quenepa could be a multimillionaire and I swear he'd still be trying to hustle people for their chump change."

"Is he still?"

"… No, he's already on set!" Sal said "He left with the crew."

"So he's been there since 4:00 a.m.?"

"Mr. D's orders."

"The clerk quit." I said.

"Really?"

"Yeah, I wonder why?"

"Too many niggers and spics, they're not use to that around here."

Sal said that so convincing, that had I not already catch him terrifying the clerk, I would've easily believed that to be the reason.

We drove up onto the castle grounds and made our way across the vast landscape. This place was absolutely gorgeous, and I was in awe when Sal pointed out about a dozen deer, galloping across the field, something I had never before seen in real life.

I looked straight ahead and imagined myself, living in this castle, and though it was huge and spooky as hell, it was an incredible sight. So much in fact, that I got butterflies whenever I saw it from a distance.

I could see the crew setting up for the day's first shot which would take place outside the front of the castle. I had no idea which scene we were doing, but Domingo always prepped me beforehand.

We pulled over to the side where the busses and other vehicles were parked and got out.

We still had about an hour before shooting, and so Sal and I headed inside to grab some breakfast.

"Wadup, nigga!" Quenepa called out from across the large room. He was sitting with a few of the dancers, including Vanessa.

"Go sit with them," Sal said. "I'm just gonna grab a coffee and go watch'em set up."

"Man, we can't take you anywhere, can we?" I said as Quenepa and I slapped each other five. Vanessa and the others started to laugh making room for me to sit down with my tray.

"Man that old cracker called the police on me!"

"What did you do?"

"I ain't do nothing. I just went into the office to say hi."

"Since when you ever say hi to white people?" Vanessa asked.

"Since them mother fuckers starting hiring me for shit like this!" he replied, and again we lost it.

"Nah for real, it was late, I couldn't sleep, and he was the only mother fucker still up."

"He said you tried to rob him."

"Yeah, I know, and he's a fuckin' liar, old cheddar cheese smelling mother fucker!"

"Don't mess this up, Q." Vanessa warned him.

"Damn, you people are tripping, you really think I'm

gonna do some dumb shit like try and rob a fucking motel that I'm staying in?"

Quenepa had a point, as it really didn't make any sense. Could the clerk have falsely accused him for whatever reason? Of course he could! He even said that no one was happy about us being there.

"So what happened? They took you to jail?"

Yeah I was there for about a half hour when Sal came and got me."

"So he bailed you out?" Vanessa asked.

"Nah, they just dropped everything and let me go. Sal said that the clerk misidentified me, said it was some tall black guy!"

"Always gotta be the black guy!" Vanessa said as she laughed and rolled her eyes. "Black, white, Chinese, I don't give a fuck, as long as they don't blame me!"

CHAPTER 15

That's A Wrap

Quenepa and I walked up to Domingo while he was giving instructions to the cameraman.

"Good morning!" He said, looking happy, and relieved that this was the last day of the shoot.

"Today we kill the bad guy and you ride off into the sunset with the beautiful princess!" Domingo said with a victorious smile.

"What about me?" Quenepa asked."

"Oh, you die!" The director replied, and then turned and gestured for me to look at the Black Knight as he rode up on his black horse.

He stopped in front of us and removed his helmet. Was there a hidden message in here somewhere, or did they purposely choose an opponent that looked exactly like Nemesis?

"King, this here is Roger, he'll playing the Black Knight."

"Howdy!" Roger said, an Oreo cookie looking guy if I

ever saw one. I nodded. For the last two days, all that was shot was me, Quenepa, and the dancers who were dressed as Peasants. I would rap, and Quenepa would respond, with the dancers, behind us.

That same scene was shot in the castle, outside the castle, on the roof of the castle, in the dungeon, during a huge feast, in the forest, through the village streets, by a lake, in the tower, where the beautiful Princess, played by Roller Girl, was held captive.

Today's scenes will be all the battling close ups of The Black Knight and myself. This video so far has been shot in such a weird order that I kept losing track of where we were.

It's been fun though and I really look forward to watching the finished product.

Today was a grueling day, the hardest of them all. Today it was a lot of running, wrestling, microphone dueling close ups. The armored suit that I had to wear was hot and uncomfortable. The friction on my inner thighs irritated my skin so much that it burned from the sweat. This suit now weighed a ton, and it took so long to put on and take off that I had to leave it on for the entire day, and my liquid intake was held to a minimum because even though the suit had an opening that allowed me to pee, I still refused because it required someone to help.

It was 3:00 p.m. and Domingo wanted to catch me literally riding off into the sunset. We had tried to catch it a few times before, but my horse riding skills were at zero, and for this shot he refused to use a double. But before we got to that, there was one last important scene that he wanted to shoot, and that was the death of the Court Jester.

When I asked Domingo, since we were shooting out of sequence anyway, why didn't we shoot this earlier? He said, *I needed your relationship to build over the last couple of days.* I didn't quite understand what he meant. Until we actually shot the scene.

It wasn't an ordinary death. It was sacrificial. The Court Jester would sacrifice his own life in order for the King and his soon to be Queen to live happily ever after.

The person whose sole existence was to keep people happy, particularly the King, would now create the saddest scene of the video.

After the epic battle between the King, and the Black Knight, where the King pierces the Knight's armor, thrusting his sword further into his heart, in victory. But as he lifts the princess up onto his horse, and is about to mount it himself, unknowingly, one of the soldier's hidden behind a tree, slides an arrow out from his quiver, and places it on the bow. He pulls back slowly, lining the arrowhead with the King's back, and as soon as he feels that the shot is right... He let's go!

It was in this scene were Q, or should I say, the Court Jester throws himself in front of the arrow, saving the King.

In this final scene I would kneel down and take the Court Jester into my arms, and hold him as his life fades away. I had never done any kind of acting in my life, so that little tear that made its way out from the corner of my eye, was real! But of course I would never admit it.

Over the last few days, I got to really know Q. I got to see him in an environment outside of the ghetto he was so accustomed to.

It was obvious, he was a victim of his own circumstances, and by giving something productive to do, some responsibility, and to trust him to pull it off, proved to be all he ever needed, to show the type of person he really is, and I was so grateful that I hadn't screwed this up for him.

"And cut!" yelled Domingo.

It didn't quite register until Quenepa broke free from my grasp.

"Damn nigga!" he said, as he jumped up on his feet. "I thought you were gonna try and kiss me or some shit!"

"Sorry man, I just got caught up in the scene!"

"Okay everybody, let's set up for the final scene!" Domingo called out as everyone scurried about getting things ready.

The shoot ended with me and the Princess riding off into the sunset, to live happily ever after.

"And cut! That's a wrap!" Yelled Domingo, as everyone applauded, and this absolute magical experience came to an end.

We were taken to the motel to shower and change, then back to the castle for what they called, the wrap party.

As we walked into the ancient ballroom, thinking it was just going to be a regular dinner, confetti cannons exploded, and balloons floated down from the ceiling.

At first I couldn't figure out what was happening, until I realized that there were more people there than had been working on the set.

Guest, celebrities and other important figures came to celebrate, but there was one guest in particular that totally made my night.

In the mist of the applause, balloons and confetti, out stepped my grandmother!

The points that Mr. D won with me at that very moment were uncountable. This entire experience would so far top anything that I've ever experienced in my life.

I met so many people that night and hundreds of photos of me with the other cast members and distinctive guest were arranged by Ciré and Donna who stayed the busiest throughout the night.

A huge screen hung high against a big open wall, where Domingo screened the video for the first time, as well as some other takes and bloopers.

The video wasn't even close to being done, but was pieced together more so like a trailer, which made it very interesting, and its release highly anticipated.

I couldn't believe just how many behind the scenes, and blooper shots there were. Like where the hell were all these cameras that caught so much of the shoot, and so much of me?

From me trying to ride the horse, to falling over in the armored suit unable to get up, eating, and even slipping a couple of candy bars into my pockets to take back to the motel.

I was a little worried about what else they might've caught.

CHAPTER 16

Birth Mark

Back home I laid in my bed, staring at the ceiling. Years of chipping paint being painted over and over, created unique shapes, that in time I've become quite familiar with.

From an array of animals and fish, to the profile of a man with a humungous nose, those shapes had a life of their own, and kept me company during some of the stormiest nights of my childhood.

I heard the squeak of my door which I left partially open for air. It was Grams, standing there with that same animated smile she's been wearing since the party.

"I didn't want to wake you." She said, popping her head into my room.

"Don't worry, I'm still wired."

"Me too," she said, as she walked in and sat on my bed. I looked at her, but all she was doing was staring at me with that big cheesy smile.

"You're acting weird, Grams!"

"I know, I can't help it," she was too cute, that all I could do was shake my head.

"You know, there were some really important people at the party." She said.

"Yeah, I know. Too bad I didn't know who any of them were."

We both laughed.

"Oh my God, every time, Donald introduced you to someone important, you just looked at them, said hi, and then went about your business!"

"Hold up a second...Donald?" I asked.

Grams looked at me with a strange face.

"Yeah, your boss!"

"Mr. D?"

"Yeah. The D stands for Donald."

"I know that, but he doesn't like anyone calling him that."

"Well, that's the name he used when he introduced himself. Actually I didn't even realize he was the same person you had been talking about all his time.

"Grams, everyone calls him Mr. D."

"Well, he introduced himself to me as Donald, and unless he tells me otherwise, that's the name I'm calling him by."

I got up, and started pulling out my clothes for the day.

"So let me ask you something," Grams asked. "When you become rich and famous, what will you do?"

"Grams, it's just one song, one video."

"I know, I'm just curious, what will you do?

I gave it a little thought and then answered.

"Well, the first thing I would do is get you the hell out of this rat hole!"

"Rat hole?" she said, throwing one of my pillows at me.

"You know what I mean Grams, this neighborhood. It's so... I don't know, just that you deserve better!

"Well, you lived here all of your life, and I've lived here most of mine."

"Right! and it's time for a change. Imagine, a big beautiful house, somewhere in the country."

"What country?"

This country... But *in* the country, like Long Island, or maybe New Jersey."

"Okay, but not too big, I'm not trying to spend the rest of my life cleaning a big ass house!"

"Oh, it's gonna be big Grams, believe that, but I'm gonna get you help. Someone to cook for you, clean, mow the lawn. I'll even get a couple of those people who know how to do nails and stuff."

Grams stared at me with a soft smile.

"What?" I asked.

"I always knew you were special."

"Special has a couple of meanings, which one are you referring to?" It took a minute before she got it, then threw another pillow.

"No, I'm serious." She continued. "I remember when I

first looked at you. You were just born. You looked at me with those big brown eyes, and it was like I could hear you tell me that, everything will be okay. An indescribable calm suddenly took over, and at that very moment, I nodded, and do you know what you did?"

I shook my head.

"You smiled at me!"

I gave Grams a moment, and watched her face once again transition into thoughts.

"How'd you do it? How'd you raise me all by yourself? No help."

"Well, being a single mother to a teenage daughter in New York City, prepared me for it. Boys were always sniffing around. She didn't like my rules so as soon as she was eighteen, she left! I didn't want her to leave, but I couldn't stop her.

I thought she'd leave for a few days and then come home, but she didn't. I went sometimes months without seeing her. I knew she was okay because I was in touch with a few of the other mothers, whose houses she would sometimes spend nights at. They knew what I was going through so they would call me just to let me know that she was okay. That helped me out so much in those days."

I watched my grandmother continue to drift in and out, her thoughts,

"What I didn't know was... she was pregnant!"

"With me?" Grams nodded a mixed smile.

"She refused to see me. I knew when her due date was,

and when she went into labor, one of the mothers went with her. They told me not to come, but assured me that they would keep me informed. I prayed for the entire twenty hours that she was in labor, and then finally I got the call. It was around 3:00 a.m. The woman who was with her congratulated me on the birth of a beautiful baby boy, seven pounds seven ounces, twenty-one inches long. I was ecstatic and immediately thanked the saints, but then the woman's tone changed, and I knew something was wrong.

When she told me that your mommy had passed away during birth, I swore, at that very moment, that I too was going to die. The entire room just started spinning. I grabbed on to the wall to try and hold myself up, and when I tried to make it to the couch, I lost my balance and fell, hitting my face on the corner of the coffee table." She said pointing to the mark under her left eye.

"You told me that was your birth mark."

"No, I told you it's *a* birth mark... yours!"

This mark represents the worst and best day of my life!

It was the day, I said goodbye to my princess, and hello to my prince.

My world was a shambles, and I didn't think I was gonna get through this. Honestly Mijo, I didn't even want to hold you."

"You blamed me?" I asked, and Grams shamefully nodded.

"And then, this nurse came in, un blanquita, very pretty. I remember her because she had these beautiful hazel eyes, and

I complimented her on them. She asked if I would like to hold you. She was concerned because no one else had come to see you, and you had yet to been even touched by a relative.

I finally agreed. She made me sit in a rocking chair, and then handed you to me. My eyes were so full of tears that I couldn't see you. You were just a blur, and instead of giving me a tissue to wipe them, the nurse used her thumbs and wiped both my eyes for me. I thought that was weird, but then I looked at you, and I couldn't believe what I was seeing.

It was like I was looking at your mommy when *she* was born, and I suddenly felt like I was being given a second chance to try this again. I'm sorry Mijo, I don't..."

"No Grams, keep on, Please."

"Suddenly the door opened and the doctor and a nurse came in, I noticed he looked mad, and he took you from me and yelled at the nurse for letting me hold you. I told the doctor that it wasn't her, that it was the other one, the one with the hazel eyes. He told me that he had no nurses with hazel eyes! In fact the nurse that was there was the only one working that floor.

CHAPTER 17

Dinner with Rey

I had a couple of days off, so of course one of them had to be dedicated to going to see Charlotte. I hadn't been over that way in over a month. I wasn't even sure if she still worked there. One thing I knew for sure was, I was going to ask her if she would hang out with me this weekend.

"Hey Rey!" Junior yelled out as he and his little friend raced toward me with their bikes, Junior of course taking the lead and skidding right up to me.

"Yo, man! I said grabbing his handlebars, but he stopped before hitting me.

"Don't worry, Rey, I got skills." He said as his friend finally made it to us, attempting the same stunt. But he was way too big for his little bike, and his weight only allowed him to slow to a stop. I played it off though, and grabbed his handlebars too. He got a kick out of that.

"Where you going?" Junior asked.

"I gotta go see someone."

"Who?

"Why you all up in my business, yo?" I said, messing up his already messed up hair.

"Porky said you were gay!"

"No I didn't!" Porky yelled back.

"Yes you did!"

First off, no I'm not gay, and secondly… I'm pretty sure neither of you even knows what that means."

"I do." Junior said. "My sister told me."

"In that case, you probably do, but to answer your question I'm going to see a girl."

"Told you!" Junior said to Porky. "What's her name, Rey?"

"Look, you guys don't need to know all that." I replied.

"Does she have big kanoobies?" Porky asked with this sort sinister smile, sending them both laughing.

I reached into my pocket and pulled out a five dollar bill, and handed it to Junior. I couldn't help but notice Porky already licking his lips.

"Thanks, Rey." Junior said .

"Yeah Rey, thanks!"

You guys go eat some Pizza, and tell Sarge I said to throw on some extra cheese.

I stood there and watched as they turned their bikes and raced off to get their Pizza.

I don't think I could ever get use to all the Nemesis propaganda that practically littered the city. From station billboards, to overhead ads, kids reading Word Up, Right On, and other teen magazines with his ugly face on the cover. His music blared through Walkmans above the rumble of the train. Newspaper articles, tee shirts, bootleg cassettes being sold on every corner. Newsstands decorated their entire establishments in Nemesis posters. It was absolutely sickening to me.

I thought about my own situation, and everything happening over at The Funky Junky. It still didn't seem real, not to mention it's taken so long just to get to this point. Nemesis's deal was quick. One minute he was sitting at the audition with me, the next minute he was a superstar.

When I got to my stop I exited the station, and walked up the block toward the library. I pushed through the heavy revolving door and immediately spotted her, doing what must be her designated job of stamping index cards. I walked over to the rack where a few Village Voices were left and took one over to the table with me.

Why didn't I just go directly to the counter beats me, it's like I have all these plans on how I would approach her, greet her. A few jokes thrown in, as well as a few compliments about how she looked. Then I would do it! I would ask her out. But it never worked that way. My entire plan would become scrambled. My nerves shot, hands sweaty. The cool walk to the counter that I had envisioned turned out to be more like a clumsy shuffle. I tossed the paper onto the table a little harder than I should've, as the entire Voice slid off the other side spilling its pages across the floor.

Kneeing above the mess I made, I tried quickly to put the

paper back together, but it was no use. I grabbed them all and threw them on that table. God, Had I been trying to be discreet I would've failed miserably.

Charlotte spotted me among the ruckus and looking surprised to see me. I sat down and began to place the pages back in order, trying my best to smooth out their wrinkles, and had I realized that my sweaty hands were smearing the ink on the pages, I would never have touched my face as much as I was, a nervous reaction Grams brought to my attention many years ago.

The lady who sat across from me followed my creepy stare at Charlotte as I flipped through the pages without even looking at them. When I gained enough nerve, I got up and walked over to the counter.

"Hey." I said. Charlotte looked up, and I noticed a slight flinch, and then her eyes glanced to the side just as Ms. Crumble stepped out from the back room.

"Can I help you with something?" Charlotte asked, loud enough for her boss to hear. "Yes, I am looking for a book." Was the only dumb thing I could think of.

"Well, you've come to the right place." She said, a bit sarcastically. "What's the name of it?" She asked.

"I'm not sure."

"Do you know the genre?"

"I'm not sure, maybe romance?"

"Romance?" She asked, her eyes bouncing between me and her boss who was tuned in.

"It's called, A date with Rey." I said trying to be cute.

Charlotte looked at me, and subtly shook her head.

"It might be in the Fantasy section. Let's go see."

She grabbed a card, and I followed her to the back of the library and into the Romance section.

"You said, Dinner With Rey?" She asked, flipping through the books on a shelf. I looked behind me and noticed Ms. Crumble staring at us.

"I heard there's a whole series, but I guess the dinner one might be a good place to start.

"And where does this story take place?"

I hadn't thought about that yet. In fact, I hadn't thought about anything, but then I remembered grabbing a bite with Sal over at a place called…

"Luciano's!" I replied.

"Luciano's?" she asked, writing it down

"Yeah, corner of 53rd and 8th."

CHAPTER 18

Promise

"How I look?" I asked Grams as she sat in her chair in the living room doing her crossword puzzle. She looked, and smiled.

"You look very handsome. What's the occasion?"

"Gotta date!" I said as I turned and looked into the little mirror on the wall to check on my hair.

"A date?" Grams asked, so surprised.

"Yeah!"

"With a girl?" I turned and looked at her.

"Of course with a girl."

Grams got up and placed her puzzle on the seat. She stood in front of me, with her hands on her hips, eyes squinted.

"What?"

"Is it that skating girl?"

"No it's not. You don't know her." I turned back to the mirror and straightened my collar.

"Oh, the girl from the library!" she said as if she just answered the million dollar question.

"Yes, Charlotte, and how do you know about her?"

"Your dancing friend told me."

"Vee?"

"Yes, Vanessa."

"Hold up! What were you and Vee, doing talking about, Charlotte?"

"Well, I always thought that Vanessa was the one you liked."

"No, Grams, not like that. You asked me and I told you, we're just friends, besides, she's gay."

"Yeah yeah, they all say that, until one day…"

"… I don't want to hear it!" I interrupted, quickly covering my ears.

"So how did Charlotte come up?"

"Well, to be honest, once I was convinced that she was gay, I kind of asked…" Grams stopped there and looked at me. I stared right back at her, trying to figure out what she might've asked Vee, when suddenly, it hit me!"

"You asked Vee if *I* was gay?" I yelled out, Grams sort of flinched a bit. I stood there, in total disbelief. "What would make you ask such a thing?" My voice was a bit loud, but not exactly yelling.

"Well, for instance, you're still a virgin!"

I covered my face with my hands and shook my head.

"What can possibly make you think I'm a virgin?"

"What can possibly make me think, you're not?"

"Oh, my God!" Grams, I don't believe this.

"Anyway, I don't think you're gay anymore, Vanessa told me about the girl in the library. She said she was real pretty."

"Vanessa never saw her."

"Yes, she did, she said she was curious, so one day she went by the library to see what she looks like."

"Vanessa, did that?"

"She's a good friend, she loves you. You never know. Maybe one day when she's not gay anymore, you two can… "

"Grams, she's been gay her whole life. She's not changing!"

My grandmother shrugged her shoulders and then gave me a kiss and sat back down. "You be careful, okay?"

She opened her crossword book and continued as if we didn't just have the most intense discussion ever.

I looked up at the clock and saw that I had about an hour to get to 53rd street, which was perfect.

"Don't go by that clock." She said.

"What do you mean?" I asked.

"It stopped!"

And at that moment I looked at the second hand and noticed… It wasn't moving.

I now only had less than a half hour.

I grabbed my jacket and dashed out of the door and down the steps. I busted my way out into the street and started jogging toward the train station, when I heard…

"Hey Rey!" I turned, and sure enough it was Junior and his little pudgy pal, Porky following behind.

"Hey guys!" I said slapping them both five. "Look, I'm in a bit of a hurry."

"Going to see a girl?" Junior sang

"Actually I am, and she's gonna be mad if I'm late.

"Are you going to do sex to her? Porky asked in a serious tone.

"What?" I asked, but then waved him off. "Never mind!"

I could tell they were waiting for me to give them some Pizza money.

"Hey guys, listen. I'm really sorry I didn't think I was going to run into you today, so I didn't bring out that much cash." The truth was, I wanted to make sure I had enough for my date with Charlotte.

Junior didn't expect that, as I've always come through for him, even when it was my last.

"It's okay Rey." Junior assured me. But still, I felt like shit.

"But I got you guys tomorrow, okay? I promise! In fact, we're gonna go together and order whole pie, just for us!"

I slapped them both five and crossed the street to get to the station.

These kids were troopers. They stood there at the corner, watching me cross. And though they acted like everything was fine, I know, I let them down.

The chances that these kids ate anything at all today, was probably slim to none, yet they were still appreciative. They were just kids, kids that were dealt a really fucked up hand. They wore the same cloths every day, smelled pretty bad, and basically spent the day begging for change, not for drugs, or alcohol, but for food.

At this point, I wasn't even thinking about Charlotte, and the fact that I'd be getting there about thirty minutes late, oh damn did I fuck up!

When I got across the street, and just before going up the steps to the subway, I turned around and noticed both boys were still there, watching me, like a meal floating out to sea.

When they saw me turn around, they smiled and waved some more. I felt like a real piece of shit. Here I was ready to spend my last dime on a luxurious meal, complete with beverages, and desert. Yet, a measly three dollars would at least get these boys through the night.

I dug down into my pocket and pulled out some singles. The boy's faces lit up, as did mine, and I waved them over. Junior didn't hesitate, he took off on his bike across the street, Porky followed closely behind when suddenly…

CHAPTER 19

Street Kid

I tried to sit calmly in the waiting room of the Metro Hospital, but my prayers were on overdrive as I awaited the doctor to come and let me know how Junior and Porky were doing. The truck driver who plowed into them paced nervously in front of me.

"I swear, they came out of nowhere." He said as he stopped and looked at me with terrified eyes. Little did he know that it was me who made them cross the street, something I will have to live with for the rest of my life.

"I wasn't even going fast." The driver, a middle aged white guy with fiery red hair, continued. A woman came over to us with a clipboard.

"Which of you are related to the boys?" The driver stopped in his tracks.

"Neither one of us." I said. "They live on my block. I was there when they got hit." The woman then looked at the driver who was a complete wreck.

"And I'm the one who hit them!" He sighed and then

collapsed into the chair and cried hysterically.

"Any family here?" she asked me. I shook my head. She looked back over at the driver, who was being real loud and gestured for me to follow her into a tiny office off to the side. I sat down while she closed the door to muffle the echoing cry.

"I'm sorry." She said as she took a seat behind her desk. "I just want to ask you a few questions, if you don't mind?"

"Sure. Anything,"

"Let's start with the chubby one. What's his name?" She asked ready to write it down.

"I just know him as Porky."

"Porky?"

I nodded.

"Do you know his age?"

"No, I don't, maybe nine, ten."

"Do you know his address?"

"Um…" I tried to think, but my head was a mess.

"You said they live on your block?"

"Yeah, but I only see them outside riding their bikes."

"So you don't know any of the parents?" I just kept shaking my head.

"What about the other boy?"

"His name is Junior." I said, watching the woman write down anything I could answer.

"I don't know his last name, but he lives in the building directly across from mine."

YES YES Y'ALL BOOK 2

"Do you know the address?"

I looked up into the air and thought hard. All the years I've lived there, I couldn't even tell you the address of the building directly across from me.

"I'm 1359, so…"

"… he's either 1360 or 1358!" The woman added. I nodded, and she wrote it down.

"His age?"

"Same as Porky's, I guess."

"Do you know anybody from his family?"

"Just his sister, Liz, she lives with him, she's about twenty."

"Parents?"

"One is dead, the other's in jail."

I went back out into the waiting room and took a seat. The driver kept getting up, pacing, sitting and then crying. He was a wreck. I guess I would be too.

The mechanical doors to the entrance parted, and in stepped two Police Officers. They walked straight to the counter and spoke to the receptionist. I saw her nod in our direction.

"Brian Collins?" One of them asked, and the driver turned and looked at them.

"That's me," he replied, raising his hand just high enough to spot him.

"Sir you're under arrest, turn around and put your hands behind your back." Brian was already a mess and he didn't need this right now.

"I didn't mean it, I swear, they rode right out in front of me." He became hysterical, as the officers placed him in cuffs and began to frisk him.

"Officers, I was there, I saw the whole thing, it was a complete accident." They told me to step back, and so I did, watching as they escorted him toward the door. Brian was losing it, giving the officers a hard time on their way to the car. I tried consoling him from a distance, reminding him that it was an accident and that they'll let him go, when one of the officers turned to me with this odd look and said,

"He won't be coming out any time soon, that kid died!"

My heart dropped like a ton of bricks, and the wind was knocked out of me.

I plopped back down into my seat as if my bones had suddenly disintegrated.

I sat there in shock, gasping for air as I watched through the glass doors, the officers forcing Brian into the back seat the squad car.

Out of nowhere, a doctor appeared in front of me, I looked up at him, trying desperately to speak. I could tell, he came with bad news.

My mouth opened, but like a nightmare, nothing came out.

"Are you related to either of the boys?" The doctor asked, waiting for me to finally catch my breath and say something.

"No," I was finally able to push out.

"Do you know them?"

"They live on my block. I was there, I saw the whole thing. Please tell me they're okay."

"Can you get in touch with their parents?"

"I've never seen their parents, those kids practically live on the street."

The doctor took a moment, looking around the waiting room.

"Please, Doctor, just tell me they're okay."

The doctor turned to me, and after giving it another moment, he answered.

"One of them isn't!"

My face fell into my hands, and I began to cry. I couldn't believe what was happening and I dreaded even more to know which kid it was, when the doctor held in front of me, his clipboard, and attached, a photo! My cry was now audible.

"Do you know his name?" The doctor asked, allowing me time to pull it together.

"Junior!" I said, shaking my head in disbelief. "That's all I know."

I placed my hands on top of my head, and took some long deep breaths, but it was no use, again I fell apart. It wasn't only because of Junior's death, but because I felt responsible. Had I just given them the money when they asked, none of this would've happened. But I was being selfish asshole, and it cost a young boy his life. A boy who at just nine years old was already dealt a shitty deck of cards.

There were a million ways that Junior could've died. He was a street kid, living in the ghetto. No parents, a piece of shit sister, who not only allows complete strangers to spend the night, but also lets him stay out till all hours riding his bike. A bike mind you, that doesn't even have brakes!

But none of those are the reason he's dead. He's dead because of me. He crossed the street to get three measly dollars to buy a slice of pizza, because he was hungry and no one to feed him.

Now he's dead. Dead and nobody knows it but me, not even his sister who will probably go days before even wondering where he's at.

I looked back up at the Doctor and asked,

"What about the other?"

Well, to be honest, had it not been for his extra layer of fat, he'd probably be lying right beside his buddy. He's beat up pretty bad, but he'll be okay."

"Can I see him?"

"Unfortunately, because of his age, we would need consent from a parent or guardian."

"Doctor, these kids come from some real shitty homes. It'll be days before anyone will even realize they're missing."

The Doctor looked at me for a moment, and then nodded.

"Room 201" He said.

I thanked him as I got up, and headed toward the elevator.

"What's your name?" he asked as I got to the button and pressed it.

"It's Rey, sir."

"Rey, do me a favor would you."

"Sure," I replied.

"Let's not say anything about his buddy. Not yet."

CHAPTER 20

Room 201

I got to room 201 and turned the knob slowly to open. I stuck my head inside and my heart dropped when I saw this poor little kid, laid out on the hospital bed. He looked what you would imagine someone would look had they gotten hit by a truck. His face was swollen beyond recognition, his head bandaged in the style of an old war hero. The rest of his broken body was in a cast.

I stepped inside and crept quietly toward the chair beside him but stopped in my tracks when I saw him move. I didn't want to wake him. His head turned toward me and I could tell that the two slits in his swollen face were his eyes, and that they were open.

I shouldn't have smiled at him, because when he tried to smile back, he was struck with a pain so horrible that his shriek made my hairs stand.

"Hi Rey." Porky struggled to say. I immediately noticed that baby teeth that once sat inside his pudgy little face were all gone.

"Hey buddy, how are you?" I replied as I approached the side of his bed and placed my hand on his shoulder.

"I'm really sorry, Rey, I didn't mean for this to happen." "It's not your fault, it was an accident."

"How's Jay doing?"

It was the question I was hoping he wouldn't ask, and though I hated to lie to him, I took the doctor's advice and did.

"Junior's hanging in there, Porky. He's just resting up."

"Did he ask about me?"

I looked at him, he was making it more and more difficult, but I played along.

"Oh yeah. He wouldn't stop asking about you."

I could see Porky's smile force itself onto his swollen face. A tear pushed its way out from the corner of his eye, but just sat there, as it couldn't make it over the mound of flesh.

I grabbed a tissue from the table and soaked it up. Porky flinched from the pain, and I whispered an apology.

"Porky, I'm gonna tell you what the doctor told Junior, and this goes for you too. Focus on getting better. If you think too much about him, and he about you, neither of you will get well.

"Okay." He replied in a soft whiny tone.

"Now, Pork, I need to know how to get in touch with your parents."

Porky tightened his eyes shut and his lips began to quiver. It seemed as if that question brought him more pain than what the truck did.

"Come on man, don't cry. You're gonna be fine."

It was no use. He cried anyway. I grabbed more tissue to pat down his eyes, and nose. This boy was in more pain than anyone could imagine. He had something he wanted to tell me, so I waited.

"They kicked me out." He finally said, within a whimper. I didn't want him to have to repeat himself, so I listened closely. "Please Rey, don't tell nobody."

"But why not, Porky, someone can help you."

"They'll send me to a home, and I'll get beat up by the other kids, and the people who work there will do bad things to me."

"Who told you this?" I asked, though I shouldn't have, as it was obvious it came from his parents.

I had to turn around and wipe my own eyes. I didn't know what to do. But whatever it was, had to be done fast.

What's your real name?"

"Victor."

"Victor What?"

"Santiago."

"Where do you live?"

"I live with Jay and his sister."

"No, I mean, where do *you* live? with your parents?"

Porky stayed quiet for a moment, then started to cry. His eyes and mouth sunk into his face, and I can hear him squeal, as he tried to hold it in.

"It's okay buddy…"

"Please Rey, please don't tell them I'm here."

"Your parents are the only ones the doctors will talk too."

"Can you just tell them that you're my parent?"

This kid was terrified for his parents to find out. I could only imagine what might've been going on there. The only good thing, though still an unfortunate, was that Porky would have to stay at the hospital, at least for about a month.

"I'm not gonna tell your parents you're here, okay."

"You promise?" He whined.

"But I can't help you, if I don't at least know where you live."

I wrote down Porky's address, phone number, his parent's names, the school he went to, everything I needed to know in order to try and help him.

"I'm gonna stop by a couple of times a day to check in on you." "Okay."

The doctors will have my number. I'm going to tell them that you're my little brother, okay, and if you need anything, they'll have my number."

"Okay, Rey."

Every time he said okay in that soft pitiful voice, it was like jabbing me in the heart with a fork. I adjusted his cover and left the room. I was about to go ask about Junior when I noticed his sister talking to one of the doctors. She didn't look a bit hurt, in fact all she was asking was for the name of the driver who killed her brother and the company he worked for. It wasn't hard to believe that all she was interested in was the huge payday she was about to receive. Junior was gone and there was nothing at all that I could do for him except pray, but as for Porky? He needed me, he needed me like no one had ever needed me before, and I would do everything in my power to make sure that I'm here for him!

CHAPTER 21

A Better Plan

Not even once had I even thought about Charlotte, and the fact that I stood her up. Not until I stepped outside and inhaled a huge gulp of the night's cool polluted air. But at this point it didn't matter, 'cause all I could think about was poor Junior, just a kid, gone forever. Chances of him even surviving his childhood was already slim, and now even that opportunity was taken away.

I could only hope that he's now in a better place, and that maybe they even have Pizza. I wondered whether this was all in God's plan, but then thought, shit, couldn't he have come up with something better?

I could only imagine what Charlotte is probably thinking. But at this point, it was hard for me to care. I couldn't get either of these boys out of my head, and it was hard to think of who might've had it worst, Junior, or Porky?

I stood across the street from Luciano's and tried to see through the glass, but the glare of the street lamps made it impossible. I crossed the street and walked just under the canopy, and of course Charlotte wasn't there, wishful thinking I guess. I turned and decided to walk down further to 42nd St. And just as I was about to cross I noticed the same company truck that killed Junior. I stared at it until it crossed in front of me and was baffled by the fact, that the driver was the same guy from the accident, Brian Collins. He had his windows open and his radio blasting as he sang along.

Was I seeing things? Or was he back on the road like nothing ever happened?

I had so much going through my mind that I couldn't even remember walking the ten plus blocks. It wasn't until I heard *my* song, Yes Yes Y'all echoing throughout the neighborhood that snapped me out of it.

I stopped in my tracks and looked around, listening closely as I tried to figure out once and for all where exactly the music was coming from. The way it filled the sky it could've been coming from anywhere. For all I knew it could've been traveling for miles and miles. I peeked into a small grocery store just to check the time. 10PM. I couldn't even pinpoint an exact time or day when the music would start. I've heard it as early as 9:00 a.m. noon time, 3:00 p.m. 5:00 p.m. and now at ten.

Last time I was on 48th street, this time I'm on 43rd. This was the oddest thing ever. Who the hell was playing my song? Where was it coming from? And like always, after a few moments of me walking in circles trying to find it, it stopped.

I continued down to 42nd Street and caught the train back uptown. I was a complete mess, my face felt numb, and my hands shook uncontrollably. There were plenty of empty seats on the train, but I chose to stand. I looked at the handful of people who sat scattered within the car. It sort of made me realize that as short as life already is, people still choose to sit as far from one another as they possibly could. The first person who would enter usually sat in the very corner, and the second to enter always sat way at the opposite end. This would continue until people were forced to sit next to one another.

Today it seemed especially sad, maybe because I realized just how precious life is. Did Junior think when he woke up today, that this would be the last day of his life?

This poor kid never had a chance. But who was to blame? We couldn't blame his sister because she had been dealt a similar hand. She was just a bit older. Was it his parents? Society? Me? What possessed me to take the money out once I crossed the street? Was that part of the plan too?

A woman stepped into the train with her son. He looked around the same age as Junior.

He was reading a comic book. I watched how his mother kept him close, her arm wrapped around him. He wore brand new white sneakers. They weren't expensive, but they were new, and clean. He wore regular jeans that she probably bought from a discount store. They too looked new and clean. They became a blur as my eyes began to flood. I didn't want to wipe them. That would attract too much attention, especially from the cute girl who sat directly across from me.

It was my stop and I got off the train, I looked at the girl through the window as the train pulled off. She glanced up and looked right at me, we both smiled at each other. Life is so strange.

I pushed my way through the turnstile and made it down the long steps to the street. My heart nearly exploded when I spotted, glistening under the street lights the small puddle of now dried up blood. The mixture of brain, skin, and bone made the tears that I held in most of the ride shoot from my eyes. I looked around in hopes that no one was near, because I had to let it out. I kept reliving the moment I stood there, digging deep in my pockets, just to pull out a few bucks so that these two boys can put a little something in their stomachs.

I wanted to so bad to bash my head against the wall. I felt so guilty. I even wished that it had been me instead. Two little boys, one beat up by a truck driving just 40 miles an hour. Multiple bones broken, cuts and scrapes. The pain that he was feeling right now was probably worse than any pain I would ever feel. And as for Junior? Shit, If God gave me a choice, I'd trade places with him right now!

I would've never in my wildest dreams thought that when I woke us this morning, that I would be going through this. This was supposed to be a special day. The day that I finally got to go out with,

"Oh shit... Charlotte!"

CHAPTER 22

My Fault

"Okay ladies that's it for today!" Princess announced at the end of our rehearsal. I'd been in a zone all day, and it was pretty obvious, however I hadn't said anything to anyone about the accident because I knew I would have a hard time not blaming myself. Princess gave me a funny look as I got up off the floor. He sort of rolled his eyes at me before heading into his office.

Everyone could tell something was wrong, but no one asked. I noticed Vanessa was taking her time changing, timing it with mine. The locker room cleared out and it was just the two of us. She grabbed her things and walked over to me as I pulled my shirt down over my head.

"You knew him didn't you?" She asked. I looked her way. "How did you hear about it?"

"Obviously you don't read the Newspaper."

I looked at her and shook my head, and then grabbed my things. It was late and most of the people had gone home already. I told her what had happened as we walked up to the spiral staircase. Then I stopped and looked at her.

"It was my fault, Vee."

"Come on Rey, you can't blame yourself."

"But I could. He crossed the street to get money from me, for pizza!" I couldn't even look her in the eyes. I dropped my head and continued.

"That was our thing. He sort of looked up to me, was always excited when he saw me. We would chit chat a bit, and then I'd give him a couple of bucks, for Pizza. That boy loved Pizza." I smiled a bit, and so did Vanessa.

"A few months ago he started hanging out with this other boy, Porky.

"Porky?"

"Well... Victor. However Junior called him Porky, for obvious reasons of course."

"The papers mentioned another, in pretty bad shape, huh?"

"If it wasn't for his size, I think he'd be..."

I couldn't even say it, but Vee knew what I meant.

"The two dollars I usually gave him, now turned to five, so that they can each have a slice, and a drink." I had to stop for a moment and keep it together. "Just sticking my hand in my pocket, made them lick their lips." Vee and I both pushed out a much needed laugh.

"You were looking out for them, Rey. That was a beautiful thing for you to do. Who does that? I bet Junior is looking down, trying to tell you that it isn't your fault!"

I looked at my dear friend, she was really special, and I was so lucky to have her in my life.

"Let me get out of here, I'm gonna stop by the hospital to check up on Porky."

"Can I come?" Vee asked.

"To the hospital?" she nodded.

"You don't have to do that, Vee, I appreciate it, but…"

"How many people do you think have come to visit him since he's been there?

We headed upstairs, and there was Sal, sitting in the lobby reading the paper.

He stood up as we entered the room and tossed the paper down on the table. It was turned to the story about Junior.

"Hey Sal."

"Hey, how you kid's doing? I read about the boys from your block, I remember them, really sorry."

"Thanks. We're actually gonna take a ride over to the hospital to see Porky."

"Porky?" Sal asked.

"Yeah, I know, but that's what they call him." Sal shrugged and smiled.

"Look, why don't I drive you two there?"

"But I have my car here." Vanessa added.

"That's fine, we'll go to the hospital, hang out with the kid for a bit and then I'll bring you back to get your car."

I looked at Vee, and she was cool with it.

CHAPTER 23

Puffy Cheeks

As we entered the hospital, Sal ran ahead and stopped the woman from closing up the gift shop. It took a little convincing as she was done for the day, but she reopened just for him. We bought it all, flowers, teddy bears, and balloons, we made reopening well worth it.

We stopped in front of room 201, as I turned to Vee and Sal. Guys, remember, he doesn't know anything about Junior. They both nodded, and we entered.

And there he was, like a big chubby baby. His huge mop of curly brown hair, matted flat in the back. His extra puffy cheeks, continued to allow him only slits to see through, and had his lips not be as swollen as they were, his mouth too would've disappeared into his face.

You could tell that he was waiting for my visit, because the minute he heard the door open, he turned his head.

"Hi Rey!" he said. The sound of his sweet voice was enough to make you wanna run out of the room crying. You could tell he was still in a lot of pain, though he didn't complain.

"Hey buddy, how are you?" I asked as we all approached his bed.

"Who are they Rey?" He asked, seeming a bit nervous.

Sal and Vee both smiled.

These are my friends, Porky. I told them what happened and they wanted to come and meet you."

"Hi Porky, my name is Vanessa." She said, gently touching his hand.

"And I'm Sal, how you doing, kid?"

Porky forced on a painful smile, and Vee caught a glimpse of his broken teeth.

"Look buddy, what we brought you, I said as Vee held up the flowers, and Sal the Teddy Bear, and balloons.

"Ouch." He cried out when his smile stretched further than it should have.

Vee, took the gifts and decorated the small table across from his bed, so that it's easy for him to see.

We stayed about an hour, talking and joking. Sal was performing magic tricks, and Porky was loving every minute of it. The only sad part was whenever he asked about Junior, everyone would look at me, which made me feel even worse as I had no choice but to lie, at least until he was better.

It was time to go, and I tried to ignore the tiny tear drop that pushed its way over his cheek. Vanessa however, grabbed a tissue, and wiped it. We said goodbye, and Vanessa leaned over and gave him a kiss, I truly believed that if nothing else made his night, that sure did. God only knows when the last time anyone ever kissed this kid, let alone kissed him goodnight.

On our way out of the hospital, Sal asked.

"So, what ever happened to the driver?"

"The police came and arrested him, made this big scene in the hospital. The man cried and pleaded for his innocence. I actually felt bad for him, though I now think he might've been going a bit too fast.

"So he's in jail?"

"That's what I thought."

"What do you mean?" Vanessa asked.

"Well, just a few hours after he got arrested, I spotted him driving down 8th Ave."

"You sure it was him?"

"Whiter than white, hair redder than red…. Yeah, I'm sure! Same exact truck too, going about the same speed he was going when he hit the boys."

"Did you catch his name?" Sal asked.

"I think it was Brian."

"What about the truck?"

"Umm, I really wasn't paying it much mind, I think it had a treasure chess or something on it."

"Treasures in Transit?" Sal asked, but I wasn't sure.

Sal knew a lot of people, and all I could think was, this guy was about to lose his job.

CHAPTER 24

Apology Not Accepted

Do you think she's even gonna talk to me?" I asked Vanessa as we sat in her car across from the library.

"Of course she is. You didn't just stand her up for no reason."

Vanessa was right, but wow, the timing couldn't have been any worst. I finally talked Charlotte into a date, and then stand her up. I stared at the front entrance and took a deep breath, and then I got out the car.

"So look." I said, leaning back into the car. "Don't go anywhere until I come out. If you see me do this," and with my fingers I ran them across the top of my forehead. "That means I'm good and you can leave."

"Wait hold up. If you do what? Vanessa asked with a laugh.

"This!" and again I ran my fingers across the top of my forehead. Vanessa was laughing hysterically.

"Come on, Vee, this is Serious."

"Like, why that?" She asked.

"What do you mean?"

"This shit," she said, mimicking my signal. "You can't just give me like a thumbs up or something?"

"Nah, she'll see that, besides I don't sweat, so that's not something I usually do."

"Look, Rey, what's the big deal? I gave you a lift."

"You're a girl, I don't want her to think anything, please, just go along with it."

"Okay, but it's no wonder you're single, Rey. You do some corny-ass shit!"

I waved her off and made my way across the street and up the library steps.

Charlotte spotted me as soon as I stepped in, her eyes pierced right through me, making it more than obvious that she was pissed. I should've thought about what to say before I came in here, but it was too late.

Had I not liked Charlotte as much as I did, I probably wouldn't have been so nervous. I could feel my heart rate increase with every step I took toward the counter, and by the time I got there, I could've sworn that she'd be able to hear it.

My mouth opened, and just as I was about to apologize, she put her finger up to her lips, and while staring me dead in my eyes, said.

"Seeing you, disgust me... Hearing you will make me throw up. So do me a favor and get the hell out of here before I embarrass us both!"

I closed my mouth, and noticed the lady beside me was listening. I then took a couple of steps back. Turned and left.

I stood outside the Library, trying to catch my breath, and without realizing it I wiped my forehead, then watched as Vanessa drove off.

"No no no, Vee!" I yelled out as I dashed down the steps, but it was too late… she was gone!

"Fuck!" I yelled to myself, and then started walking uptown toward 42nd to catch the train, because I needed a little time to think. I walked past a newspaper stand and was sickened even more by the amount of Nemesis memorabilia displayed. From magazine covers and Posters, to the ugliest fucking Bobble Head I had ever seen in my life.

This was crazy. This guy was becoming Rap's Superhero, while my life seemed to be stuck in quicksand.

Half of me couldn't wait for everything to finally take off, but the other half of me continued to question whether or not any of this was even a good idea. Why did he blow up practically overnight, while I continued to struggle?

I regretted so much that I didn't agree to write for him, I at least would've been getting a nice paycheck. I should've known just by the name, Funky Junky that this was some corny white boy shit. I was so tired of it. Mr. D had me running around looking like a fucking clown, rapping some corny ass lyrics that he wrote himself, wearing dresses and this stupid hair style, that made people stare no matter where I was. What was I thinking?

How was I even sure that Nemesis wasn't somehow a part of this whole scheme? I couldn't put anything like that past Mr. D, he could be an evil genius for all I know, and this could easily have been his plan from the start.

I felt myself picking up speed, my heart pounding inside my chest. What the fuck was going on? Who was I? What was happening to me? Who are all these people around me? Mr. D, Sal, Quenepa, Roller Girl, even Vanessa. I could see Mr. D doing something like this. Going all out and changing my world, just so it doesn't interfere with his.

I grabbed on to the pole of the stop sign at the corner and shut my eyes tight. I felt like I was about to pass out, and everything was starting to spin. I wrapped myself around the pole even more and took deep breaths trying to gather myself. Finally, the sky stopped spinning, and the air became cool again. I took a few more breaths before letting go of the pole. I was a bit scared to walk, so I just waited a few moments until finally, I felt better, and took a step into the street, when a car skidded beside me honking the horn like a maniac. I turned and to my surprise it was Vanessa, and she was laughing hysterically.

"I'm sorry, I just couldn't resist it!" She yelled out her window, referring to her scaring the shit out of me.

"What are you doing here?" I asked, and that's when she held up my wallet. I patted my pockets and realized that it was in fact mine, so I took it.

"You left it on the seat."

"Thanks."

"Where's your girlfriend?" She asked. I just shook my head. Vanessa's smile faded.

CHAPTER 25

Bigger Than The Beatles

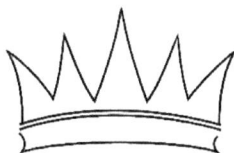

I opened the door and stuck my head in.

"You wanted to see me?" I asked. Mr. D was on the phone and waved me in with a huge welcoming smile. He gestured for me to close the door and then yessed the person he was talking to over the phone. I entered the office, and headed straight to one of his bar stools, passing up on the beanbags.

As I sat there, my eyes explored his office for any new items that Mr. D might've picked up. He was huge collector of strange and unusual things, so-called conversation pieces that would have you conversing for years.

And there it was! Sitting on a shelf along with a few other new items he picked up from God knows where. This one, weirder than all the rest. I got up and walked over for a closer look. It seemed to be some kind of the skeleton hand, human I'm sure. It was professionally mounted on a beautiful mahogany stand with a glass cover, though the question I had when I saw it was, what the fuck was it holding?

It looked like a piece of paper. Rolled up, like maybe a note or something. That alone made the hand even much more interesting.

"King, what's up my man!" Mr. D said as he walked over to me and shook my shoulder. It's been a rough couple of days, so I just sort of shook my head.

"Hey, I heard about your little friends, I'm really sorry about that."

I knew it had to be Sal that told him, but that was fine, it saved me from having to go into any detail.

"If there's anything you need, you let me know, okay?"

"Thank you." I replied.

"So check this out." He began. "We're ready to drop this song."

"Drop it?" I asked.

"Release it, King."

"Oh, okay, you had me a little worried there for a moment. "Your grandmother was right, you are a bit square."

"My grandmother told you that?"

"It's okay though, square is good. But never mind that. We're about to launch the biggest thing since The Beatles. In fact, this is gonna be bigger than the Beatles!"

"The Beatles?"

"Yeah, the Beatles."

"So people actually liked them?"

Mr. D looked at me like I had two heads.

"King, The Beatles were huge man, seriously huge!"

"I just never got into them… White boy shit, no offense!"

"Well, buddy, keep in mind, you can't excel in something in which you don't know its history."

I don't normally disagree with Mr. D, as I've learned over the last few months, that he knows a lot of shit, but this time I didn't agree with his theory.

"As much as I hate to even bring up what's his face." I began.

"I'm pretty sure he didn't have to learn about The Beatles, and look how big he's become."

"You're talking about Nemesis?" Mr. D asked. I nodded. "Like I said. you can't excel in something, unless you know its history."

I was trying to figure out what Mr. D was trying to say, but I wasn't connecting. I watched as he went over to his desk, picked up an article that looked like it was clipped out of a newspaper and brought it over to me.

"What's this?" I asked as I took the article.

"Read it," he said with a gesture. I took a moment, and then finally looked at it, realizing that it was the same exact article that Grams was trying to get me to read.

"It's an interview of Nemesis, I heard about it."

"That's right, and I think you should read it."

I'm sure it's no different than any of the others he's done."

"Have you ever read any of them?" Mr. D asked. I looked at him for a moment, and then answered.

"Nope."

"I didn't think so."

"But what does this have to do…"

"Read it!" He said, and then took a seat beside me.

I exhaled like a kid being told to take a bath, and then looked down at the article.

It took a minute for me to focus, and though the article was nearly an entire page, I ended up reading it in no time.

"And?" Mr. D asked when I handed it back to him.

"And what?"

"What did you get from it?"

"Besides him being an arrogant asshole? Not much!" Mr. D just looked at me, disappointment hanging from his face.

"That's not arrogance, King, it's confidence."

"Can we get to the point 'cause I really don't like that dude.

"You don't like him because you feel he took your spot over at Frontline!"

"I don't know what you're talking about!"

"But it wasn't your spot to be taken. You had the same opportunity that he did. The difference was… He went for his!"

"How do you know all of this?"

"I pay attention!"

I exhaled like a real brat. I could tell Mr. D was becoming annoyed.

"If you one day ever decide to read it, you'll learn that what Nemesis has, didn't come easy.

He got the spot that he rightfully deserved. He's a college graduate, King, with a Masters in Music. You cannot get a Masters in Music without knowing Music History, Music Theory, and every other boring ass subject that has to do with music.

He's a classically trained Pianist, and can play various instruments, not to mention he can read and write notation. So whatever you or anyone else has to say about this guy, sorry, he deserves what he's getting. He's put in the work. Now if you ever run into him, ask him about The Beatles. I bet he can tell you anything you wanna know."

I was silent, nothing to say. I read the interview, but I guess my mind only registered what it wanted to. When will I learn not to argue with Mr. D, in fact, this argument was a bad one, as it exposed how truly inferior I was to this guy. Mr. D was right. He did deserve this and probably more. How would I even surpass the success he was currently experiencing? Did I just help him realize the bad investment her made?

I looked at the boss man, again humbled. His eyes softened a bit. I guess he's been wanting to have this talk with me for some time now, and he finally got the chance.

"King, Sept 3rd is Labor Day. We're releasing your video along with the song. Two weeks after that, you will be available for performances."

"That's less than a month away."

"I already spoke with Princess, he promised you'd be

ready."

I looked at Mr. D and nodded, then watched as the doubt I thought might've been growing on him, vanish, and his smile widening, the way I was so used to seeing it.

A new confidence suddenly glistened from his eyes, and seemed to be telling me, that regardless of the skills, and talents that Nemesis might've possessed, I will still in fact... Be King!

CHAPTER 26

Revolving Doors

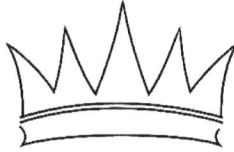

With so much happening around me, I still couldn't get over Charlotte. I never even had a chance to explain what happened. I decided to give her another try and headed for the Library.

I pushed my way through the huge revolving door, and immediately our eyes met, except hers added to it, a roll. I walked over to the counter and just as I got there she stepped away and old Ms. Crumble stepped forward.

"How can I help you?" She asked. I didn't hear her at first as I was focused on Charlotte, who had gone over to the book cart with some books.

I was looking at the Librarian yet she still hadn't registered.

"Hello!" She said, snapping me out of my weird trance.

"I'm sorry. Do you have any books on The Beatles?"

"The band, or the insect?"

"Um, the band!"

"Follow me." She said as she made her way out from behind the counter.

I followed the old woman to the back where she pointed to a entire shelf full of books on The Beatles.

"If you have any questions, I'll be in the front."

I watched as the stereotypical librarian turned and walked away. I had no real desire to read about The Beatles, or any other artist for that matter. In fact, I hated to read, I found it boring as hell. From where I stood, I could clearly see the front counter, as well as Charlotte. She didn't look at me once. I took my time, grabbing books from the shelf and opening them, only to pretend to read, while instead, I stared over toward the front where Charlotte stayed busy.

The Librarian scared me when she popped out of nowhere.

"Did you find what you were looking for?" She asked, and at that moment I held up the book that was in my hands and nodded. "Well come on and I'll check you out."

I watched as the woman walked off and I just closed the book and followed. I had no idea what I had in my hand, this just happened to be the one I had at the moment.

She took the book from me from over the counter and read the title.

"This is a 1st Edition." She said as she pulled out the index card from the back and stamped it. I had no idea what the hell she was talking about.

"Is that a good thing?" I asked.

"Well it's in its purest form. If you want to really learn

about The Beatles, you made a good choice." She handed me back my library card, along with the book.

"You have it for three weeks. Next!"

I stepped away from the counter and looked at the book again. It was pretty thick, had to be at least 500 pages.

"Beatles, The Authorized Biography 1st Edition. By Hunter Davis" I said to myself.

The most I've ever read was a Right On Magazine. A book this size, if I really did decide to read it, would definitely take me more than three weeks. Three months might be more like it. Maybe even three years.

I looked back over at the counter and caught Charlotte staring at me, but then she quickly turned away, and so I left.

CHAPTER 27

Visiting Porky

It was a nice day, and the sun would be setting in a couple of hours. I decided to walk up to the hospital, to check in on Porky. While there I would also check up on the status of Junior, find out where his funeral might be, or if they'll be one at all.

I still couldn't believe this kid was dead.

I got to the hospital and signed in to see Porky. "Excuse me, the receptionist asked. Are you a relative?"

"Yes ma'am, he's my little cousin." I said, trying to think quickly.

"And what's your name?" she asked, looking in the log book.

"Reynaldo Rosario."

"Do you think you can put us in touch with his parents?"

"You mean to tell me, they haven't even been here?"

"Not at all, according to this, just you, and a couple of people that came with you."

"Yeah, and those were just friends of mine. I could go by their house tonight."

"Would you please? I mean, it doesn't make any sense. I called Child Services, but I guess as long as he's in here, they're not too concerned." I nodded, and thanked her, but before walking off I asked.

"By the way, the other boy, that was in the accident?"

"Yeah, poor thing," The receptionist responded.

"Do you know what's going on with him?

"Supposedly his only living relative is a sister, and she refused to deal with any of this."

"What?"

"I know."

"So what happens now?"

"It already happened … He was cremated!"

My head began to spin. This poor kid couldn't live a decent life, nor die a decent death. I was furious, had I known his sister would've done this I would've stepped up.

I continued to the elevator and took it up to Porky's floor. As I approached his room, a nurse stepped out.

"Hi." I said to her. She placed her finger up to her lips.

"He just fell asleep. Poor child's been in pain all day."

"Can I go in and see him?" The nurse knew I was the only one coming to see him, so she smiled and stepped aside.

I walked in, and as always, a knot began to develop in my throat. This poor kid can't even get his parents to come see him. What if *I* wasn't around?

I took a seat over on the yellow leather lounge chair beside his bed. I sat back, and got comfortable. There wasn't even a TV in his room. All I could do was stare at the pale green walls.

I reached into the bag and pulled out my book on The Beatles and decided to give it a whirl. I started first by looking for pictures, there were several, however, I didn't know anything about the group, so the people in it were strangers to me.

After reading all of the captions under the photos, reading the back and inside cover, I turned to the first page of the book, and began...

CHAPTER 28

The Box

"Hi Rey," Porky said, waking me up. I looked around, as I had forgotten where I was. I sat up and rubbed my eyes knocking my book onto the floor. I picked it up and placed it on the seat when I stood up.

"Hey Buddy!" I said, pleased to see Porky more responsive than usual. It had been a week since the accident, and already most of the bruises on his face were gone as was the swelling. "How you feel?" I asked as I placed my hand on his shoulder.

"Hungry!" He replied, and I laughed.

"Well, that's good to hear, what about some?"

"Yeah!" He replied excitedly.

"No!" The Nurse said as she walked into the room to check on Porky."

"I figured he was hungry..."

"He can't eat any junk yet. We need to make sure his body is getting the right nutrients so that it can heal itself."

The Nurse continued as she stuck a thermometer in his mouth while wrapping his arm to take his pressure.

"Sorry man." I told him, watching as his smile suddenly flipped upside down.

"He's doing really well." The Nurse said as she continued to check his vitals. "It's so sad, that the other boy didn't make it." Porky's eyes shot up to the nurse, his eyes brows arched high. I looked at the nurse with wide eyes as if to say, you dumb bitch! But she didn't catch it.

Porky looked at me, dropping the thermometer from his mouth.

"Who's she talking about, Rey?" he asked in his thin whiny voice. The Nurse looked at me, finally realizing that she done fucked up.

"I'm so sorry." She said to me, before rushing out of the room. I turned and looked at Porky, trying to figure out how to tell him that his best friend was dead. But he knew already, and his eyes started to flood and his lips quivered. Porky dropped his head back down onto the pillow and pulled the covers over his head, and cried.

There wasn't anything I could do about it, but just let him cry. I grabbed my book, and left him alone to weep for his buddy. As I left the room I ran into the Nurse who had opened her mouth.

"I don't know what to say." She said apologetically. And though it was a careless move, she did save me from having to do it.

"He was gonna find out eventually." Was all I could tell

her, before continuing toward the elevator.

I inhaled the cool night air as I stepped out of the hospital and over to a pay phone and decided to let Grams know where I was.

"Don't worry about it Grams, I'll grab something... I will... Okay, love you too!"

I hung up and was about to head back when suddenly I heard Yes Yes Y'all echoing across the sky. This was crazy. I was way up town and could hear it. Now wasn't the time to go chasing it, as Porky was expecting me back up. Instead I decided to take a seat on a bench, and just listen.

As much as I hate to admit it, the music was in fact beautiful, not to mention, difficult to tell whether I was listening to it live, or was it a recording?

The vocals were smooth and melodic. It was nothing compared to the way I would rap it, but it was an interesting version. How I wanted so bad to find out where it was coming from, who was singing it, playing it. How did they get it, what were their intentions?

A bus pulled up in front of me and opened its door. I shook my head at the driver, and with an attitude he pulled closed the door and drove off. Once the bus was gone, I noticed... so was the music!

I headed back into the hospital and up to Porky's room. I stuck my head inside and saw him just sitting there, staring out at nothing. I walked in and sat back down in the yellow lounge chair which faced him. We both sat there, silent, just thinking.

"He was my best friend." Porky finally said, still staring into space. "We said that when we grew up, we were going to have a Pizza store. He wanted to name it, Junior's, I didn't mind.

"What do I do now, Rey?" Porky asked his eyes sadder than any eyes I'd ever seen. I didn't want to baby him so I just sat there and watched.

"I don't even know what happened to my bike."

Last time I saw their bikes, they lay mangled in the middle of the street, a memory that will haunt me for the rest of my life.

"Junior built my bike for me." Porky said. This I didn't know, but was impressed when I heard. He became silent again, and then turned to me.

"Did you get to see him, before…" he didn't want to say the word. I shook my head. "They wouldn't let me in. He was a fighter I heard. He tried to hang in there. He really did.

The door to the room opened and the Nurse who had accidentally revealed Junior's death stuck her head in.

"Can I come in?" She asked. I nodded. "I just wanted to say how sorry…"

"…It's okay miss." Porky said, in a soft and soothing tone. Not only did he look like a Cherub, he was seriously beginning to sound like one.

"I was there when he passed on." Porky looked at me, and then back at the nurse. He wanted me to pass a message to his best friend. I'm trying to remember the name he called him, started with a P.

"Porky!" he yelled out all excited.

"Yes! That's it, Porky.

"That's me!" he said with a huge smile.

"Well, Porky, he wanted me to tell you that he thought of you like a little brother, and then he told me to tell you that everything in the Magic Box is now yours."

"The Magic Box?" I asked, confused about what was going on.

"The Magic Box, Rey! It's where me a Junior keep all the cool things we find."

At first I thought the nurse was making this all up, but apparently, she wasn't!

CHAPTER 29

Five Dollars

It's been a few days now, and though I have the release of my record coming up, the only thing I could think of is Porky, his pudgy face and red cheeks. His curly bed matted hair, and his smile filled with broken baby teeth. I never had a little brother, but if I did, I assume, this is how I would feel.

It was bad the way Porky had to hear about his buddy, but I was glad that part was over.

Now his mind and heart could heal along with his body.

As I turned the corner of my block I immediately noticed a girl walking with a bike. As I got closer, she looked at me, and I realized, it was Liz, Junior's sister. She saw me, but acted as though she didn't. I couldn't blame her though, she looked cracked out, I wouldn't want to see anyone either.

She was always an odd girl, even when she was younger. Grams use to see her in the streets at 2:00 a.m., when the girl was no more than Junior's age.

I watched as she dropped the bike off at the trash, and then turned and walked away. It was Junior's bike, and the tires were both severely twisted. I never really looked at it before, as Junior was always on it. But it was a really nice looking bike. It was a Huffy, rebuilt from pieces he'd gathered from the garbage of the neighborhood buildings. It had a sort of chopper look to it, with the extended front fork. The tire in the back was thicker and bigger than the one on the front. It had a back bar that came up to the base of Junior's neck, and a five speed stick shift on the body. The only thing it didn't have, were breaks!

I watched as Liz disappeared inside her building, and then went over to the garbage.

It took a moment to decide before taking hold of the bike and pulling it from the trash.

The tires were so badly twisted that I just picked up the whole thing and was about to carry it across the street when I heard someone yell out.

"Hey, leave that alone!"

I turned, and it was Liz, hurrying down the stoop. I placed the bike down and waited until she got to me.

"You threw it out!" I told her as she came up to me and grabbed hold of the handlebar.

"No I didn't." She replied.

"You just put it in the garbage, I saw you!"

"You saw me put it *next* to the garbage. That's my brother's bike." She spoke a mile a minute but only looked into my eyes once. She kept swinging her body around, her arms following along.

"Listen, I know what happened to your brother." Liz

remained quiet a second, then responded.

"I told him don't be riding in the streets."

That remark made me wanna punch this bitch dead in her face.

"Give me five dollars." She suddenly blurted out. Her eyes looking out into God knows where.

"What?" I asked

"Give me five dollars and I'll give you the bike." She said, as she reached down and picked up a white cigarette butt, looked at it and then tossed it back down. I pulled five dollars from my wallet and gave it to her. She let go of the bike.

"For another five I'll suck your dick!" She then said, still not making any eye contact with me.

I didn't even answer her. I just took the bike and left.

CHAPTER 30

Baby Giant

Grams was sitting on the couch doing her crosswords when I came in. I stood the bike against the wall, and then went over and gave her a kiss.

"Why are you bringing that garbage in here?" She asked, gesturing to what looked like just that.

"Remember the boy I told you about that…"

"Ay Dios," she said, making the sign of the cross. "what are you doing with it?"

"I don't know, his sister threw it in the garbage. I just couldn't…"

The horror on Gram's face as stood there staring at the mangled bike was indescribable.

"Bendito," she sobbed. She closed her eyes and said a quick prayer. "How's the other boy?" She asked as I passed her a tissue.

"He's hanging in there. Today he found out about his friend."

"Poor baby."

"He took it better than I expected."

"It hasn't hit him yet." She assured me.

"You think so?"

"I know so." Grams continued, he's still in shock about the whole situation. But once he's out of there, back in the streets, that's when he's really going to feel it."

"Back in the streets, Wow." I replied. "Junior was a real street kid, tough, knew how to get around. Porky on the other hand… I'm not so sure."

"And still no word from his parents?"

"Nothing."

"Look Mijo, you can only do so much for him, so you have to let the system step in and do what they think is best."

Grams came over and gave me another kiss.

"You have a special heart, mijo," she said. "Just pray for him. He's going to be okay." I looked at Grams and nodded. "I'm going to bed now."

"Okay, bendicion," I said, but I don't think she heard me, and watched as she slowly headed to her room.

CHAPTER 31

Good Clay

"Lights dim, and… end!" Princess said as he directed the rehearsal of our full performance. We all stopped out of breath as Mr. D, and a few others from the office applauded. I looked at Quenepa and patted him on the back, and then turned around and applauded the dancers. Vanessa looked at me and smiled.

Mr. D stood up and walked over to us as he continued to applaud. He gave Princess a nod requesting permission to address his class, Princess smiled and stepped back. Mr. D took his time to look and smile at each and every one of us, his way of giving us our individual props before addressing us as a whole.

"Okay everyone, take a seat," he said, gesturing for us to sit on the floor, and that we gladly did, as we were exhausted.

"First off, I have to thank Princess for once again, a spectacular job." Mr. D applauded, and we all followed.

Though he could be a dick at times, he was without doubt great at what he did, and it showed in our performance.

"You guys, and girls who have been dancing since you were probably infants." Everyone laughed. "Are so special and so incredible, which is why you were chosen for this project. We auditioned at least a thousand dancers, and you were it! We didn't do second and third call backs, we met you, spoke to you, and then watched you dance. A few of you fumbled during your audition and probably kicked yourself all the way home." Emerald raised his hand as did another at the back of the room. Everyone laughed.

"But we called you to join us, because we saw in you more than just great dancers. We saw magic, a magic that we would've never been able to develop. Nurture, Maybe! Develop? No way! That had to come from inside you, and now we want you to take that magic, and perfect it.

"Quenepa!" He said, now addressing him directly. You were successful in the streets, I know, I watched you. That might've been something the streets perfected, but it wasn't something the streets developed. That was already in you, yes, that same magic I spoke in regards to them.

There are plenty of kids in the street, surviving, due to their hustle. But there was always something special about you. Where this opportunity leads you, none of us knows, but if you stay open to it, nurture it, and protect it, it will take you very far in life. Just like a bird must leave the safety of its nest in order for it to learn to fly, you too must leave the nest of the streets." I looked over at Quenepa, his eyes were flooded, yet his macho-ism wouldn't allow him to wipe'em.

"King!" shouted Mr. D! I immediately turned to him and he smiled. "I don't think that even *you* can see the magic that *I* see in you. Or that anyone sees in you for that matter." I looked at him and slightly shook my head. "A sculpture cannot be made out of ordinary clay. You understand what I mean by that?" I gave it a moment, and then nodded. "It has to be the right clay, because the better the clay, the better the sculpture, and that's what my talent is, finding the right clay. Trust me, it's taken me a long time to learn how to decipher between the good clay, and shit that looks like clay." We all laughed, including Princess who just stood back with his arms across his narrow chest.

"You see, good clay is rare, rich and thick. You can feel the power of it when you squeeze it. It obeys your commands without question, and molds to whatever your hands direct. Good clay even smells good.

"Now shitty clay!" again everyone started to laugh "Is nothing but waste. It is the stuff the body excretes after it took from it all the good stuff. It's light and airy, sometimes even brittle. You can try and mold it, but no matter what, once you're done it's still going to look like shit. Oh, and did I mention the smell?" Every one of us busted out laughing. Even Princess couldn't contain himself any longer.

"You were made from the good clay, King, I want you to know this. Your abilities are limitless, and what you will give to your audience will be like no other. Perfection will become your trademark, it is for what you will mostly be known, and therefore perfection is what you must always seek." I nodded, as did others around the room.

If *she* screws up," Mr. D continued, pointing at Lily. "The headline will read KING SCREWS UP! You guys are all in for one hell of a ride. Work hard, rest hard, eat right, stay away from drugs, alcohol, boys, girls… whatever you're into, and you will all set yourselves up for life!" We all looked around at each other.

"I want to introduce you all to someone who is going to be extremely important to you in just a couple of weeks. He's worked for some of the biggest booking agencies in the country and abroad, he left all of that to focus on just one act, and that is you!" Mr. D pointed directly at me.

Ladies and gentlemen, let's welcome Mr. David Donovan!" We all applauded as this pretty young energetic looking fella stood and walked over.

"I am totally excited." David said in his English accent. "I have been a Booking Agent for nearly 20 years. I am 44 years old in case any of you are wondering. I've worked with the best of the best. I have booked, managed and organized some of the biggest concerts throughout the world. I was still in my twenties when I made my first million, and I've added a million to my net worth every year since. I am not telling you this to brag, I am telling you this so you will know that making money was not the key factor in me taking on this position."

This guy was just as impressive as Mr. D was. His charisma and drive were incredible.

Just hearing him speak was so inspiring, that it made his job sound like the best job in the world.

"I have placed to the side a roster of over two hundred artists, so that I may focus on you and you alone. So far from what I can see, my decision was a good one, but rehearsal and the real thing are two different animals, so none of us know for sure what really to expect until you are at The Coliseum in front of twenty-five thousand people." We all looked at him, and then at one another.

"I say the Coliseum because that will be your first performance, and yes, it will be in front of twenty five thousand people!" We all got excited. David waited till we settled down.

"Now the reason I'm telling you all this, is because whatever it is you are doing now, you must triple it. You will have three days off before the show to recoup, rest and heal, but once you are done at the coliseum, don't think it's over, because from there you will head out to California and will be hitting just about every city in that great state." I raised my hand, and David nodded to me.

"First off, Mr. Donovan…"

"Please, save the Mr. For this guy." He said Thumbing toward Mr. D. David will work just fine.

"I'm sorry. David. Why are we doing our first show at the Coliseum?"

"Well, for a couple of reasons. First off… its home for most, if not all of you. Am I right?" We all nodded. "We don't want the world to see you before your friends and family, so they're all invited, just have your list in to me by next week. Secondly, how many of you have ever flown to the West Coast?" Only Lily and Jini raised her hand.

"San Francisco?" He asked, and sure enough, she nodded. "Six hour flight with a three hour time change will add to an already stressful event. I want you all to at least be comfortable on stage and have a good feeling. All the shows will be more or less the same, slight changes in stage size, but other than that, you do one, you do them all.

I have an entire year already booked for you, and it will begin two weeks after the release of the video, which is actually in two weeks and three days.

Your schedules must be cleared. Don't plan anything. No birthday parties, weddings or funerals. In order for this to be successful, it will have to take precedence over everything else. Anyone who cannot commit needs to stand up right now, and exit this room. Everyone looked at each other, then suddenly we heard movement happening toward the back, it was one of the male dancers, standing up and gathering his things. We all turned and looked at him. His eyes were flooded, and we waited for him to speak.

"My mother's got cancer," was how he began. He wiped his eyes, and continued on, "she only has a couple of months left, and I need to be with her."

David nodded, and the dancer got up and went into the dressing room to empty out his locker.

"Anyone else?" David asked. Everyone looked around at each other, except me, I couldn't get that dancer out of my mind.

Here's someone who worked probably all of his life just to get where he's at, and now he has to let it all go, and though I understood, and would've done the same. It didn't seem fair.

"Can we fill his spot?" David turned and asked Princess.

"Not a problem" Princess assured him.

"So!" David began looking out at us. "Come tomorrow, during practice, start to envision twenty five thousand people, watching you perform. If any of you have any questions, Mr. D blessed me with a fabulous corner office, feel free to come by. However, if you see me on the phone... Come back at another time!"

David turned and gave Princess back the floor. He then waved goodbye as he and Mr. D left the room.

"Okay people, pack it in." Princess said. We all got up and headed to the dressing room when out walked the dancer who was going home to be with his mother.

Everyone went up and hugged him, but it was too much, and so he broke away and rushed across the room and out the door. I chased after him.

"Excuse me!" I called out. He stopped and turned to me. "I'm really sorry..." he began to say, but I cut him off.

"...It's okay man look, go take care of mother, for as long as she needs you, and whenever you feel you're ready to come back, I don't care how long it takes, you come back, your spot will be waiting.

CHAPTER 32

Tux and Gowns

I have never in my life worn a Tuxedo, but I have to admit, I looked good. Mine was a special tuxedo of course, as Antonio would say "Made for a King!" A shimmering purple jacket, trimmed in satin gold, with a black shirt and tie. The pants were also black with the same satin gold that trimmed the jacket, running down the side of my right leg. My shoes were black leather, so shiny that I can see myself as easily as I could in a mirror.

Though I understood the colors, I was happy that the style was a bit calm, believe me, I expected some craziness.

I stepped out into the living room, and was in awe of how beautiful my Grandmother looked, in her gown. It was purple as well, but with a gold laced sweater over it. Woven within the sweater were these black stones that would glisten under the lights of the cameras. But the thing that stood out the most was the long gold rosary I bought her. Dangling from around her neck, I could tell, she loved it!

It was the release party for my video, which was

premiering at the Ziegfeld Theater in Manhattan, Grams was my date for the evening, and I wouldn't have had it any other way. This was going to be a spectacular event, but of course it would... look who was throwing it.

"He's here!" Grams sung out when she heard the horn.

"Ready?" I asked her, and she smiled the biggest smile I've seen in years, then grabbed her matching gold purse and followed me to the door. I held it open and watched as the most important person in my life... stepped out.

"Oh, my God!" she said as we stepped out of the building and Sal was there, holding open the door to a purple stretch limousine.

"Really?" I asked, gesturing to the vehicle.

"You two look amazing!" Said Sal, as he bent forward and kissed Grams on the cheek.

"You look so handsome." She told him, before getting into the car.

"Big day," he said before closing the door behind us.

Grams sat in the side seat, I of course to the back facing forward. It was the only way I was sure not to get sick. I watched as Gram's eyes scanned the whole interior of the limo, from the bar to the glowing lights. This ride alone would've made her day, as it was probably so far the most excitement she's had in a very long time.

"What do you think?" I asked her.

"I'm speechless. Is this what you ride in everyday?" Grams asked.

"Not quite." I replied.

"We can fix that!" Sal said looking at us through the mirror. I laughed and shook my head.

"Nah man, I already attract enough attention." I replied, pointing at my hair. We all laughed.

"Oh, and the bar is stocked, so help yourselves." Sal yelled out from the driver's seat.

I grabbed a bottle of wine and held it up for Grams to see,

"or something stronger?" I asked her, but she was good with the wine.

It was a beautiful night. The sky was clear and comfortable, and the city looked extra beautiful from where we were.

We turned off the avenue and up into a street where we ran into a bit of traffic. I tried to look out, figuring there must've been an accident or something.

"You think we should back out?" I asked Sal.

"Why would we do that?" he replied.

"To get away from this traffic,"

"That traffic belongs to you." He said, just as a police officer directed us to pull over which is when I realized we were in front of the Ziegfeld Theater.

"What the hell?" I said to myself.

"Oh my God!" had become Grams catch phrase of the night, because that's all she kept saying.

CHAPTER 33

Bulbs like Gunfire

The door next to me opened, and the first thing I noticed was a red carpet, leading from the car to the entrance of the theater. A gentleman also in a tuxedo held open the door.

"Welcome Mr. King!" The man said as he guided me out of the car. I stepped out in complete awe in what I was seeing. Flashing lights lit up my entire space, blinding me to where it all seemed like a dream.

The gentleman then leaned forward to help Grams out, but I politely intercepted. I wanted the honors.

"Try not to look at the lights." The gentleman whispered, pulling me away from doing just that.

The display signs on the sides were posters representing the video, made up to look like a movie. I stopped and looked at it. It was then when I caught hold of the cheering going on behind me. I turned and looked at the massive crowd that filled the street. Grams looked up at me, as I stared out at the scene, my mouth partially opened.

"They're waiting for you, sir." The gentleman said to me, as Grams tugged on my arm, and whispered.

"Come on!"

As soon as we stepped inside there was Mr. D, standing with a few of his associates, all decked out in tuxedos and evening gowns, holding glasses of champagne.

When we were spotted entering the theater, everyone began applauding, with smiles on each of their faces, the biggest being on Mr. D's.

"This is it, King!" He said to me, his proud smile, smiling prouder than ever. He stepped forward and gave Grams a kiss on the cheek.

"You look absolutely astonishing!" He told my Grandmother, making her do something that I thought was impossible... Blush!

We shook hands as Mr. D introduced me to the others he was standing with. Though he would never explain to me, what roles any of them played, it was obvious, the roles were indeed important.

A waitress approached us, and from her tray, Mr. D took the glasses of champagne and beginning with Grams and I, handed them out. He then stepped up on the first step of the staircase we stood in front of and asked for everyone's attention.

The entire lobby, including the help quickly quieted down and turned to Mr. D.

"Excuse me, everyone!" He announced, loud and commanding. Everyone turned his way. Mr. D held up his glass, and all followed, including Grams and I. The lobby was silent, and still, that not even the help moved about. He looked out, his eyes connecting with everyone else's. Until finally, he said it!

"Long live the King!" and at that moment, as if it had been rehearsed a thousand times, everyone repeated his toast, and in one smooth action shot back their drinks.

"Now let's go watch the birth of a Superstar!"

Everyone applauded as the crowd made their way into the theater. Grams looked at me with such pride. I smiled at her, and then threw my arm around her and we walked in. "This way Mr. King." The Usher said as Grams and I stepped into the theater. With his flashlight he guided us to where three seats with reserved signs sat front row center. On both sides were all my people, Princess, Quenepa, Vanessa, Jacq, Lily, Emerald, Sal, Roller Girl, Domingo, and Antonio.

They all stood up to greet me and give Grams a kiss. The highlight of the night so far was how wonderful everyone made her feel.

The Usher removed the signs, and guided us in its place. Mr. D sat beside Grams and took her hand… I held the other. I looked behind us and couldn't believe all the people who had come to watch the video. It was like the premiere of a major motion picture… and I was the star!

One man ran around the theater snapping photo after photo of the people entering. Many of which were high profile actors, artists, and politicians, while another was taking pictures of only me from different angles. It seemed weird at first, but when I looked to Mr. D, and he nodded and smiled, I got it, and then turned, and smiled at the camera.

I leaned to the side to tell Grams to do the same, but I was too late… She was already cheesing it up.

Someone came up to Mr. D and handed him a microphone. He stood up and turned toward the back as everyone began to quiet down.

"What a great turnout." He began, as his eyes scanned the audience. "You have to open up many oysters, just to find that one pearl. And folks, I believe I found him!" The audience began to cheer. "And I want to thank you all for coming to help celebrate. His name is King, and in the world of Hip Hop… that he will be!"

You are all about to witness something spectacular, a legend in the making, so please sit back, relax and be amazed!" Everyone applauded as the curtain opened and the lights dimmed.

What was happening in front of me was beyond my wildest imagination. This wasn't a typical three minute music video. This was a major motion picture! So many of the questions I wanted to ask while on the set were now being answered, and it all finally made sense!

The look and feel of this thing was amazing, and once the music started, not even I was able to stay in my seat. The entire audience stood, as did the hairs on the back of my neck.

I looked at my grandmother, and she was crying. I quickly looked away, so that I wouldn't have to watch with blurry eyes.

Normally I would've thought that this was just another

Mr. D scheme, to create a buzz. But it wasn't. This shit was real. I know it was. I could feel it!

The music faded as we watched my image along with the Princess played by Roller Girl, ride off into the sunset.

The video ended and the crowd roared with a standing ovation, as they continued to applaud every credit that scrolled the screen. The video came to an end and as the curtain closed, the lights dimmed back on.

I was in shock, this could no way have been my life right now. But when I glanced to the side and saw Grams standing there applauding and crying, I knew this was no dream.

Mr. D took me by the shoulders and turned me around to face the audience. I looked up and out at everyone. Flashbulbs going off like gunfire. I smiled, and mouthed the words… Thank you!

CHAPTER 34

Secrets

We all then got into a string of limousines, ours of course the most elegant and driven by none other than Sal. We headed to a restaurant for dinner, how ironic was it, that it just happen to be the same restaurant where I once worked for just a couple of hours before running off. Though I didn't think anyone would recognize me, I in fact did catch the manager staring, trying I'm sure figure out from where he knows me.

The place was closed off to the public, reserved only for those who attended the premiere. Our table consisted of me, Grams, Mr. D, Domingo, Ciré, and Sal. It was obvious that Mr. D looked at Sal as much more than just a driver, as he himself was always treated as VIP. Not to mention, I loved having him around.

"I just wanna say thank you." I told Mr. D from across the table. He smiled and nodded. "This was all so beautiful." Grams added.

"Domingo, Mr. D was right. You are a genius!" I told our

director. "Well, I had a great palette to work with." He replied.

"Can I tell you guys a little secret." I asked them. Everyone gave me their undivided attention. Even Grams, as I'm sure she thought she knew all of my secrets.

"I once worked here." I whispered, loud enough for my table to hear.

"You did?" Mr. D asked. I nodded.

"I don't remember you ever working anywhere." Grams replied. Everyone started laughing.

"Remember, I came home wearing that crazy uniform?" "Oh my God, yes!"

"Did anyone recognize you?" Ciré asked.

"I was only here for about three hours before I quit."

"Three hours?" Sal asked.

"Yeah, I took the job to try and help Grams out a bit."

"Well. It was a nice thought, I guess!" Grams said.

"I couldn't take it. that guy right there." I said pointing at the maitre'd. "He was so mean, to everyone, and for no reason. Look at him." And at that moment we can see him pinching the arm of one of the waiters.

Mr. D didn't say anything, and raised his hand for the manager to come over.

"Yes sir." The Manager asked. Mr. D gestured him to come closer, and we all watched as Mr. D whispered into the manager's ear.

Sure, no problem sir, right away!" The manager replied,

before heading to the back.

Mr. D looked at all of us and smiled.

"Ciré, why don't you take King around to meet everyone, until the food comes?"

"Sure," Ciré replied and then got up and gestured for me to come along.

We made our rounds from table to table, thanking everyone for coming to the Premiere. I couldn't believe how many celebrities had showed up, and the photographer was there the whole time, catching it all.

The food arrived, and now I knew why this particular restaurant was rated number one in all of New York, and even though we were all having a blast, I still couldn't help but wonder, what the fuck did Mr. D say to the manager?

CHAPTER 35

Dance Castle

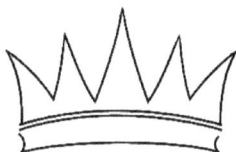

I swore that after the dinner, the festivities would be over. And though I was having the time of my life, I was exhausted. Little did I know, even more was planned.

We headed over to the Dance Castle, New York City's hottest night spot. The treatment we received from this place was beyond VIP, to the point where I had to ask Sal if Mr. D actually owned it. He said no, but I was having a hard time buying it.

I knew I still had a few of hours left in me, but my concern was Grams, but that changed when I looked over and caught her dancing with Princess.

Four waitresses were assigned our section, and if I had to guess, I would say that there main order was to keep all of our glasses full, because it seemed like no matter how much I drank, my glass remained full.

I was never much of a drinker, Grams, however was another story. She was having one helluva night, and I could only imagine the helluva hangover she was gonna have the next morning. And yeah, she was acting a bit of a silly, but that was fine. Shit, she deserved it. I've never seen her have so much fun, and I felt guilty.

Grams danced with just about everyone we were there with, but Sal seemed to be her favorite, because those two danced the most. I even imagined them as a couple, as Sal wasn't that much younger than she. But that stupid thought did nothing but get me nauseous.

Sal was an older gentleman, but only in age, 'cause even with the thinning of his platinum white hair, he had a youthful aura about him.

From the way he spoke to the way he dressed. He was in great shape, better shape than I was for sure. He had this sort of cool thing about him, and the streets respected him. One thing I do admit though, I was glad he was on my side.

"What's up stranger?" Vanessa said as she stepped up beside me sipping on her little pink drink.

"Hey." I replied the two of us looking out at Grams and Sal. "She's so cute." Vanessa said with a smile. "You see any sparks between those two?"

"Oh God, no!" I replied, and we both laughed. I gave Vanessa a hug.

"What was that for?" She asked.

"I'm just glad you're a part of this with me."

Vanessa smiled, when suddenly I felt someone grab me from behind and pick me up. I broke free and turned, surprised to see it was Quenepa.

"Hey man!" I said to him giving him a little push. It was

surprising though how strong he actually was. Like a little bulldog.

"Wadup, Vee?" He said, slapping her five.

"Where you been man?" I asked as he had disappeared about an hour ago.

"Man, I was getting my dick sucked!"

"What?" I asked.

"Yeah, that shorty I was chillin' with before, she sucked my dick!" I glanced over at Vanessa.

"And that's my cue!" she said before turning and walking away.

"Come on man, why you gotta say that in front of her?"

"She's a fuckin' dike, I figured she'd like that shit."

"She's still a woman."

"Whatever, she probably went to go look for her, so she can get her dick sucked too."

I just shook my head, and we both started to laughing, when suddenly a photographer jumped in front of us and took a succession of photos. Quenepa struck a bunch of quick poses. We both busted out laughing. The photographer thanked us and walked off.

"I could get use to this shit." He said.

"Well, good, because I have a feeling we're you're gonna have a pretty nice run."

"Some mother fucker even took a picture of me taking a piss." Q said.

"For real?"

"Yeah."

"Maybe it was for his private collection?" I joked.

"Ladies and gentleman!" the DJ said over the house system. "Get ready for the debut of The Funky Junky's hottest new release, by their hottest new artist, and remember, you heard it first, right here at The Dance Castle.... I Am King!

And at that moment, I heard it. The way people will hear it from this point on. It was the extended club version and I could tell it was my song even though the beat and bass were different. I watched as the dance floor quickly filled to capacity, Grams and Sal disappearing in the crowd.

"Oh shit!" Quenepa said as he smacked me in the back before dashing out onto the dance floor.

"My first dance to this song has got to be with The King himself." I heard someone say.

I turned, and it was Roller Girl.

"I don't know..." I said, like the shy kid at the school dance.

"...I didn't ask you!" She interrupted before pulling me onto the dance floor. The crowd seemed to open up as we made our way through to the middle. Everyone was smiling and laughing, dancing and jumping up and down to the music. It all seemed in slow motion, my music, muffled in a sort of dream-like state.

I was feeling it, really feeling it! Roller Girl placed her hands on my shoulders and we stared at each other as we both moved to the music. I kept feeling pats on my back and people yelling out my name.

I was just waiting for Grams to come wake me up, but she never did, 'cause she was out there too. This was real…. This shit was all real!

CHAPTER 36

The Sleep Over

I forced my eyes to open, and immediately my head started banging. Did I really drink that much? Lying on my back I placed my hands over my face and rubbed. I don't even remember getting home. I sat up when suddenly out from under the covers beside me emerged Roller Girl. She scared the shit out of me.

"Good morning." She said in a tired and crackly voice. I looked around, confused. "What are you doing here?" I asked her, and she started laughing.

"I told you that you weren't going to remember anything" Was her reply. I jumped up out of the bed, not realizing that I was completely naked. Roller Girl's eyes latched on to my joint, so I grabbed the pillow and covered myself.

"What the hell happened?" I asked, as if everything after our dance was completely erased from my memory. "Does my grandmother know you're here?"

"I don't know, she was a bit wasted herself. All I know is

her and Sal dropped us off."

"Dropped us off?"

"Yeah, and then they went for breakfast."

"Are you fucking kidding me?" I asked as I scrambled to find something to put on.

"Oh God, please no," I prayed out loud, as I put on a pair of shorts and a tee and rushed out into the kitchen.

"Good morning sleepy head!" Grams said sitting at the table with her paper and a cup of coffee. My eyes quickly scanned the room. She got up and gave me a kiss.

"You're here by yourself?" I asked suspiciously, Grams looked around the room and then replied. "Claro que si."

I exhaled in relief.

"So," I began. "How was your night?"

"Oh my God, the best night ever!" She replied. I kind of didn't like the way she said it though. Grams went over and poured me a cup of coffee.

"Do you remember any of it?" I asked her.

"Of course, and I'll never forget it." She replied putting my cup down on the table and then sliding over the milk and sugar.

"So um, you and Sal…"

"He is an absolute sweetheart," she said, I kind of didn't like the way she stared up into the air when she said that. I took my seat at the table.

"So you two, kind of… Hung out, huh?"

"Hung out? No, not really. After we dropped you off, we

decided to go to the diner for some breakfast."

"And then?"

Grams looked at me, catching on to the interrogation.

"And then we had wild passionate sex in the back of the limo!"

"What!" I said as I jumped up from my seat, knocking my coffee over on the table.

Grams broke out laughing, as she grabbed some paper towels to clean up my mess.

"I'm joking! She said, as she quickly cleans up the mess, though still laughing. "After we had breakfast, he dropped me off here, and then went home." Grams explained, shaking her head. I exhaled the biggest sigh of relief.

It wasn't like I wouldn't like to see Grams meet someone and fall in love, but not with Sal, that will be too weird.

Grams poured me a fresh cup and then sat down across from me. I wasn't even sure if she knew that Roller Girl had spent the night.

"Oh, and look at this, Rey!" Grams said opening up to an article in the paper. "They're talking about last night." She continued. "Wow look, and there's your picture."

I took the paper and briefly read the article, that's how small it was, barely five lines. "What are you talking about? I'm not even mentioned, and that's not me, that's just a random guy that was at the club."

"Of course you are," she replied pointing out to where it said, *A Night Fit For A King.*

"It's a publicity article promoting their club, Grams."

"Well, you look at it your way, I'll look at it mine. Either way, I'm very proud of you, Mijo, and you deserve everything that's happening, as well as everything that's about to happen!

This tiny article did more damage to me than if it didn't exist. After watching the entire city get plastered with photos and full stories about Nemesis, this was no more a public display of my failure.

I suddenly remembered I still had Roller Girl in my room, and needed a way to get her out. I was embarrassed to even hold a girl's hand in front of my grandmother, let alone this!

"Do you want breakfast?" Grams asked, just as I was about to head back to my room,

"Um sure." I replied. This would at least keep her in the kitchen while I try and get Roller Girl out onto the fire escape so that she can go up on the roof and then walk across and come down from the other side of the building.

As I stepped out of the kitchen, Grams called me back.

"Yeah?" I asked sticking my head into the kitchen.

"Ask Mary how she likes her eggs." I swear, wanted to disappear into the fuckin' wall.

Roller Girl was just getting out of bed when I entered the room. I have to admit, she was just as perfect without clothes. I know I slept with this girl, but I was embarrassed to tell her I didn't remember a thing.

"My Grandmother wants to know how you like your eggs?"

"Aw, she's so sweet, but I can't stay." I had hoped that the relief I felt from her not being able to stay didn't show, and though I tried to play like I was sad, I don't think she bought it.

"Do you mind if I take a shower?" She asked.

It was good to know the girl was clean, but this was one day she would've gotten a pass.

I was about to point in the direction of the bathroom when…

"I know where it's at!" she said, and with a smile, and her balled up garments, she creeped across the hall to the bathroom. All I was hoping for was that she didn't run into Grams, when suddenly…

"Good morning Ms. Rosario." I heard her say. I rushed behind my door to listen in, and couldn't believe that they were having a conversation. All I can could was visualize Roller Girl, standing in my hallway, butt naked talking to my grandmother.

"Did Rey invite you to have breakfast with us?"

"He did, and thank you, but I really have to get home."

"What about Coffee?" Grams then added.

"Um," Roller Girl began to think, and I began to pray, and just when I thought she'd decline again, grams helped push her through.

"It'll be done any minute, and you can take it to go."

"No, please God…"

"Okay, thank you!" She finally said.

"Fuck!" I huffed, punching the air.

I stayed in my room, and listened as Mary finished in the bathroom and was heading out. There was a knock on my door and I figured it was her saying bye, but I was wrong, it was grams.

"Your friend is about to leave," she said.

"Okay, tell her I said bye."

"I'm not going to say tell her that. Be a gentleman, and at least walk her to the elevator!" Grams ordered, obviously annoyed at my behavior.

"Are you sure you don't want to eat a little something before you leave?" Grams asked again as Roller Girl entered he kitchen.

"No, thank you, I really have to get going."

"Let me call you a cab?" I said, as I walked in behind her."

"No that's okay, King, I have to make a few stops, trust me, I practically live on the subway, but thank you." I looked at her and she assured me that she would be fine. Grams handed her a coffee in a Styrofoam coffee cup complete with the lid. Roller Girl held it up, impressed.

"He makes fun of me when I take them home and wash them." Grams said referring to the cup. I couldn't believe she told her that. Roller Girl looked at me and smiled.

I got up and walked Roller Girl out into the hallway. She turned and looked at me, she was so beautiful, her eyes looking extra blue.

"I don't know what to say." I told her.

"That you had a good time, maybe?"

I scratched my head, as I wouldn't know whether I did or didn't, but of course I wouldn't tell *her* that.

"I had a great time," I finally said, and so she smiled.

"Look, Roll..." I was about to come straight, but she stopped me, and placed her finger up to my lips, replacing it then with a kiss.

"I'll see you at the office!" She said before turning and stepping into the elevator, sipping her coffee as the door closed.

I went back in and sat down at the kitchen table, adding sugar to the coffee that was probably already cold. Grams took her seat across from me, preparing hers as well. I could feel her staring at me, but I didn't want to look up.

"So, you went for breakfast with Sal?"

"Little twenty four hour diner in the city." She said, and then took a sip. I gave it a moment before proceeding.

"And then where did you go?" I asked as I took *my* sip.

"Nowhere, he dropped me off here."

I looked at her, and she shook her head.

"He's a very nice man... But not for me!" She said. I believed her, Gram's dating days had been long over, and she seemed to have no interest in men. We both remained quiet for a moment, when finally she broke the ice.

"So Mary's a really nice girl."

"Who?"

"Mary! Why do you keep saying who?"

"I don't call her Mary."

"Well you were sure as hell calling her Mary last night!" My eyes dashed up to Grams, and she started laughing.

"Come on, you're a grown man now.

"Not around you I'm not!"

"I just have one question," she said. I was so scared to allow her to ask it, but she wouldn't let up, so I gave in.

"Was she your first?"

I dropped my head into my hands in disbelief that she was asking me this.

"Are you seriously asking me that?"

"I just need to know, Mijo."

I knew if I answered that question either way, it wouldn't be the end of it. I finished my coffee, got up and placed my cup in the sink.

Grams sat there, still waiting for me to answer, but I knew better. I went over, kissed her, and went back to my room.

CHAPTER 37

Pop Stands for Popular

As I ascended the steps of the train station, I spotted a young couple were coming down. They were engulfed in heavy conversation when suddenly the guy took a quick glance at me, turned away and then turned back. I didn't recognize him, but he nodded, so I nodded back.

I got up into the station and stepped up to the token booth. The guy behind the glass who has worked there for as long as I could remember smiled at me for the first time ever.

"Hey! How's it going?" He asked, yelling out from behind the thick bulletproof glass. "I'm good thanks." I replied, looking at him strangely.

"Two please." I asked, referring to the amount of tokens I needed. Standard practice was to wait till he received the money before passing the tokens through the opening. But he passed them to me beforehand, and when I went to pay him, he shook his head.

"Don't worry about it!" He yelled out. I wasn't sure if I heard right so I moved in closer placing my ear in front of the intercom attached to the window.

"I said, you're good, go 'head!" He said with a smile even wider. I stuffed my money back into my pocket and thanked him a bit hesitantly, before and proceeding toward the turnstile. Was this some sort of joke, or maybe even a trap? It was too strange to make sense out of. I dropped the token down into the slot and pushed through. I looked back at the token booth and can see the clerk telling something to the person next on line as they both watched me go up the steps.

Just as I got there, so did the train. I stopped and I entered the middle car, the one with the conductor, a habit that Grams had instilled in me since I first started riding solo. She always said it was the safest car. As I stepped in, most of the seats were full, and even when they weren't I usually enjoyed standing by the door so I can watch my dilapidating city swoosh by.

After the doors closed and the train pulled from the station, I could see this girl from the reflection of the window, I wasn't sure but she seemed to be staring at me. I casually turned around, sure that if she was, she wouldn't be by the time I turned all the way around, but I was wrong. She was still there, staring at me. Like if she knew me. I tried to place her face into my memory bank to try and remember where I might know her from, but nothing came up. She didn't exactly smile at me, but her eyes seemed very inviting so I pulled the most subtle smile ever, one that most wouldn't even catch, but she did, and returned one much bigger. I got nervous and turned back to the window.

I've never really had girls look at me that way, so I wasn't use to it, and sure as hell didn't know how to handle it. The train stopped and the girl got up and walked toward me. My heart raced as I didn't realize while she was sitting just how fine she was. The ass on her was beyond description. She stood beside me waiting for the doors to open. She stood so close in fact that I could tell what shampoo she used, Grams used the same brand. Okay okay… so did I!

"Have a good day." She said as the doors opened and she stepped out. I watched that booty as it seemed to put on a little extra bounce just for me. She glanced back knowing for sure I was watching, but I quickly turned away. Don't ask me why!

I was never much of a flirt, and I can't recall anyone ever trying to flirt with me.

I must've forgotten just how unusual my hair style was because I couldn't understand why suddenly I was getting all of this extra attention. Girls were smiling at me, and guys nodded. One guy even said what's up and shook my hand. I had no idea who the hell he was. This shit was getting weird.

I got off at my stop and when I turned around the train was already pulling off, I saw a man sitting there, he was holding up the newspaper as if he was reading it, but really wasn't. Instead he was looking at me.

I left the station and walked down the block toward the hospital. More stares and nods greeted me, as well as smiles from young pretty girls and a few eye rolls from the blue haired ladies staring at my hair.

Just outside the entrance of the hospital was a Newsstand. I figured I'd grab a few candy bars for Porky, he'd love that, but when I approached the stand, my heart suddenly hit the ground when I spotted on the front page of the Daily News... My picture!

I grabbed the last two copies when to my right I noticed the New York Post had a similar front page, but with a different photo.

"Hey! This is you, huh?" The Indian guy tucked deep into the booth said with a smile as he held up the front page. I didn't even know how to answer him because though it was my photo, what was it doing on these papers?

Along with a few candy bars, I grabbed two of the Post, one to read, the other to save, and when I went to pay, the clerk grabbed another and asked if I would sign it.

"Excuse me?"

"Please, for me, one signature." He said gesturing to other autographed photos he had hanging up, one of them of course being that of Nemesis.

I was so nervous and my mind was so fogged that when I wrote my name it was in print and I signed it, Renaldo Rosario. I handed it back to the man along with the marker he lent me. He looked at it with a smile. My handwriting sucked, so it didn't matter what I signed. Nobody would ever be able to read it anyway.

On my way into the hospital, people nudged those they were walking with when they saw me. It was no longer a mystery as to why I was suddenly getting all of this attention. But I still didn't know how to handle it, and therefore pretended as if I didn't notice.

I entered the hospital and went straight to the front desk to check in. After doing so, the receptionist compared my name to her log and then shook her head.

"I'm sorry Mr. Rosario, but Victor was moved to the Children's Ward this morning, and it's only immediate family. It's for the safety of all the children, I'm sure you understand."

"But there isn't any immediate family. I'm the only one that ever comes to see him." The receptionist looked at me for a second, then went through the log once more, but this time, starting back from when Porky first arrived.

"Give me a second please," the receptionist said before leaving and returning with what I believe was her supervisor.

"Oh, my God!" the supervisor said the minute she saw me. "Please, go right up Mr. King, fourth floor."

"But that's Mr. Rosario," The receptionist tried to correct, but the supervisor just waved her off, not once taking her eyes off me.

CHAPTER 38

Life As You Knew It

The moment I exited the elevator I could hear the kids in the far distance. I didn't need directions, I just followed my ears. As I approached the huge double doors I took a peek through one of the two narrow windows on them. The scene sort of reminded me of a scene from one of those old orphanage movies, where the kids were out of control, jumping on the beds and throwing things across the room.

It was a huge room with at least eight beds on each side. I scanned the area in search of some sort of adult supervision, but found none. My eyes fell upon a couple bullies standing over Porky, as they took turns hitting him with their pillows. The others kids stood around and laughed. Porky just sat there, with his good arm up he did his best to try and block the blows.

"Quit it!" He yelled out after each time a pillow whacked him across the face.

Immediately I stormed through the doors.

"Yo!" I called out, furious! The boys so caught up in

their cruel game didn't notice me, and got in a few last whacks, before dashing to their beds, the others who were merely spectators slowly backed away.

"Rey!" Porky yelled out with the biggest smile ever, his eyes flooded with tears. I rushed over to Porky and took him into my arms.

"You okay, man?" I asked as my eyes stared out at those little assholes.

"I'm okay, Rey."

"How long has this been going on?" I asked him, trying to control my anger.

"They were just playing." Was all said, as he looked out at his oppressors. Suddenly one of the nurses barged into the room.

"Sir, sir!" She began, with a stern and demanding voice. "No one is allowed in here!"

"That must include you, right?" I asked her, being as sarcastic as I possibly could.

"Excuse me?" She replied, even snottier than when she came in.

"Where were you?" I asked, quickly turning the tables.

"I was right across the hall."

"Oh, so I guess you didn't see what was going on in here, huh?"

"Sir, if you don't leave, I'm going to have to call security."

"You know, that might be a good idea, because if security's here, then maybe kids wouldn't be getting bullied."

"Nobody's getting bullied, the nurse shot back in her own defense, as she walked over and grabbed the phone.

"Yes, can you send security up to the children's ward please. We have a bit of a problem," she said, before hanging up.

"Rey, it's okay," Porky pleaded.

"You cannot leave these children alone." I scolded.

"I was only gone for a few minutes!" The nurse insisted.

"And within those few minutes this boy was bullied!"

"Hey, that's King!" One of the kids yelled from across the room. "I told you he was my friend!" Porky yelled back.

Two more nurses entered the room after hearing the racket, along with the supervisor from down stairs.

"Is there a problem here?" The supervisor asked.

"Yes there is Ms. Homes. This gentleman came in here causing a problem."

"Come on now, don't lie! This boy was being bullied and no one was around to help him!" "Where were you, Ms. Johnson?" Ms. Homes the Supervisor asked.

"I went across the hall to make a quick phone call." She replied.

"We went through this before. You are not to ever leave this room without someone to relieve you... ever!" Ms. Homes scolded, in a low but stern tone.

"Why are you on me, when you should be on him for being in here?"

"He wouldn't be in here if you had been here to stop

him!"

"You're King, the rapper right?" One child stepped up and asked. "Michael, go back to your area." Ms. Johnson ordered.

"Look." I interrupted the nurse and her supervisor. "I just want him in his own room." "We can't do that, sir." The supervisor replied.

"Why not?" I asked.

"Well, first off, the private rooms are kind of expensive and not covered by, you know...."

"I didn't ask you all that. I asked if you could put him in his own room, I'll pay for it."

I watched as the two bullies walked up to Porky and started talking to him. I kept a good eye on them because I had no idea what they were up to, but it looked like they were just talking to him. I saw Porky laugh, and then so did they.

"Rey!" Porky called out to me.

"Wudup kid?"

"Can you give my friends your autograph?"

"Friends?"

"Yeah, Jose, and Javier!" I looked at the two bullies who suddenly seemed like ordinary little kids."

I looked at the two kids, trying to shake off the branded image I had of them beating Porky with their pillows. I really didn't wanna give them an autograph, instead I wanted to stab'em with the fucking pen. But I knew Porky had to be here for a while, so I decided to try and do whatever I could to make his stay here as comfortable as I possibly could, and if that meant kissing up to these two little assholes, well then, that's what I was gonna to do!.

"Sure." I said. "What do you want me to autograph?" I asked, and watched as the two boys rushed off to their sections and came back with crayons and sheets of drawing paper.

"Jose?" I asked one of the boys.

"I'm Javier." I nodded and began to write. *To Javier, Thank You For Being So Nice to Porky, and not letting anyone mess with him. Your Friend… King!* Javier read it to himself and smiled.

"Thanks!" He said, and then went over to Porky and showed him what I wrote. Next was Jose. I took his and wrote the same exact thing, when suddenly, the entire Children's Ward lined up, each with their own piece of paper and a crayon. The supervisor was about to break it up, but I stopped her. She smiled at me, then whispered something to the nurse who nodded and went and sat at her desk. She just happened to have the Newspaper sitting on her desk, and it was then that she figured out who I was.

The kids all started asking me questions. I felt bad because I wanted to spend this time with Porky, but when I looked at him, he seemed to be enjoying every minute, so I sat up on his bed, and began to answer whatever questions I could.

I was amazed at the questions I was being asked, many pertaining to the video, which I was told had been playing over and over on one of the music video shows on TV.

It was kind of cool, and I was actually having a good

time, so long as none of them ask me to Rap.

"Hey, King! One of the kids yelled out. "Say a Rap for us!"

All the kids started to cheer on the idea. I was way too embarrassed, and tried to excuse myself out of it, when I hear Porky in his sweet little tone say.

"Please Rey!"

This kid gets me every time. I looked over at the door, never realizing that practically the entire hospital personnel had come up to the room. They too began to cheer me on, leaving me absolutely no choice.

I thought about rapping Yes Yes Y'all, but let's face it. That's not what they wanted to hear.

It would be the first time I'd ever Rap *I Am King* outside of a recording or video production, and was blown away by the fact that these kids knew the song, and every word of it.

Had I let them, these kids would've had me Rap the song several times, but I didn't want people to start hating it. The supervisor had brought in a camera, and asked if it'd be okay if she took some pictures.

"Sure!" I replied.

I figured we'd take a few group photos and that'll be it. But I was wrong. They even sent someone out to buy more film. I had to have taken at least a hundred pictures, but you know what? I actually had fun.

Photography was the Supervisor's hobby, and she was actually really good. She took so many cool photos that I couldn't wait to see them. One of the coolest ones, was of me laying in Porky's bed while him, Jose and Javier, all wearing over-sized lab coats and stethoscopes, stood around me like I was the patient.

I ended up staying for about three hours, and they let me order pizza for the kids. I called Sarge's of course.

Ten pies came through the door with plenty of soda and juice. Suddenly, one of the kids called out to me, and when I looked at him he pointed up to the TV, and there it was, my video.

Everyone sang along as did many of the nurses, patients, and even a few doctors who stopped by to meet me.

It was getting late and the party was about to be over, when one of the nurses came up to me.

"Mr. King, we were able to secure a private room for Victor, would you like to see it?"

"Wait! Is he leaving?" Jose asked as the entire ward quieted down. I looked around and noticed everyone was watching.

"Well, he'll still be in the hospital." I replied, when suddenly all of the kids stood up in protest against Porky leaving the Children's Ward.

I looked at my little chubby friend, and he seemed surprised at how everyone was reacting to him leaving.

"Come on, Pork. Tell them you wanna stay here." One of the kids begged. I watched as Porky looked across at all the other children, and then back at me with pleading eyes.

"Can I stay, Rey?" he asked. I looked at the nurse and she shrugged her shoulders, leaving it up to me.

"You think you'll be alright?" I asked him. Jose, who was actually the biggest kid in the room answered for him.

"He'll be alright, King! I'll make sure."

I wasn't this kid's father, brother, or even an uncle. Shit, I was barely a legitimate friend. But with his parents paying just enough attention to keep the checks coming, everyone looked toward me for his better interest.

"Okay, cool. You could stay!" And just then the entire ward broke out in applause and cheer. I went over to Porky, gave him a hug, and snuck a whisper into his ear.

"If you have any trouble at all, you tell them to call me right away, okay."

"I will, Rey, I mean, King!" Porky said, and then smiled.

"Nah man," I said to him, shaking my head. "We're family... You call me Rey!" Porky liked that, smiling his mouth of broken teeth.

"Can I take one more picture of just the two of you?" The supervisor asked. "Sure." I replied, throwing my arm around my little buddy.

As I exited the hospital I was bombarded by a succession of camera flashes. At first I didn't realize what was happening, and then it dawned on me, that someone had alerted the press of my visit to the Children's Ward.

"King, so what made you visit the Children's Ward?" One reporter asked as he shoved a microphone into my face, his cameraman shooting over his shoulder.

"I went to see a friend." I replied.

"Word has it that that the kid you went to see is

homeless, how did you meet him?" Another reporter asked as his cameraman shot from the side.

"Well, word gave you some false information because, he's far from homeless!"

"So is it true." Another reporter interrupted. "That you were the one responsible for the accident that..." and at that very moment, I felt someone pull me from the chaos that was starting to close in on me.

"Don't say another word!" Sal said.

"What are you doing here?" I asked him. But he didn't answer. Sal was focused on getting me out of that hospital, quickly and safely.

I did exactly as he asked, a bit worried about the crowd that seemed to be growing by the second.

We made it out and I immediately spotted his car. Holding me firm by the arm, he picked up speed, walking through reporters as if they weren't even there.

Sal opened the door and practically tossed me inside.

I sat there, scared to death as reporters and people holding markers and papers in their hands for autographs. They were banging on the window, so hard in fact that I thought it would bust at any minute. Slowly Sal began to pull away. I turned and looked out the back window in disbelief that we actually made it out of there.

My heart was pounding a mile a minute and I was still out of breath. "You okay?" He asked, looking at me through his review mirror.

"I don't know," I replied, Sal laughed.

"How'd you know I was there?"

"The whole country knew you were there."

"Huh?"

"I figured on your day off you were just going to relax at home, had I known you were going out I would've picked you up."

"I just wanted to see Porky." Sal looked at me again through the mirror and shook his head with a smile.

"Kid, when artists visit children hospitals, nine out of ten times it's for publicity."

"But I wasn't..."

"I know!" Sal interrupted. "Kid, you gotta understand. Life is no longer gonna be as you know it. All this, jumping on a train, and just going wherever and whenever you want, isn't gonna fly well, believe it or not... This is what you signed up for!

CHAPTER 39

King Everywhere

It was 7:00 am when I stepped out of my building. We were putting the final touches on our show, and would work from early in the morning to pretty late at night. Sal waited as usual, leaned up against his sedan, except this time, it wasn't just a sedan.

"What's this?" I asked him as I gestured to the black stretch limousine behind him. "We can't have you riding around in that little thing anymore!" Sal replied as he stepped over and opened the back door. Our normal car wasn't a little thing at all, unless of course you compare it to this one, which was definitely much bigger, and more beautiful. There was no more trying to roll under the radar, because this shit would attract attention from blocks away, especially if those blocks belonged to The Bronx.

I was kind of use to the Sedan, but like Sal said. I signed up for this shit.

Just as I was about to get in I glanced across the street, and noticed practically every window in the building had in it, someone looking out. I turned around and looked up at *my* building, and yep… Same thing!

"You'll get used to it." Sal told me as he guided me the rest of the way in, closing the door behind me.

Once inside, I didn't dare roll down the window, but I still glanced up at the surrounding buildings and noticed more and more people watching. Between the limousine, and all the publicity I've been getting, there was no more hiding this. The News had done such a great job of explaining everything that everyone pretty much leaves me alone. Instead they just watch from a distance.

"How you're feeling?" Sal asked, adjusting his mirror to look at me.

"Hard to explain," I replied as Sal pulled away from the curb.

"How you're sleeping?" He asked. I just shook my head.

"Man, I've dreamt of this most of my life, and now that it's almost here. I'm kind of freaking out.

"Well, let me freak you out a bit more, and let you know, this shit ain't *almost* here… "

I looked at Sal, and waited for him to say it.

"It's here!"

I sat back in my seat and watched as the city swooshed by wondering if that was a metaphor for my career. It did come pretty fast, the question was now… How long will it last?

My day dreaming kept me from realizing that we were driving a different way to The Funky Junky, I sat up and looked out at the crowded streets of New York City. I took a double take of someone I saw step into one of the stores. I swear it looked like Ciré.

Sal pulled over at the corner of 42nd street and Broadway, and then stepped out of the car. He walked over to my door and opened it.

"What's going on?" I asked.

"I just want to show you something." He replied.

I stepped out of the car, looking at the blank look on his face.

"What?" I asked again.

"Look around."

And when I did, I nearly fainted from what I saw. The heart of New York City was covered with advertisements of my up-coming Tour which was of course titled The Royal Tour. Suddenly, Sal gestured for me to look up at the huge screen above Times Square and I had to grab on to something when I saw my music video suddenly begin.

Pedestrians stopped in their tracks and looked up at the big screen. My eyes scanned the area and I swear, nobody moved. The lump in my throat was practically choking me and my eyes seemed to have sprung a leak.

This couldn't have been real, this just had to be a set up. It was way too perfect. My eyes bounced from the screen to the people, some stood there with smiles, others danced. Little kids rapped along as they knew all the words, when suddenly I heard someone call out.

"Oh my God, there's King!" I turned and spotted a small group of white girls, coming my way. Their blue eyes opened wide as two of them fumbled inside their bags for cameras.

One asked permission to take my picture, while the other just started shooting. It was a little embarrassing, but flattering as well. Sal leaned up against the car with his arms folded, enjoying my discovery of this new found fame.

A policeman on horse clippity-clopped his way up to Sal who was obviously parked where he wasn't supposed to. I glanced their way and watched as the officer got off his horse and shook Sal's hand, but of course, Sal knew everyone, and if he ever decided to run for Mayor, he'd win by a landslide.

One by one the girls took turns posing with me as others stepped up, also pulling out their cameras, as well as pens for me to autograph whatever they could get their hands on. Napkins, flyers, and maps, one girl even asked me to sign her tee shirt, just above her breast. Her friend on the other hand, told me to just sign her breast.

In no time the corner where I stood was congested with people who by now I was convinced were fans. The policeman had radioed in for some assistance, and before I knew it there were at least half dozen cops all working to keep the crowd under control.

Whether they were there all along, or had just driven up, I did notice there were three News vans parked across the street, their antenna mast towering high above the crowd.

I glanced over at Sal and he pointed to his watch as if to say, we gotta go. I looked at the never ending crowd that seemed to blanket the entire corner. These people were waiting for a chance to meet me, get an autograph, or take a picture. How do I just stop what I'm doing and walk away.

That would be impossible. I shrugged my shoulders at Sal and he laughed, as did his police friend.

Finally, two of the officers walked up to me and pulled me away from the crowd, escorting me back into the limo. No sooner that I was in, Sal began to slowly pull off. I looked out my window, and sure enough, there he was, Ciré standing at the edge of the sidewalk smiling at me.

The officers held back traffic as Sal pulled from the curb. He waved thanks to his cop buddy, and then took off, probably faster than I thought he should've been going.

Looking back I was in awe of the massive crowd that began to fade in the distance. I turned and looked at Sal through his mirror. We stared at each other for an unusually long moment until finally, we busted out laughing!

CHAPTER 40

Afro and Bermuda

I sat in the living room with Grams watching the News. I was all over it. The trip to the hospital somehow put me over the top, I couldn't believe it. Grams got up and answered the phone.

"Hello? Yes, one moment please," she stretched the long coiled line across the living room and handed me receiver.

"Who is it?" I asked her as I rarely got any calls, especially this early in the morning.

"Something Magazine, I couldn't understand them."

"Hello?" I said into the phone. "Yes... Yes..." I gestured to Grams to get me a pen and paper, so that I could write down an address.

"Okay, see you then." I hung up and looked at my grandmother. "That was Right On Magazine," I told her.

"What is that?"

"Only the hottest Teen Magazine in the country. They want me to come in for an interview."

"Oh how wonderful, my baby is going to be in a..." The phone rang again, and again she answered.

"One moment please." She said handing me the phone.

"Hello? Yes, this is he. Who? Really? Umm, I guess I can go to *you*. Sure." I grabbed the pen and paper again and wrote another address, this one was for a Cable Access TV show. I got up and rushed to go get ready.

In less than an hour, I was able to secure six appointments. Three magazines, two Newspapers, and one TV show that wanted to interview me live.

It was my day off, and I had planned to go see Charlotte, as I was sure that by now she'd seen me on TV, or read about me somewhere.

I was kind of excited to hit the street. I was enjoying my new found fame, the autographs and pictures, the smiling girls and every guy who came up and shook my hand.

I stepped out into the living room, and Grams handed me a piece of paper. "What's this?" I asked.

"So many people called you while you were in the shower."

I looked at the paper and could hardly decipher Gram's handwriting.

"I'll call these tomorrow," I said as I dropped the paper into the vase on the shelf. "I told you, that is not for garbage, coño!" Grams yelled out.

"I don't want to lose it." I said and she waved me off and continued watching the News.

"Ay Reynaldo, mira eso!" I leaned to the side to see what

she was talking about. It was Porky, and they were asking him questions. Grams got up and put up the volume so we can hear.

"King?" Porky said to the reporter, he's like my big brother.

"And how long have you known him?" The reporter asked.

"Since I was a baby!" he lied with the straightest face I'd ever seen. Grams looked at me for confirmation, but I shook my head and smiled.

"Since you were a baby?" The reported asked.

"Yeah, he use to take me to eat pizza."

"Really?"

"Uh huh, and he bought me my bike."

"Wow, so he really *is* like a big brother to you."

"Oh yeah, even better than a big brother, because sometimes big brothers can be bullies, but not King, he's the best big brother in the world."

Grams looked at me and I just shrugged my shoulders. Half of me had wished that Porky hadn't lied so much, though the other half was glad he did.

"And what do you think about his music?"

"Oh he's the best! He's even better than Nemblis." Porky said totally butchering his name on national Television... I loved it!

"You mean, Nemesis?"

"Yeah, King is way better than him."

"Well Victor, thank you very much …"

"Oh, can I say one thing please?" The reporter stopped her crew from moving and gestured Porky to go ahead.

Porky's eyes dropped to the floor as he gave himself a moment to think. He then looked up at the reporter, but she gestured for him to look at the camera, and he did. His chubby cheeks were their natural red, his curly brown hair full and in need of a trim, and those eyes, big and brown, sucking in anyone who might be watching, as he spoke in his shy soft tone.

"King is the nicest person I know. He comes to see me all the time, and brings me things. He's my bestest friend in the whole world… The End!"

And with his eyes still glued to the camera, he smiled his broken baby teeth.

The camera then turned to the reporter, catching her as she patted her eyes with a tissue, then suddenly switching over to a commercial.

I was choked up, but Grams totally lost it.

"Poor baby," she cried, as she wiped her eyes and blew her nose. "Next time you go to the hospital I want to go with you." I told her okay and then gave her a kiss. However, I was a bit concerned, Grams had an incredible heart, and I could see her really falling for this kid, and though it was a beautiful thing, it would now be another person she would always be worried about.

"I have a lot of running around to do today.

"Is Sal driving you?"

"Nah, I usually don't bother him on Wednesdays, I'll take the train."

"Wait, didn't you *just* go through this with him?"

"Yeah but, I kind of like the attention, besides, everyone's really nice to me, it's just a few autographs here and there, no big deal."

I gave Grams a kiss, and then took the stairs as the butterflies in my stomach didn't allow me to even wait for the elevator.

I pushed my way out into the street and immediately noticed that there were more people outside than normal. Everyone turned to me when they heard the door to my building open. I smiled, and immediately watched as everyone began walking toward me. The scene sort of reminded me of The Living Dead. You know the part where the Zombies get a whiff of their next meal.

I wasn't sure if I should keep going, or run back inside, until suddenly they started to applaud.

I shuffled down the stoop and was greeted at the bottom with hugs and handshakes

"Rey! What's up brother?" One of the older kids on the block said, as if he was an old friend. I've known him my whole life and in just that one sentence he said more to me than ever before. We shook hands, and he even threw in a quick hug.

"That was so nice what you did for those children." The Cat Lady from across the street said, as another stepped up and placed a Rosary over my head, and watched as it dangle over my chest. I took it in my fingers and lifted it for a closer look.

This wasn't some Rosary she bought at the neighborhood Botanica. You can tell it was an antique, made of wood and gold. I turned and looked at the woman, who I've known all of my life, yet never having spoken to.

"It's been in my family for almost a hundred years." She proudly said.

"Oh, Ma'am, thank you, this is beautiful. But really, I…"

"Please." She interrupted, stopping me from removing it from around my neck.

"I was always worried about what would happen to it once I'm gone."

"But I'm sure you must have someone…"

"Please." She said again. Eyes telling me that this meant a lot to her. I thanked her, and gave her a hug.

"Son, you's 'bout to get a whole bunch of pussy!" Sang Mr. Brown, the old man who's been sitting on the same ol' milk crate in front of his building for over forty years.

"That's disgusting!" said the woman beside him, backhanding his chest.

I thanked everyone as quickly as I could, and then excused myself from the chaos. I hurried toward the subway, and made my way up the steps when I noticed there was a bit of a line at the token booth.

I wasn't that hard to miss, so of course the clerk noticed me right away and waved me over. I really didn't want to skip anyone, so I pretended not to see him, but then he pulled his microphone to his mouth.

"King! King! Come on!" he yelled, much louder than he probably should have.

Everyone looked back at me, a few smiled when they figured it out, but the rest of them weren't happy at all.

I stood there, not really sure what to do, when the guy in front of me, one of the unhappy one's looked at me and said.

"You might as well go ahead, he's not going to stop."

I thank him and apologized to everyone as I made my way to the booth.

I figured I'd get my tokens quickly and then get out the way, but the clerk kept asking me questions. I glanced back at the growing line, and apologized some more.

The responses were a mixture of *"It's okay, King!"* with *"Hurry the fuck up!"* becoming even more agitated when the train came.

"Listen, I really gotta go!" I told the Clerk, and he immediately tossed two tokens in the dish, and then waved me off when I tried to pay.

I rushed up the stairs and practically dived through the closing doors. I laughed to myself, surprised that I had made it, though the guy behind me who didn't, gave me the finger.

"Hey, it's King!" I heard someone yell out. It was a young girl in a Catholic School uniform. She and a bunch of her friends ran up to me jumping up and down, and screaming, surrounding me while pulling pens and paper out of their bags. Some who were sitting, gave up their seats to also come over, while others stared, trying to figure out who the fuck I was.

I spent the entire ride talking and signing autographs. It was fun, but also a bit exhausting. I knew the stop these girls had to get off on, and they didn't, instead they road with me the entire way.

"You girls are gonna be late for school," I told them.

"They'll get over it," one of the girls replied, while the others laughed.

They were cool, and funny as hell, but I was becoming uncomfortable, as a couple of them held on to my arms, while the train kept knocking them into me. Thank God it was my stop. I said goodbye, and quickly got off the train, praying that none of them would follow, and they didn't, though one of them did stand at the window and throw me a kiss.

I rushed up the steps and on to the street at 42nd. I reached into my pocket to pull out the address of where I was supposed to be, but instead pulled out a piece of paper with the name and number of one of the girls, probably the one who threw the kiss.

I balled up the paper and tossed it into the trash, and then checked my pockets again until I found what I was looking for.

My first stop was Street Beat Magazine, located on 43rd and 8th, I checked the address again as I was a having a hard time finding this place. I stood at the corner and looked around. I had to have passed this place, because the numbers weren't making any sense.

A couple of guys standing on the corner across the street

had been watching me for some time now. From the corner of my eye I caught one of them nudging the other before they both finally crossed and walked up to me.

"Wudup, Home Boy!" One of the guys greeted, a Tall and skinny Puerto Rican kid with a huge afro, and a fist shaped pick sticking out from the top, a look I haven't seen since the 70s. His partner, also Puerto Rican wore a Bermuda.

"Yo, I know you from somewhere, right?" Afro asked while Bermuda played Look-Out.

Both guys wore jean jackets, Bermuda had his sleeves cut off, obviously to show off his muscular biceps, and when he turned around I recognized the emblem on his back. They were *Los Perros*, the same gang that Quenepa was down with, and the ones that Sal seemed to have in check.

"What's up with your Do yo? Afro asked touching one of my points with his finger. Bermuda overheard him and started laughing.

"Do you know where this place is at?" I asked, showing him the paper while trying to sound as cool as I could.

"Yo, that's that white kid that be doing the rapping!" Bermuda yelled out from where he was standing!"

"Oh shit, that's right!" Afro confirmed, laughing into his hand as he looked me up and down.

Afro snatched the address from my hand and read it. "Yeah, I know this place!" he said.

"Okay, cool," I replied, waiting for him to help me out, but he just stood there, staring at me. My eyes shifted over to Bermuda who was still at the corner, looking as suspicious as fuck!

"You mind telling me where this place is at?" I asked.

"Yeah yeah," He said, sort of snapping out of some kind of weird trance.

"It's right up there," he pointed, and though that didn't seem right, I thanked him anyway and took back the paper with the address. Shit, I just wanted to get out of there.

I managed to walk a mere five feet when suddenly Afro called out.

"Yo home boy!" his arms extended out to his sides, I turned and looked in a way as to ask, *what?*

"You come to me asking for information, I give it to you, and then you step, that's it?"

I gave a slight laugh and nodded as I dug into my pocket and pulled out two dollars, Afro stared at it, like it was a foreign object.

"Fuck is this?" he asked, his partner, who didn't say much, held his post, suspiciously on the lookout.

"I just needed you to point me in the right direction."

"Nigga, I ain't just point, I damn near escorted you to the fuckin', and you handing me this shit? is you crazy?"

"Look, I don't want any trouble..." I began to say, removing my wallet from my back pocket when all of a sudden, out of nowhere, Bermuda punched me in my stomach sending me instantly to the ground.

It took a while to catch my breath, as I watched both guys come and stand over me. I tried to remind them of who I was, and that I was cool with Quenepa and Sal, but they weren't listening, and instead sent a Combat Boot straight to the side of my head... everything went black!

CHAPTER 41

The Basement

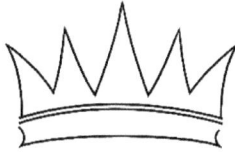

The pain didn't even wait for me to move, it struck upon the mere opening of my eyes. At first I couldn't tell if I was looking up at the sun, or a light bulb, but as a few seconds passed and my eyes adjusted, the later was confirmed. It hung unusually high, just below what looked like a concrete ceiling with a several pipes running in different directions.

The room was damp and dusty, and the musty smell was as if water had accumulated in some corner and sat for years.

Just the thought of moving my head sent a sharp pain ricocheting throughout my skull, and though my eyes and ears felt as if they were about to burst, I needed to know where the hell I was.

Turning to the left was a bit less excruciating than the right, and from there I was able to confirm the fact that I was in the basement of some tenement. I turned to the right, and this time realized that someone actually lived here.

It had all the fixings of a small studio apartment, its furniture an assortment of the neighborhood's trash.

An antique dresser stood against the peeling wall, a cracked and dirty mirror on top. An old card table in the middle of the room with four unmatched chairs seemed to make up the dining room, while in the corner, sat a toilet, out in the open. And though it was clear that no plumbing was attached, the roll of paper and stack of magazines were proof that it was indeed being used.

I attempted to sit up, realizing that what I was laying in was a hospital bed, one that smelled like someone died in. There were no sheets, and the pale green mattress was hot and sticky.

I quickly sat up, grabbing my head with both hands until it stopped spinning, and though I couldn't remember of how the fuck I got here, I knew for sure, I better get out.

Several doors lead to the room I was in, but none I could tell were the exit. I got up from the bed and held tight till the room stopped moving, when suddenly I heard.

"Good morning sleepyhead!"

I quickly turned toward the voice, and nearly fell over when I saw who it was.

Quenepa walked into the room with this huge smile, and a Baseball bat twirling in his hand. I didn't know how to read this, 'cause if anyone could be unpredictable, it would be him.

"Q? What the fuck is going on, man?"

He didn't say anything. He just continued walking until he made his way directly in front of me, placing the bat now on his shoulder. With one eye on Q, and the other on the bat, I asked him,

"Where am I?"

"Wrong place, wrong time!" was all he said, positioning now his slugger as if to hit a home run.

It seemed like the pain I felt just moments ago had completely vanished, as Q's too familiar smirk and whitened knuckles had me ready to leap, when suddenly, he busted out laughing!

The acoustics that surrounded us, made his laugh loud and animated. He dropped the bat from his shoulder and dragged it over to the nasty ass recliner, and threw himself on it.

"Yo, you a funny dude." He said, laughing and pointing the bat in my direction.

"So, where am I? What am I doing here? I asked. Q pushed out the last few laughs he had left, then once again became serious. He looked up at me, with his head tilted, and mouth shaped like he was about to throw up, he said,

"Nigga... You got jumped!"

My memory was back, so he wasn't telling me anything I didn't already know. The question I had was, what the fuck was I doing *here*?

"So, what is this place?" I asked, smells like pure shit.

"This my crib, yo!" He replied.

"Wait, you live here?" I asked, though I shouldn't have laughed.

"What you expect, a penthouse?"

"Well, no, but, damn, Q" when suddenly, a huge rat came

out of nowhere and dashed between us. I jumped on that bed so fast that bashed my head against the cement wall.

"Man, they don't do shit, but try to eat all your food!" He said, waving it off. I got back off the bed, checking my skull for blood, there was none.

"Hey man," I began. "So, the two guys who jumped me…" Q threw his finger up to his lips, then got up from his seat and grabbed hit bat.

"Come on," he said, making his way through an opening in the cement wall that looked as if it was made with a sledge hammer. I caught a glimpse of another rat from the corner of my eye which hurried me through.

Upon entering the room, I immediately spotted the two guys that had jumped me. Tied down into chairs and placed back to back, a single light bulb dangling above them. I stepped in further and without getting too close, I gasped. Had it not been for the Los Perros jackets and the huge afro, I would never have recognized them.

"What's going on?" I asked.

"Are these the guys that fucked you up?" Q asked. I looked at them, and nodded. Quenepa leaped forward, and with all he had, bashed the bat into Afro's face.

"Whoa!" I yelled as I watched, what looked like his jaw fly across the room and slam into the wall. A huge rat appeared out of nowhere, and grabbed the entire chunk of blood, bone and teeth, lifting it completely off the floor, and carrying it into an uncovered drain hole.

Quenepa then stepped over to Bermuda and held high his

bat.

"Wait!" I yelled out as I stepped in front of him holding out my hands.

Quenepa rested his bat on his shoulder to hear what I had to say.

"It really wasn't that serious, Q, for real man. He got a good shot in and I was out." "Man, you don't know these fools, King. They would've killed you and left your ass in the street. Just so they can read it in the papers."

"But look at them. They're fucked up already, what more can you do?"

"I wanna do to them what they were about to do to you."

"But why, Q? It's over man. You got them good, and I appreciate it, but please... don't kill them, you'll have to live with that for the rest of your life."

"I learned how to live with that shit a long time ago." He replied. I looked in his eyes, and God knows I saw the blood.

"Yo!" We both turned as we heard someone called out from way at the other end of the basement.

"Yo yo!" Quenepa yelled back, when suddenly stepping through the opening was Sal. "Sal!" I said, so relieved to see him. I knew if I couldn't talk sense into Q, he could. He walked up to me and took my face into his hands to examine it.

"How you feel?" He asked.

"I'm fine, but you need to talk to Q, man. I mean, this shit is crazy." I said, gesturing to the mess in front of us. Sal slowly walked around the two guys. I could tell he knew them too.

"Put that shit down." He said to Quenepa. At first hesitant, he finally did as he was told and let the bat drop to the floor.

I exhaled the biggest sigh of relief and when suddenly, Sal pulled out his 44 and shot twice, once into each of their heads.

"Oh, my God!" I yelled out, the ringing of the shots echoing violently in my head. I couldn't believe what I had just witnessed.

"Oh, my God. Oh, my God!" I kept repeating, gagging in between.

"Why did you that?" I cried, tears exploding from my eyes. I started pacing the room, frantic. He didn't say anything.

I glanced over at the two bodies, a large piece missing from each of their heads...I threw up.

"Aw come on, man. Fuck!" Q cried out. "Not here."

"Let's get out of here." Sal said. I started following.

"Yo, who's gonna clean this shit up?" Q asked referring to the vomit, yet he had two dead bodies in the middle of his apartment. And at that moment, two rats ran out and started gobbling it up.

"There you go!" Sal said, gesturing toward the feast. I quickly turned away, as I felt another gag session about to erupt.

CHAPTER 42

You or Them

I stared out the window for a good portion of the ride. I could feel Sal watching me through the mirror as he drove, until finally, I looked his way.

"You're okay?" he asked. How could he even ask that question?

"No man, I'm not! This shit is bad, Sal, real bad!"

"King, you don't know these streets. You don't know those guys. This wouldn't have been over, and the chances of you ending up like them were high."

"But you killed them."

"After what Q had already done to them, believe me. This shit wasn't over, and it'd be you they'd be after. Was either you or them!"

"But how did he get them, I mean, in that room, tied up, I mean, I don't understand"

"Q's been down with Los Perros since he was a baby. Don't let that little mother fucker fool you, ever!"

"How'd he even get them there?" I asked. Sal laughed, then looked back into his mirror, his serious face, now turned eerie.

So he spotted his boys from a distance, doing what they normally do... fucking people up. He went up to get in on the action when he realized it was you. He stopped them before they were able to finish you off." My eyes shot up to Sal's. "Yeah... you ain't supposed to be sitting here right now!"

He told them that he could get some money for you, and convinced them to bring you over to his place.

Once you were safe, he ordered one to crack the other and tie him up. Once it was done, Q, came up from behind and cracked *him!*"

I couldn't believe what I was hearing. I've watched movies about this kind of shit happening, but never did I think I'd ever be a part of it.

"But what if the cops find out?" Sal laughed again.

"First off, the cops don't give a fuck about these clowns. As far as they're concerned, that's just two less assholes they'll ever have to deal with."

I looked up at Sal, and though he didn't say a word. His eyes did! And at that very moment, we both knew... I would never say a word about this to anyone.

As we drove on to my block, we noticed the streets were full of people. Like the way Moses parted the sea, Sal slowly drove through the crowd until we made it to the front of my building.

"What's going on?" I asked myself as Sal pulled over. My

heart began to race as I realized the crowd had thickened around the entrance of my building. I began to panic, as all I could think of was Grams. I tried to get out, but the door was locked.

"Yo, open this door!" I yelled to Sal. He turned around and looked at me.

"My Grandmother's up there"

"I know, but you have to calm down and listen to me. If you go out there, that crowd's gonna rush us."

"But my Grandmother!"

"I know, I'm gonna go up, make sure she's okay, then I'm coming out to get you.

Just then we heard this loud bang, and when I turned, it was someone banging on the window, and as more people approached the more banging that would occur. I swore the windows would bust at any moment.

"Don't worry, a bullet couldn't break that."

Sal got out and stood in front of the car. I could tell he was saying something to the crowd, but I couldn't make out what, though whatever it was, it had them stepping back and away from the entrance of the building as he made his way in.

Those who were standing around the car were cupping their eyes against the windows trying to see inside, but these windows were heavily smoked, and as long as the lights inside stayed off, they couldn't see shit.

I could hear them talking outside. *I see something!* Someone said as others tried to move into his spot. I turned to my left, and saw one young girl just staring, as if she was actually able to see me, but there was no way.

"I love you, King." She said, still staring right at me. I raised my hand and waved, knowing damn well she couldn't see me, but I wanted to make sure. She didn't wave back, but I could've sworn she smiled. A loud bang on the roof snapped me out of my little trance.

I looked toward the entrance, praying that Sal would hurry the hell up. This wasn't anything like what I expected. I've lived here my whole life, and most of these people I've never even seen before, in fact, I don't even think any of them were from here.

At least twenty minutes had already passed, and I could only think the worst. What the hell was taking him so long?

With my hand on the door handle, and my eyes glued to the entrance of my building, I prayed.

"Please God!"

I would give him just a couple of more minutes, then I was going in.

More hands smacked the car and faces covered the windows, making it nearly impossible to see out.

"Fuck out of here!" I suddenly yelled out.

"Did you hear that?" Someone outside said to another.

I gripped the door handle even tighter and stared even harder toward the entrance. I began to count to ten. "One…" A few teenagers stood beside the car and began to rock it, nearly knocking me over. "Four…" I could feel the car lifting as more people joined in. Were these people really trying to tip over the limo?

"Seven..." By now the limo felt vulnerable, like rolling it over was about to become a reality. "Ten!" I grabbed the handle and pulled it up...

But it didn't open!

"Fuck!" I yelled out trying my best to balance myself. Sal had locked me in. I pressed a few of the buttons hoping to bring down the window or at least the partition so that I could get to the main controls, but everything was disabled. In fact, this shit just became a deathtrap.

I didn't know what to do, so I just started yelling, but all that seemed to do was bring over more people. Why were these people trying to flip over the limo? I braced myself, ready for the inevitable roll.

I laid flat on the backseat and placed my feet up against the door so that when it tips, I'd be standing, when suddenly, the car dropped and silence took over. Slowly, I sat up and noticed everyone moving away from the car.

The door suddenly opened and I yelled, cocking my fist up over my shoulder when I noticed it was...

"Grams!" I said grabbing and hugging her.

"Are you okay?" I asked her, "What happened?"

"People kept knocking on the door, asking for you." She replied. "I told them you weren't here. Then one girl said she didn't believe me and her and her friends pushed their way inside. I started yelling at them but they wouldn't listen. They started checking the whole house. When they were leaving other people started coming in. They went through everything, Mijo." She said, crying hysterically.

"Did anyone hurt you?"

"I got knocked down trying to stop them, so I crawled to the corner and just stayed there."

I couldn't believe what I was hearing, why were they doing this? If I was there, what were they gonna do?

"They went into your room and started taking things, I'm sorry!"

"There's nothing to be sorry about, and anything they took could be replaced, all that matters is that you're okay."

"I locked the door," Sal said looking at us through the mirror.

"What do we do now?" I asked Sal, "We can't go back there."

"Mr. D already took care of everything."

"What do you mean?"

"He has an apartment all ready for you."

"But I didn't bring anything, no clothes, no nothing!" Grams cried.

"Please, don't worry about any of that," Sal assured us.

As we drove, the street lights lit up the bruises on my face, as well as my dilapidated Do. Grams looked at me with a sadness that I would never forget. She didn't say anything. She placed her head on my shoulder, and just cried.

I felt horrible for having put her through this. She's lived here most of her life, and all of mine, and now there was no way we could ever go back.

I glanced up at Sal's mirror, and noticed he had been

watching us. His eyes shifted back to the road.

CHAPTER 43

The Apartment

The moment we entered the block on East 67th Street on the Upper East Side. Known to its residents as Lenox Hill, and to the rest of us as The Hill, I already felt like an unwanted guest. Just walking through this block was enough to scare people into calling the authorities, and though I was pretty white for a Puerto Rican, for this neighborhood, I wasn't white enough.

Grams would get less of a hassle walking through this hood, because of her age and dark skin, she would immediately be written off as somebody's maid or a nanny to one of their brats.

As we pulled up in front of a beautiful building with a burgundy awning and a uniformed doorman, the butterflies in my stomach began to take flight.

The doorman came up and opened the back door before Sal could even get over to us.

"Welcome Ms. Rosario, Mr. King." The doorman pleasantly greeted as he helped Grams out from the back seat.

"This here's Rodriguez," Sal said as he walked up to us. "If there's anything you need, you call downstairs, and he'll take care of whatever it is you need."

"Señora," Rodriguez greeted Grams, tipping his hat like an English gentleman. He was late fifties, short, chubby, and with a thick graying mustache.

"The bags are already upstairs." He said to Sal, who smiled and patted him on the back. Rodriguez led us into the building and into an elevator which seemed to have been waiting for us. He held open the door as we stepped inside and then placed a key into the control panel, turned it, and then hit top button that simply said PH, which I had no idea what that stood for… until we got there.

Stepping out placed us directly into the most luxurious apartment either of us had ever seen.

"Oh, my God," said Gram's her favorite line seeming more appropriate now than ever. Our eyes scanned the massive interior, with an emphasis on a window that took up an entire wall, and featured a perfect New York City skyline.

"There are four bedrooms, you can take whichever you like." Sal said, before gesturing us to follow him into the kitchen.

"What am I supposed to do with all this?" Grams said, referring to a kitchen that was bigger than our last apartment.

Sal pulled open the refrigerator and showed us that it had already been stocked.

"Everything in here is fresh, bought today, and the cabinets have everything you need to cook. Your biggest challenge will probably be, figuring out where everything's at."

"And if there is anything else you need." Rodriguez added. "No matter what time. I am here every day from 7:00 p.m. to 7:00 a.m. From 7:00a.m. to 3:00 p.m. is Valencio, and from 3:00 p.m. to 7:00 p.m. is Fernandez."

"Great guys, you'll love them all," Sal assured us.

"Buenas noches," Rodriguez said with a slight bow, before placing his hat back on and leaving.

"I'm sure you two are exhausted," Sal said. "Look, Mr. D got this place especially for you, so you two relax and enjoy it."

"But, how did he know?" I asked, but he just looked at me, and laughed. "Goodnight." He said.

I walked Sal to the elevator, where he pointed to a key on the wall and showed me how to lock the elevator from coming up. I nodded my understanding of how it works and then looked at him.

"What a day!"

"But you're safe." I nodded.

"You're gonna be here for a while," he said. "At least until after the tour, so that you know your Grandmother will be okay."

"But we have all of our things…"

"Don't worry about any of that. We'll take care of it. I promise. Now there are three bathrooms in here. Pick one, and take yourself a nice long relaxing bath. Shits changing, King, so you have to change with it." We looked at each other for a moment, and when the elevator door opened, he patted my shoulder, and stepped inside.

"When the door closes, lock the elevator."

I nodded and once the door closed I did as instructed.

I stepped into the living room and spotted Grams out on the balcony, staring out at the beautiful evening sky.

"So beautiful," she said as I walked up and stood beside her. "So, how long do we stay here?" She asked.

"For as long as we want, I guess" I glanced at her from the corner of my eye to see her reaction... There was none!

Though I wanted so bad to know her thoughts, I didn't push it. I just took her, without warning away from her home, the home that she not only lived most of her life, but rather the home where she raised me.

Then suddenly, she took a deep breath, filling her lungs with the cool night air. I watched as she held it in and closed her eyes. Until finally, she exhaled, following it with the biggest and most beautiful smile.

CHAPTER 44

First Date

I now understood what a goodnight feels like, not to mention the importance of a great mattress. I've slept on the same one for as long as could remember. So long in fact, that my body has left in it a permanent indentation.

The aroma of Gram's Bustelo, help make this new spot feel a bit more like home. I got up, pulling my tighty whities out of my ass as I stepped out into the hallway toward the bathroom. I could see Grams digging her way into the fridge, so I decided to sneak up and scare her, but when she turned around and screamed, so did I when I realized that it wasn't my grandmother at all.

"Oh, I'm sorry. I thought you were my grandmother!" I said to the young lady with the long black ponytail peeking out from behind the huge refrigerator door. Her big brown eyes and full lips made me forget that I was standing there in nothing but my Fruit of the Looms.

"That's okay Mr. King... My name is Rosie." She said stepping toward me with an extended hand. I took hers into mine and we stared at each other for a moment.

"You can just call me Rey. Mr. King, really isn't necessary"

"I could probably drop the Mister. But King is the name that I was instructed to call you by. And I need this job." She laughed. I stood there, like a fucking creep, just staring at her. I just couldn't take my eyes off her, she was stunning.

So… What are you doing here?" I asked, with a little laugh. She laughed again.

"I guess they never told you."

"Told me what?"

I'm the housekeeper." She replied.

"Housekeeper?"

"Yes."

"What is that, like a maid?"

"Um, yeah you can say that, except it's with a more acceptable title."

"Sorry." I replied.

Rosie reached down into a laundry basket and handed me a towel to wrap myself.

"You know, it's nothing personal, Rosie, But, I'm not sure if my Grandmother would be down for all of this. I mean, this is her shit. This is what she does, and she loves doing it. Last thing I ever want t do is make her feel useless.

"Are you talking about *that* Grandmother?" Rosie said pointing toward the balcony. I turned and looked, and couldn't believe what I was seeing, Grams was out on the balcony, laid out on a beach chair.

"What the fuck!" I said to myself as I headed over her way.

Peeking through the glass sliding door, I noticed that not only was she laying there in a bathing suit. She was reading one of those Romance novels with the shirtless Fabio on the cover, while sipping on some fruity looking concoction that had one of those little umbrellas in it. And it was just 10:00 am!

"What are you doing?" I asked as I slid open the door and stepped out.

Grams turned to me and gave me the biggest smile. "Hey! Pull up a chair." She replied in a mood I found totally unrecognizable.

"No, I'm good. What's going on?"

"Did you meet Rosie?" She asked, ignoring my question.

"Yes I did." I replied.

"So what do you think?" She asked with a sort of sinister look on her face.

"I'm not! And she's the Housekeeper!"

"I know. Isn't that wonderful?"

"You're okay with that?" I asked

"Hell yeah, I'm okay with that, did you see the size of this apartment. It's like ten times bigger than what we had." Gram's eyes looked down at my towel. "Why are you wearing that?"

"It just feels weird having her here."

"This is her job, Mijo. What do you want to do? Fire her?"

Just then, Rosie stuck her head out onto the balcony.

"Excuse me, um, breakfast is ready."

"Okay, thank you, Rosie." Grams said, and then got up and threw on a robe. "Can you imagine? Someone making *me* breakfast?"

Grams made her way past me and toward the kitchen, while I detoured to my room.

I came back just as Rosie was serving the food. I had thrown on some shorts and a tee shirt that Sal had picked up for me from the apartment. Rosie's eyes gave me a quick scan and then she smiled, and continued laying out the breakfast.

"You're going to eat with us, right?" Grams asked Rosie. "Oh, no, I can't Senora…"

"Can't what? I asked. "Eat with us?"

"Rosie, go grab yourself a plate and come join us, Please. I promise, no one will know." Grams assured her.

She was hesitant at first, but then did as Grams asked, taking a seat directly across from me.

"You made this?" I asked Rosie, referring to the coffee.

"Yes, it's Bustelo, that's what you like right? I can make another pot if it didn't come out good. "Rosie said getting up from her seat. "No, no! Rosie, please."

"But it's really not a problem."

"No… It's perfect!"

"Perfect?" She asked.

"Yeah, In fact, since you're up." I held out my cup for a

refill. Rosie nodded with a smile.

"Sure." Rosie replied as she grabbed the pot and refilled my cup. Gram's brows arched as she smiled, and then took a bite of her toast.

"So, how long have you been working for Mr. D?" I asked.

"My mother use to work for his father, many years ago. She took care of his house upstate. I practically grew up there."

"She's retired?" I asked.

"No." Rosie replied, her eyes dropping back down to her plate. "She passed away."

"Oh, I'm so sorry." Grams said. "What about brothers or sisters?"

Rosie just shook her head, when suddenly, the doorbell rang. Rosie jumped up, dumped her food into the trash, placed it into the sink, and wiped her mouth before rushing to answer the door. Grams and I just looked at each other.

"Good morning, Mr. Sal." Rosie greeted, stepping to the side so he can enter. Sal didn't even acknowledge her.

"Would you like breakfast?" Rosie offered.

"Just coffee." He replied. Rosie nodded, and headed back into the kitchen.

"So, how was your night?" He asked us.

"Man, I slept like a baby." I told him.

"Very good," he replied then turned to Grams, "and what about you?"

"It was difficult." Grams replied.

"Really?" Sal said as he and I looked at her.

"Yes, I'm too used to lumps in my mattress!"

We all started to laugh as Rosie placed a cup of coffee in front of Sal, and took our plates from in front of us.

"Today you have to go to the office and go over your wardrobe with Antonio." Sal said before sipping his coffee.

"I wonder what kind of crazy shit he made for me this time?"

"Hey, what's up with that language?" Grams said as Sal laughed.

"There's still so much to do before we leave." I said.

"And you only have two days to get it together." Sal added.

"So you're leaving Thursday?" Grams asked.

"No, we leave on Wednesday." Sal replied. "It'll take us a few days to get to California, and then we'll work our way back from there."

"I'll be gone four weeks, Grams. You'll be okay?"

"Oh yeah, I'll be fine."

"Rosie, will be here from breakfast until dinner time." Sal explained.

"Oh that's not necessary." Grams added.

"Ms. Rosario, it's fine, it's her job."

"Yes, it will be my pleasure, Ms. Rosario." Rosie added.

"Okay, but please, call me Dora." The two of you.

"Okay… Dora." Rosie said and they both smiled.

"Ready to go?" Sal asked me.

"Not really, but let's go!"

As I was leaving the kitchen I couldn't help but catch Rosie, on her toes, placing dishes high up in the cabinet. I immediately pictured her in heels, staring longer than I should've, because she caught me.

CHAPTER 45

Popular Porky

"Hey Rey!" yelled my little high pitched buddy, limping his way across the room. It was the first time I'd seen him out of bed since the accident.

"Hey man, look at you." I said with a proud smile. Porky loved the attention, so he added a bit more exaggeration to his limp, to make it look good. I can see his eyes glancing off to the sides to see who's watching us, and of course... everyone!

"How you doing?" I asked as I put my arm over his shoulder, and helped him back to his section. It was remarkable how all of a sudden his limp switched legs.

"I'm doing okay, Rey. I started walking again yesterday.

"Hi King!" One of the other kids yelled out from his bed across the room. I waved.

"Doctors said I might be able to go home soon!" Porky continued.

"Really? that's great man!" I replied

"Hey King!" Another kid at the back of the room also

called out. I waved again.

Though I smiled and gave Porky an excited hug about the good news the doctor gave him, deep down, I just wasn't that happy. All I kept thinking about was, where would this poor kid go? Back to that house of assholes, where nobody gives a fuck about him? Though I don't wish anyone to ever have to go to the hospital, for Porky, I kind of wished they'd keep him, at least until I got back from this tour.

This place was clean and safe. He had friends, and I'm able to come and see him pretty much whenever I want.

All the other kids surrounded us. I greeted them all with handshakes and hugs. Doctors and nurses came by to say hi. One kid dragged over a chair for me to sit down, and though I was a bit in a rush, I thanked him and sat for a few minutes.

"Hey King, sing your rap for us will you?" One of the kids yelled out from his bed, "no, not today!" I replied, but the others didn't let it go, and kept asking. I looked down at Porky, and his big brown eyes were practically begging, until finally…

"Okay… just once!"

The entire room exploded in cheer.

I caught myself beat boxing the intro. Some of the kids joined in, a few did way better than me. No sooner than I started to rap, those kids not only joined in, but actually took over.

Word for word, they did it all. From facial expressions, to dance moves. They had it down pat!

What impressed me the most though, was the fact that,

the video didn't play all the time, you basically had to watch the channel all day, and hopefully catch it when it came on.

The funniest however was when Q's part came up and at least three of the kids rapped along to that part perfectly. I considered bringing him by to meet the kids, I'm sure they would've loved that, but I had second thoughts.

I was enjoying their performance so much, I felt like I was in a scene from Little Orphan Annie, and when the song was over, I just had to stand and applaud them.

I glanced toward the door, only to find it jam-packed with doctors and nurses, so many in fact that I feared the rest of the hospital may have been left unattended.

"Bravo!" I cheered, as did the rest of the staff, for what was clearly a spectacular performance, by a room full of some truly spectacular kids.

"You guys were incredible." I kept saying to them. The head Physician stepped up beside me with a big smile.

"They really are." Replied the head Doctor as he walked up and stood beside me.

"These kids got a helluva future ahead of them," I said. The doctor however remained silent. I looked at him, and he gave me a sort of sad smile when suddenly one of the kids came up and wrapped his arms around my waist. A knot developed in my throat, and when more kids came up and joined in on the hug, I fought hard to keep it together.

"How did you guys learn all of that?" I asked them, trying to refocus.

"They've been practicing everyday Mr. King." One of the

nurses said as she walked up to the TV and ejected a VHS tape that said on it, KING.

"How'd you get that?" I asked the Nurse.

"They made me stand by the TV for over an hour watching music videos, and as soon as yours came on, I recorded it… I hope that was okay."

I looked at the kids and smiled with watery eyes.

"Wow, you guys are the best. Thank you so much, you really made my day."

"Can they eat Pizza?" I asked the nurse in a whisper.

"I'd be happy if many of them ate anything at all." She replied."

"And there's a girls ward?" I asked.

"Yes there is. Well, for now at least. Would you like to visit?" The Nurse asked.

"Can he go with us?" I asked, gesturing toward Porky. The Nurse looked at the Doctor. "Sure." He said. "But get him a wheelchair."

I made a call to Sarge's and ordered seven Pizza Pies, and sodas for the kids and staff as they got Porky settled into the wheelchair.

We went to the other side of the wing where the girls were. It was like I was looking at a female version of the boy's ward, little girls of all ages, sizes and colors. Whereas many of the boys wore baseball cap, many of the girls wore pretty scarves.

The Nurse was about to introduce me to them. But the

moment one of them saw me, she screamed from the top of her lungs, and then pointed and yelled my name.

The screams were so loud that Porky covered his ears. Trust me, I wanted to do the same, but I didn't want to hurt their feelings. The Nurses tried to quiet them down a bit, but I begged her to let them.

The hospital photographer came to the room. You know the one who takes the pictures of the new born babies?

One at a time, in small groups and as a huge group photo, we must've taken about twenty pictures. I glanced over and spotted Porky talking to this one little girl. I wanted so bad to tease him, but didn't dare.

Porky was now, not only the most popular patient in the Boy's Ward, he was now the most popular patient in the entire hospital. Everyone spoiled him from this point on, but no matter what. Porky remained that sweet and kind little boy that everyone would've eventually fallen in love with anyway.

Once back at the boy's ward, I told Porky that I was leaving on tour, and that I would be away for a bit. He turned sad for a second, but then brightened up when I told him that on my way back, this would be my first stop.

The Nurses had promised me that they would bring him over to girls ward once in a while so that he could say hi.

When the Pizza arrived, I ate a slice with the kids. The Nurse looked on in amazement as all of the kids, not only took a slice, they were actually eating it, many for the first time in a while.

When it was time for me to leave, I whispered in my buddy's ear, and though a bit of sadness did take over for a moment, Porky's new found popularity, made it much easier.

Everyone wished me good luck on the tour, and just before exiting the ward, I turned around, expecting to find Porky, sitting there, staring at me as I was leaving, something he usually did. But this time, it was different. The eyes that normally followed me out the door were now preoccupied with his Pizza, and friends. It was a bittersweet moment, but would make my trip much easier to deal with.

But just as I stepped past the door, I heard him call me. I stuck my head back inside the room and looked at him.

"Hurry back, okay?" He said. We smiled at each other, and then I nodded and left.

CHAPTER 46

And We're Off

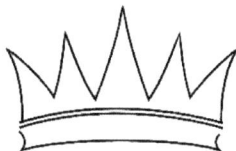

It was 5:30 am when Sal and I rolled up in front of the Funky Junky. The scene was similar to that of the video shoot. Three buses parked at the curb. Mr. D walked out of the building with EDDIE, our Tour Manager. They spotted us and walked our way.

"Good morning!" Mr. D greeted all bright-eyed, as if he'd been up for hours. "Hey King!" Eddie said, as we shook hands.

"So how are we looking?" I asked.

"Looking great!" replied Mr. D. "Everything's on schedule, everyone's here ..."

"...Everyone except Quenepa," Eddie interrupted. Mr. D Looked at his watch then out toward the corners, hoping to spot him in the distance.

"Anyone know how to get in touch with Quenepa?" Mr. D asked.

"I know where he lives, but he doesn't have a phone." Sal

replied. "I could go see if he's there, but I'm gonna be about thirty minutes.

"Fuck!" grunted Mr. D. It was the first time I ever really seen him get angry. I watched as the creases in his forehead deepen, giving the situation some serious thought. And though this could be bad for the tour, for some reason, I knew Mr. D would come up with something, and just as I thought, he said "Okay, I got it!" But then suddenly, Eddie pointed out into the distance and there was Quenepa, jogging toward us. I was glad to see him, but also curious as to what Mr. D had in mind.

"Brother, this ain't good!" Sal said to him as he approached us.

"Come on man, everyone here either has a ride, or gets a ride. I gotta fuckin' walk twenty-five blocks."

"Why didn't you just take the train?" I asked him.

"Cause I didn't want to risk getting busted."

"Busted for what?" Sal asked.

"Jumping the turnstile! them mother fuckers would hold me for hours, just to be assholes."

"But we gave you train fare," Sal said.

"Man, I spent that shit. Besides, I ain't never paid to ride a train in my life, and I ain't 'bout to start now. Shit, I still gotta rep to uphold!"

"Okay guys, let's get the fuck outta here." Mr. D commanded, rubbing his hands together like a mad scientist.

"Oh, what about my ..."

"...I got'em!" Sal interrupted, then pulled my bags from the trunk, and gave his car keys to one of the assistants to park it in the garage.

"Well, this is it!" Eddie said to Mr. D. They shook hands, and then Eddie left to make sure everyone was on their assigned busses.

"So I take it, you're not coming?" I asked Mr. D.

"I have a ton of work to do while you're gone. He replied. We both remained silent for a long moment.

"You're gonna do great, King!" He assured me, placing his hand on my shoulder and giving it a little squeeze.

"Can you check in on Grams for me?"

"We got that all covered. You don't have to worry about a thing."

"Man, I don't even know how to thank you."

"Oh, that's an easy one. He replied. Rock the fuckin' house!" I laughed and nodded. We then shook hands, and I boarded my bus.

Sal brought my bags to the back of the bus, and into a private room that was apparently mine.

"Wow!" I said, as I stepped up onto the bus.

"Nice huh?" Sal responded, settling into the driver's seat. "Your own rolling castle." "Who else is riding with us?" I asked.

"It's just you and me, buddy, as usual." He replied, straightening out his side view mirrors.

"That's crazy." I responded.

"What is?" Sal asked.

"I mean, those other buses are packed and we got all this extra room."

"They're good. Trust me. Now sit back and enjoy the trip. You have a TV, radio, magazines. You can also go in the back room and sleep, or just jerk off the whole trip if you like.

I walked over to the huge lounge chair up against the window and settled myself in it.

Busses three and two pulled out. We followed behind. I could see Mr. D still standing in front of the building watching as we drove away.

It was the strangest feeling. Here I was sitting within the epitome of luxury, as the slums of my great city swooshed across my window. Crackheads littered the wee hours of the morning, as rats and stray dogs ripped the garbage bags put out on the curb.

The life that I have been dreaming about for as long as I could remember was becoming a reality, but how long will it last? The only one that could answer that question was Mr. D.

He took an ordinary kid from the street and pretty much turned him into an overnight sensation. He could've done this with practically anyone, as I couldn't even credit my success to any of my songs, as I have yet to even use them.

So much I haven't even had the time to think about. But I guess during this trip, that's what I'll do, because God knows, I don't wanna fuck this up.

We drove only about thirty minutes so far, and it already felt like hours. I reclined my seat and just did my best to relax and enjoy the ride.

"That's the idea!" Sal yelled out from the driver's seat as he looked up through the rearview mirror.

"I could really get use to this." I said.

"I bet you could." He replied with a laugh.

I've been pretty anxious about this whole ordeal and haven't really been getting much sleep at night. Now we have one hell of a ride, so in between me trying to make sense of this all, I'm gonna try and get some much needed sleep.

I closed my eyes, and between the hum of the bus, this incredibly comfortable recliner, and the air conditioning. I couldn't help but start to dose.

What was happening to me was still a fog, like it wasn't even real, and all I kept waiting for was for Grams to finally come and wake me from this awesome dream.

"Uh oh!" I heard Sal say. I sat up and watched as the busses in front of us began pulling over.

"What's going on?" I asked.

"I don't know." Sal replied as he followed them to a stop.

"What's wrong?" Sal asked Keith, one of the other drivers, standing on the bottom step of our bus.

"Fucking AC's down." He grunted. I felt bad because though ours was working fine. "Did you let it run?" Sal asked.

"It's been running since we left. Tommy's checking it now."

I could see Tommy, the driver of bus number three, who

was also a mechanic going in and out of the bus. Finally, he closed the hood and walked over to us.

"What do you think?" Keith asked as he approached.

"That compressor's fried.' Tommy replied wiping sweat from his forehead. "I've never seen no shit like that in my life."

"Think you can make it to the next service station." Sal asked.

"How far is it?" Keith asked.

"Hour… Give or take." Tommy added.

"I don't know about that. It's already an oven."

"Fuck!" I heard Sal say as he slapped the steering wheel.

"Give me a second." He said and then got up and walked over to the phone hanging on the wall across from me, and dialed.

"Hey, we have a problem." Was how he began.

"Bus 2's AC is dead." He said, obviously speaking to Mr. D. "Yeah he did that, but Tommy said the compressor's fried. Yep!" I watched as Sal listened to the instructions being given to him, and then gave him our location. "How long, do you think?" He asked, and then responded with an "Oh boy!" as he looked at his watch, making it obvious that it wouldn't be soon. "Okay, got it. Call you later."

Sal stepped off the bus.

"They're sending over another bus." He told the other drivers who, along with Eddie the road manager, all stood right outside the door. I sat up to watch what was going on.

YES YES Y'ALL BOOK 2

Keith was really upset, as he now had to tell everyone that they had to wait, in the 98 degree heat for another bus to come. Unload, and reload.

"Can you take any of them?" Eddie asked Tommy.

"I don't know, maybe two or three." Tommy replied. "But that's it."

"Nah, that won't work." Sal said. "All that's gonna do is piss everyone off."

I noticed that no one even suggested they come on this bus meanwhile I had all this extra space.

"Hey, we're dying up in here!" One of the dancers yelled out the door of the bus.

"Tell everyone to get out, get some air." Sal ordered.

I watched as at least fifteen people poured out of the bus like molten lava. I could hear huffs and puffs as they realized that it was even hotter outside.

"Guys guys, listen up!" I heard Sal say as he stepped over to calm everyone down. "Your bus is experiencing some technical difficulty. But, they are sending over another one, and it should be here in about ten to fifteen minutes."

Sal was bullshitting them, trying to keep them calm, at least until we were out of here.

"I don't know if I could wait that long." Said another one of the dancers. I watched as Quenepa tossed a pillow on the ground and laid down like if this was normal. And for him it was. I knew this because I'd been in his basement apartment, or whatever the fuck you wanna call it.

"Are you waiting with us?" Vanessa asked.

"No, we can't. We have to keep moving. I'm not allowed to stop, neither is Tommy. But don't worry, you guys will be right behind us." Sal patted Keith on the shoulder and nodded to Tommy to let's go. Sal got back up on the bus and closed the door. I looked at everyone just losing their minds, as I sat in this cool comfortable bus about to leave them behind. I watched as Bus Three drove off, and as we were about to follow I asked Sal.

"Stop!" I said. Sal looked up at me through his mirror.

"What?" He asked.

"I said stop!"

"There's nothing we can do King. Besides, Keith can handle them." I got up and rushed to the other side of the bus and looked back at those who I was now calling my friends, and watched as they became smaller as we distanced.

"Stop the fuckin' bus!" This time I yelled. Sal looked up at the mirror, then pulled over and stopped the bus.

"Open the door." I said as I made my way to the front.

I got off the bus, and began walking toward my dancers.

One of them saw me coming their way and said something that made everyone else look.

"Guys, there aren't a lot of seats, but there's plenty of room. Just grab what you need for the trip, and the rest of your things will meet up with you there.

Everyone got excited and ran back on the bus for their belongings.

"You too, Keith." I told the driver.

"Thanks King, but the Captain never leaves his ship. I'll catch up to you guys."

Once everyone got their things, I waved them to follow me back to my bus.

As we approached Sal stood blocking the entrance.

"You sure you wanna do this?" He asked me. "It's gonna be tight." Everyone stood behind me in silent, waiting for my reply.

"It's the only way I want my family... Tight! Now move the fuck out the way!" Sal looked at me, smiled and then stepped off and to the side, as everyone applauded and got up onto the bus. The burst of oooh's and Ahh's as the cold air blasted upon them entering, let me know, that I'd done the right thing.

Sal and I were the last to enter, but before we did, he looked at me.

"You did good, kid!" He said, with a proud smile and a pat on my back.

Q was laid out on my recliner.

"Hey asshole!" Sal yelled to him. He looked up as to say what. I jumped in.

"Get some rest!"

Q looked at me, smiled and then laid back down.

I however, took the best seat on the bus, the one on the floor next to Vanessa. She wrapped her arms around mine, and placed her head on my shoulder, as Skye, one of our dancers, took out her guitar, and started playing.

CHAPTER 47

On The Road

We were having such a good time on the bus that we didn't even realized that we had made it as far as Ohio when our bus suddenly pulled off to the side of the road.

"What's going on? Quenepa asked from the comforts of my recliner, when beside us pulled up the replacement bus. Sal got up from his seat and turned to the back.

"Okay Sweat Hogs, get the fuck off my bus!" Skye immediately stopped playing, and everyone became quiet. Sal pulled open the door and let the other driver in. They shook hands.

"How's the Air conditioning?" He asked. The other driver looked to the back and replied.

"Make sure you bring your bring blankets!" Sal smiled at the other driver and then turned back to us.

"Come on folks, hurry it up!" Sal called out with a double clap of the hands. Nobody looked enthusiastic to go anywhere, and they dragged their asses to even get up.

"I'm claiming my spot now!" Quenepa said and then dashed through the bus and out the door. I looked at everyone as they gathered their things. Vanessa kissed me on the cheek as she headed to the door. A few had already stepped outside.

"Thanks." I said to Skye as she picked up her guitar and headed out. Roller Girl walked up to me and patted my back. I still couldn't get over how little she was without her skates on.

"Try and get some sleep." She said, continuing to the front. She was the last to leave when suddenly I dashed past her and to the door.

"Hold up!" I yelled out. Everyone stopped and turned to me. It was so hot out, well over a hundred degrees.

"I don't think I could make this trip without you guys." "Fuck you talking about?" Sal asked from behind me.

"I don't need a lot of room. Could you guys please ride with me?" They all remained quiet and looked at each other, when finally, Vanessa made the first move, and turned back toward me.

"Let's do this!" She said with a huge smile, and one by one, they all gathered back on my bus. Vanessa reserved the recliner for me, and when Quenepa got back on after realizing that the bus was turning back, he caught a fit when he saw me sitting in it. Everyone laughed. I looked at Sal, and he was smiling.

"What do I do now?" The other driver asked Sal.

"Just follow!" Sal replied. The driver stepped back as Sal

closed the door and started the engine. Bus 3 pulled off, replacement bus number 2 followed behind us all.

After so many hours, I was tired of singing, joking and playing cards. Instead I grabbed one of Sal's maps and sat back to track our route. I had never even left New York before, and now I was traveling across the country. We had just crossed from Missouri into Kansas, and all I kept thinking about was the Wizard of Oz. It looked exactly as I had expected. Flat open land for miles and miles. No wonder Tornado's loved spinning through here, there's really nothing in its way. My eyes remained glued to the distance, and though I didn't say anything, I was sort of hoping we would come across a Tornado.

Hey, where are we?" Vanessa asked, seeing that I had the map.

"Kansas!" I said and immediately Skye began playing on her guitar Over the Rainbow, while everyone else began to sing. I still couldn't get over on how talented these individuals were. From what I had learned this wasn't just a group of dancers. each person in here possessed a wide variety of talents that most had been developing since they were toddlers.

From Ballet to Gymnastics, Beauty Pageants and Musical Recitals, these kids had done it all. In all honesty, I was the least talented of them all, and except for a few good laughs during my training they were all very supportive and encouraging. Shit, even Quenepa had talents beyond my own.

There were thirteen of us on the bus, including Sal. I looked out at them all as Skye continued to play, and everyone sang along. Skye had a coolness about her, sort of hippy-ish in fact. Her olive complexion gave proof to a black father and Puerto Rican mother, though her white attitude was still a complete mystery.

Emerald, always the show off, stood up and began to vogue. At first look, a dancer would be the last thing you'd think he was. Totally opposite of Princess, this guy was short and chubby, but his dancing skills were incredible.

Besides the emerald eyes that brought compliments from anyone who noticed them, the rest of him was a bit hideous. Because of that he was never really that popular, whether in school or in his neighborhood, and being Gay certainly didn't help.

He became interested in dance when he and his mother use to take his older sister to ballet class. He found himself memorizing their lessons, and then going home and practicing. It was his sister who caught him one day, and then talked him into joining.

This didn't sit well with dad, and eventually became the essence of a divorce. But Emerald by then was too obsessed with his new found passion to give anything else much thought.

His awkwardness in the regular world was in complete contrast to his life in the dance studio, therefore he spent countless hours working on the only thing that made him happy, and because of that, he was one of the best.

His un-dancer-like appearance seemed to be genetic, because everyone in his family looked similar, including his sister who dropped out of ballet a couple of months after

Emerald joined.

Jini was this cute Japanese girl who had been living in the U.S. for only about a year.

She hardly knew any English, yet knew every word to my song. And as for her dancing? Absolutely incredible! I remember Vanessa telling me that Jini was a classically trained pianist, but despised that talent for whatever the reason.

Lily was Puerto Rican with a very slight accent, and though she was born and raised in the Bronx, her parents never learned English, which made Spanish her first language at home. She was beautiful, looked more like a model than a dancer, and with a master's degree, she was no dummy. This girl had a lot going on for her, why she chose to dance for me? One day I plan on asking.

Then there was my homegirl, Vanessa. She lit up any room she entered, and people loved being around her. But life for Vee, has not been easy, and if being gay, black, and female, were actual strikes, she wouldn't even have any left.

Vee wasn't one to open up to just anyone, and the moment she felt you digging too deep, she'd immediately shut you down.

With Vee, all you needed to do was be patient, and listen, and in time she would reveal quite a bit, and from the moment her and I first met, I knew right then and there, that we would be friends for life.

My eyes continued to each of the remaining six dancers who rode with us. They were all really cool with me, and fun to be with. I felt extremely lucky. I placed my head back

YES YES Y'ALL BOOK 2

against the headrest and closed my eyes. Life was good, and from what I could see, it was gonna get even better.

It was 6:30 in the morning when we got to California, and everyone was still asleep, everyone except me, and Vee.

"Are we here yet?" She asked from where she laid on the floor beside me. I nodded.

"Thank God." She said, and then turned over and went back to sleep. Lily woke up and crawled over, and leaning on my leg she looked out my window.

"Wow. I can't believe I'm really here." She then looked up at me. "It was always my dream to live here." She said.

"So why haven't you?" I asked.

"My parents, they're old you know."

"It'll be an exciting change for them."

"Nah, they moved from Puerto Rico to the Bronx in the sixties. Pretty much everyone else followed. My whole family lives in the Bronx."

"So you know they won't be alone."

"No, they'll never be alone. My brothers and sisters are there too,"

"Brothers, *and* sisters?" I asked.

"Seven of us, and I'm the baby." She said with a cute smile and finger up against her dimple. I laughed.

"Okay, you fucking rug rats, wake up, we'll be at the hotel in about ten minutes, and please, go brush your fucking teeth, this fucking bus smells like the number seven train.

CHAPTER 48

Dear Mijo

It was Friday morning as we exited the bus and gathered into the lobby of the Holiday Inn.

Roller Girl was already there, and surprisingly back on her skates. She had a small box and from it handed us our keys, instructing us to drop off our things and be back in the lobby in thirty minutes for sound check. Apparently everyone was doubled up, except, Sal, and myself. Quenepa was paired with Emerald and wasn't at all happy about it. He kept telling Emerald that it was nothing personal, but continued until finally, he got his own room.

We all squeezed into the elevator, but when the doors wouldn't close, the clerk made half of us step out. Everyone seemed to be on the 4th floor, except me, Sal and Q, *we* were on the 6th. After over forty hours of driving, I'd become pretty close with my dancers, and now at the hotel, we were being separated once again.

Upon entering my room, I flicked on the light and stood by the doorway. Counting the motel we stayed at for the video shoot, this would be only the 2nd hotel I had ever stayed at.

This was cool as shit though. I had a huge bed, TV, nice bathroom. It even had a Coffee maker. I threw my bag on the bed and pulled out my clothes and started putting them in the draws. I didn't bring much, a few pairs of Lees, shirts and why I packed a Kangol, I don't know because ever since I got this hair style I can't wear them.

In my bag was this little pouch. I didn't put it in there, so the only culprit would be Grams. I unzipped it noticing that she had packed it with the necessities that I was too excited to even remember. Toothbrush, Soap, Deodorant, Razor and only Grams would remember to send along a small bottle of Egyptian Musk.

A sheet of notebook paper was folded inside the pouch, and when I opened it, the familiar handwriting made me smile. It was a letter from Grams, and taped to it was a ten dollar bill.

Dear Mijo. By the time you read this you will already be in California. I just wanted to say how very proud I am of you. Not just for the music thing but more importantly, for the man you have become. The world is opening up and welcoming you to all it has. Take it Papi, and please don't worry about me, I am fine, and relaxing in this gorgeous apartment. In fact, I'm out on the balcony getting some sun as I write this. I love you beyond words. Que Dios te bendiga.

Grandma.

Suddenly, there was a knock on the door.

"One second!" I yelled out as I tried my best to dry my eyes. I opened the door and it was Roller Girl. She looked me dead in the eyes.

"Are you okay?" She asked.

"Yeah, I'm fine." I replied looking away and sniffling.

"Well I just wanted to make sure your room was okay."

"It's perfect, thank you." Roller Girl stepped further into my room and closed the door behind her.

"She adores you, King." Roller Girl said out of nowhere.

"I feel guilty leaving her behind. I mean, if anyone deserves to travel around the country, it's her."

"You're right. And that's what vacations are for. What she's doing right now is what she prefers to do. Believe me, King, she doesn't want to do all of this. Besides, right now she's ecstatic, so let her be." Suddenly there was a knock, and Roller Girl opened the door.

"You ready?" Sal said, his suspicious eyes bouncing between the two of us.

CHAPTER 49

West Coast Arena

I stepped onto the humongous empty stage. The knot in my throat was practically choking me, and I was scared to blink as my tears were on edge. I watched as the stagehands scurried like madmen, rolling across scaffolds, and other equipment. I knew what the set would look like from the many drawings we've seen over the past several months, and now it was all coming to life.

I couldn't believe how far off I was when I use to try and imagine what this day would be like. This was some real shit. So real in fact that I felt out of place. Like what the fuck am I doing here? I kept waiting for Mr. D to come up and thank me for my time, before letting me go.

The dancers all dropped down and began stretching around me. I was still in shock, and therefore just stood there mesmerized.

"Let's go Sunshine!" Princess called out to me clapping his long skinny hands just under his chin. "The last thing we need is for any of you cramped up and shit."

"Get down and stretch!" Vanessa said in a loud whisper, as she pulled her head to her knee.

I sat on the floor, and with my legs spread out, I too began to stretch. Each direction that I turned, I spotted something new and exciting. From the colorful lights, dangling above us, to the huge mixing board, where at least a half dozen pony tailed white guys stood around fussing. A stretch to the right had me looking straight out at the endless amount of seats.

"Okay, that's it, up!" Princess commanded. "Without any music we are going to walk through the entire routine. I want everyone in position." By now my heart was racing, and I swore I was going to have a heart attack.

"Sunshine, are you ready?" Princess asked. I took me minute to answer, and when I did, all I could do was nod.

"Well then, I need you in position."

I stood there, frozen, my eyes scanning everyone around me as they waited for me to at least move. But for the life of me, I couldn't remember what that position was that I was supposed to be in. My mind had gone completely blank. I glanced to the side where the dancers were, and saw Vanessa's finger gesture for me to turn around, and at that very moment, it all came back. I turned my back to where the audience will soon be, and before I knew it... It was all over.

We ended with applause for one another, but I still can't remember anything. Princess strolled through our ranks, making to each of us, small suggestions. He talked about covering up mistakes, and assured us that, no one would notice. It was the first time that he spoke to us in a more civilized manner, and didn't bash our every move. In fact, his entire prep speech was positive.

We went through the routine a few more times while the set was being put together around us, and just as we were finishing up, a group of people suddenly entered the venue. We all looked, and realized that it was Nemesis and his entourage coming for sound check.

I could see a few of my star struck dancers get excited. Vee looked at me. She knew how I felt about him, and therefore paid him no mind.

"Okay, everyone, let's stay focused!" Princess shouted, though it seemed more so for Nemesis to hear. I saw Princess starting to revert back into the old him, once again becoming demanding and rude.

Princess glanced back, as if to see if Nemesis was watching. But he wasn't, and that seemed to bother him.

Nemesis and his crew took seats in the first row, and watched us. I was so embarrassed, and could hear small burst of laughter and mumbling.

"Sunshine!" Princess yelled out, and I turned to him. "You need to get your head in the game."

"Did he just call that nigga Sunshine?" I heard Nemesis ask one of his buddies, this one an Albino. He wore a short white afro, along with a pair of shades in a red frame. The albino laughed. "What is this, the fuckin' fruity loop tour?" Nemesis added, and from there on the jokes continued.

I wanted so bad to just jump off the stage and start fucking everyone up, but by the size of these ten guys, I'd surely end up in the hospital, or even the morgue.

It was becoming very distracting and loud, but nobody knew what to do. I had no idea that we were the opening act for Nemesis, and now we either had to take his abuse, or be thrown off.

Suddenly, out of nowhere stepped Sal. We all began to slow down staring in his direction.

"Hey, look who it is, Numb Nuts."

"Fuck you say, white boy?" Albino said as he jumped up from his seat, followed by the others. Nemesis stopped them.

"Let me handle this shit." He said stepping past them and in front of Sal. Who immediately pulled out his gun and shoved it directly into Nemesis' mouth, in one smooth and graceful move. It was like something out of a movie. I didn't think this was a good idea, but it caught everyone's attention for sure.

"Now you fucking Gorilla's listen to me. If I ever, hear any of you disrespecting anyone on that stage, one by one your asses are going to go missing. Now I'm saying this in front of plenty of witnesses, which means that I don't give a fuck!"

Sal turned his attention back to Nemesis, as he stood there with the gun barrel practically down his throat.

"They're here to open up for your ugly ass." Sal said low and stern into Nemesis' face. "Now you can either be nice and appreciative, or don't say shit. Your choice! But if you ever disrespect them again." Sal pulled him closer, cocked the gun, and whispered. "I will make sure this bullet rips up your insides before it finds its way out of your ass. Nemesis nodded and Sal uncocked the gun, and slid it out from his mouth and wiped it on Nemesis' clean white tee.

"Now get the fuck out of here until they're finished."

Nemesis looked at us, and then at Sal. He didn't say a thing, just gestured his boys to follow. Just as they were leaving the Albino looked up at me and mouthed, *you're dead!* I don't think anyone noticed, so I just did my best not to look scared.

CHAPTER 50

Opening Night

I stood on the stool talking to Roller Girl, while Antonio put the finishing touches on my outfit, and Roberto and Gina touched up my hair and makeup.

Gus, the photographer had already taken at least a few hundred pictures of me. I thought that Bus three was just our equipment. Come to find out, it also housed much of Mr. D's staff.

We had more people with us than even the headliner. Didn't make much sense to me, but I'm sure Mr. D had a reason.

"Going to need you side stage in ten." One of the runners said, sticking his head into our dressing room.

"Thank you." Roller Girl said and then turned to me and smiled. "This is it!" I smiled back, except mine was a bit nervous.

"Okay, that's it!" Antonio said as he stepped back for a better look. I was able to see myself in the large mirror across from me. I stared, and it was as if I was looking at a complete stranger. Gus jumped out in front of me and quickly snapped at least another twenty pics.

"Ready?' Roller Girl asked. I nodded and stepped off the stool.

Antonio wished me luck as I followed Roller Girl out of the dressing room and into the corridor.

I could only look forward for some reason, I could hear my dancers complimenting me, as they stepped out of their dressing rooms, but I was unable to respond.

Gus had rushed ahead of us, and walking backwards, he continued taking pictures.

It was like a dream, and it seemed as if I was walking in slow motion. The rumble that shook the tunnel as we walked, I realized was in fact, the audience.

As we approached the stage door one of the security guards immediately opened it. We stepped through and stood off to the side of the stage out of view.

We all gathered around Princess for some last minute reminders, as Gus continued to snap away.

I glanced up at the host, a personality from the local radio station. I can hear him setting up our introduction.

Vanessa put her arm over my shoulder. I looked at her and her smiled soothed my nerves.

After the pep talk, Princess told us all to bring it in closer. We did, and as he got down on one knee, we all huddled around him, when suddenly, he began to pray.

"Dear Lord, you have given us, not just the talents to express ourselves, but also the drive to bring us to where we

are. We thank you for everything you've given us, and tonight we dedicate this show to you, in Jesus' name, Amen!"

Everyone repeated the Amen, though mine was a bit delayed.

And then, for the first time, I heard it, my name, being introduced to thousands of people.

"Give it up for, King!!!"

The applause in no way represented the amount of people that were in the seats, as the place was jam-packed. The dancers rushed up on stage and got into position, remaining there until the music began. It seemed to take forever, but when it finally did, and the audience heard it, they got up on their feet and applauded with a thunderous roar. They had no idea who I was, but they sure as hell, knew the song. And there it was… My cue!

I got up on the stage and headed to my microphone that stood front center on a stand. I could hear a few laughs but no sooner that I started rapping did they stop, and instead stood up to sing along.

My biggest fear was forgetting something, whether it was my words, or my moves, but it was as if I wasn't even in control anymore. Like my body was moving on its own, the words just flowing from inside me. I couldn't forget anything. It was all so natural to me. I felt comfortable up here, and I could feel a connection with the audience, like they were family, my family! I looked out into the crowd, my eyes meeting the eyes of so many, each person seemed so familiar to me, like I knew them, whether in this life, or another.

The moves that I did with the dancers flowed like water and for the first time I truly felt like the leader. I stepped to the front of the stage where several people stood with cameras, both still and video, shooting my every move. I spotted Gus, he was *my* guy and I made sure to get him some really cool shots.

One girl almost threw me off when I noticed she was crying. I didn't know why, all I thought was that something was wrong, but I continued when I saw at the other end of the stage was another girl. She too was crying, but mouthing the words to my song at the same time. I saw someone raise something in the air. It was a tee shirt, and it had my picture on it. I had never seen that before, and figured she had it made and when I acknowledged it, out of nowhere, more Tee Shirts began popping up from the audience. Hundreds, maybe even thousands. I did my best to acknowledge them without interrupting my routine.

Our show came to a close, and what I thought was going to be a long and grueling performance, flew by like a flash of lightening, much of it I couldn't even remember.

We settled in our closing pose to a crowd whose applause was deafening. The lights lit the audience and I couldn't find one person still sitting.

I didn't know what to do so I just ran off the stage, just to find at the bottom of the steps was Mr. D…. And my Grandmother!

Immediately I grabbed and hugged her. I looked at Mr. D and said Thank you. Princess called out to me and when I turned to him he pointed back to the stage.

"They want you!"

I didn't know what I was supposed to do, so I just went back onto the stage to an even louder cheer. I bowed and said thank you, and then turned to my dancers and waved them up.

CHAPTER 51

What A Surprise

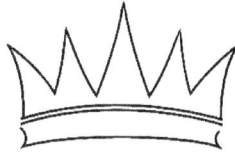

What Mr. D did by attending my first performances *and* Bringing Grams, was beyond anything else I could ask for. He closed the circle for me and I will never forget that. After the concert we were to go back to the hotel, change and head to the After Party being held at an exclusive club not far from the venue. Mr. D and Grams stayed behind as they had an early flight back home. I was satisfied because I offered to take her with us to the next three cities and she laughed at me. She was happy to have been there for the first one, but that was it, she said it was too loud. That was obvious as she stood side stage with her hands over her ears... So cute!

Sal and I pulled up in front of the Paradise Lounge and I was in awe of the massive crowd that stood on line to get in. The entrance to the after party was part of the VIP package that I heard was as high as a thousand dollars a ticket, and very exclusive. I knew that Nemesis had become a huge artist. Though this was all beyond what I imagined. This shit was crazy!

Sal walked around and opened my door, but when I

stepped out, the already loud crowd that stood on line became much louder and then left their places on line and dashed toward the limo. I got scared and froze, and Sal pushed me back into the car and shut the door. He stood there, a barricade between the crowd and the door, literally pushing people away.

I noticed people began to make their way around the car to the other doors, but thank God, they were locked.

I could see the people trying to move Sal out the way to get to me, but he stood firm and unmovable. I didn't know if I should lock the door he was leaning on, or leave it open. What if he needed to get away from them too?

I heard some yelling, and looked around to try and figure it out, and though I couldn't, I did notice the people getting back on line, and then spotted several huge bouncers in black Tee Shirts.

The door opened up and Sal quickly waved me to come out. The bouncers surround me and then led me through the entrance.

We continued through the club to a staircase that led up to a top section being used now as our VIP. Another monster standing in front with his arms crossed stepped aside and unlatched the velvet rope.

The upstairs VIP area was like a whole other club, except you can look off the side at the people dancing below.

"Would you like a drink?" A waitress said as she stepped up to me. "Uh um, Pepsi?"

"A Pepsi?" She asked, and I nodded, "With?" She

continued.

"Ice?" I replied.

"One Pepsi… with ice, she giggled, before she turned and walked away. "Ladies, and gentlemen," announced the DJ as he lowered the music. I leaned up against the banister overlooking the crowd, when suddenly I was hit by a spotlight.

"As promised," he continued, My smile so wide that my cheeks began to hurt. "The Paradise Lounge would like to welcome…" I raised my hand, ready to wave out to the crowd below, when I heard… Nemesis!"

I quickly used my waving hand to pretend that I was fixing my hair. My wide smile flipped upside down, and slowly I stepped back from the banister.

I continued following the spotlight as it flashed across the balcony, finally landing on Nemesis, who to my surprise, was standing just to my left. He too was waving. He had been watching me all along, and gave me a sarcastic grin.

I turned and walked to the bathroom to try and hide from the humiliation. Locking myself inside one of the stalls I just stood there, trying to get over what just happened while listening as a couple of guys in the stall next to me sniffed cocaine.

"Also joining us in the VIP," I could hear the DJ continuing in the distance. "is none other than… King!"

"What?" I said to myself, as one of the guys in the other stall confirmed.

"He said King!"

I couldn't believe it. The roar of the crowd literally shook the stall I was in. In fact, it sounded louder than Nemesis'.

By the time I made it back to my section, the excitement of me being in the house had died down and the crowd was back to dancing.

"Yo! Where the fuck were you?" Quenepa asked, the rest of my crew standing with him.

"I was in the bathroom."

We all came together, talking and joking, having a great time. A few of the dancers were dancing around us, and everyone was drinking, when Roller Girl came up to me. I was glad to see her and gave her a hug. I saw Vanessa look my way and smile.

As Roller Girl and I got into a little conversation, she started dancing in front of me. I laughed when she tried to get me to join her. I declined, until my crew circled me into submission.

I danced until I was soaked in sweat. The waitress handed me another drink, Rum and Coke was the only one I knew, and I was already on number four.

I stepped out of the circle and made my way back over to the banister for a little air and to check out the crowd below. I never realized how much I'd been missing. This club shit was fun.

"Sup kid!" Quenepa said smacking me on the back as he stood beside me and leaned over the banister.

"One too many drinks," I replied.

"You drinking that old man shit, you gotta hit this!" He

said holding up a bottle of Hennessey.

"Nah, that's alright." I said, shaking my head as I watched Q chugalug right from the bottle.

"This is nuts!" I said to Q as I looked out over the club.

"Bitches are fine up in here," he replied. I smiled in agreement. "Shit, I bet you can probably get any girl you want up in here." I didn't respond, but I sure as hell was listening. I looked down into the crowd and started spotting all the big asses, wondering if what Quenepa was telling me was true. Could I really get any girl up in here?

I turned to look at Quenepa, and spotted him leaning over the banister with a tassel of saliva hanging from his mouth.

"Fuck you doing?" I asked just as it broke loose and plummet to the crowd below, landing smack in the center of some guy's head.

He reached up and wiped it off with his hand. Realizing what it was, he immediately looked up as Q and I jumped back out of sight.

"Yo, you hit him." I said as I watched Q drop down on the small couch laughing hysterically.

"Oh my god, that shit was perfect!" He laughed.

"That shit was nasty, yo." I replied, though also laughing.

We both peeked off the banister and the guy was nowhere to be found. Quenepa leaned over again.

"Come on man, stop that shit." I told him. But it was too late, another string of saliva swung from his mouth until it snapped free and we watched it hit a girl on the wrist. She didn't even notice. We both jumped back and I couldn't help but start laughing. I couldn't believe that this shit was even entertaining me.

We peeked back over, and Q looked at me and nodded.

"Nah man, I ain't doing that shit."

"Don't be a pussy," he replied, but this time he had stopped laughing.

I looked over the banister and began to load my mouth with the disgusting ammunition. Q smiled and pointed to a bright shiny target... Some guy's bald head.

I glanced back at Q, who was now getting excited. Looking like a child up to no good. I looked back down, took aim, and let go. Mine didn't stretch the way Quenepa's did, but it was thick and just as nasty, and when it missed its intended target, splashing instead into some girl's drink, it knocked the entire cup right out of her hand.

Again we jumped back laughing hysterically. We gave it a few seconds before looking back over, but when we did, we were busted! We jumped back again, unable to stop laughing when we noticed Nemesis and his boys had come over to our section.

"Are you two fucking spitting on people?" Nemesis asked. I kept quiet and just looked at the floor, I was so embarrassed.

Quenepa on the other hand wasn't, instead, he jumped up and stepped forward, placing his forehead up again Nemesis' chest.

"Yeah so what, you got a problem with that?" Q yelled

out, grabbing the attention of practically everyone in the VIP. I couldn't let this get out of hand, besides, we were guilty. I grabbed Q by the arm and tugged on him a bit, but this boy was like a cement statue, I couldn't budge him.

"Man, come on Q, chill out."

"Nah, fuck that! This ugly mother fucker wanna come up in here and question me on some bullshit? Fuck you nigga!" Quenepa said even louder, his finger gesturing toward Nemesis. The streets had definitely made Quenepa into some type of monster. Standing well under five feet, while not one of Nemesis' eight boys were under six. Q showed not an ounce of fear, me on the other hand, shit, I ain't want no trouble!

"What's going on here?" I heard Sal say before even seeing him. He stepped in between us and looked at both sides. "Are you guys serious, tonight?"

"This mother fucker don't know how to mind his own business!" Quenepa said. Chin up and chest out.

"They were spitting into the crowd, Nasty bastards!" Nemesis responded. Sal turned and looked at us.

"Serious?" Sal inquired. Immediately, I nodded! Q however denied the whole thing. "Ain't nobody was spitting. Mother fucker, maybe if you pop some actual lenses into them corny-ass Cazels you'd be able to see, bitch!" I stopped nodding though it was too late Sal had already heard me confess.

"I'll take care of it." Sal said to Nemesis and his boys, gesturing them back to their section. They turned and walked off, and just as they approached their section, Albino looked back, and for show, yelled out.

"Pops ain't always gonna be around, yo!" The Albino said with a smile. Sal turned and looked at him. The Albino's smile widened before throwing Sal a kiss. Sal just stared at him. His blue eyes latching on him like a guided missile. Nemesis noticed and grabbed his boy, shaking his head as if to say, *don't fuck with him*! Nemesis remained quiet while his people were making fun of the incident. Albino stood there, just staring at me. I looked away and pretended not to notice, but when I looked back, he was still staring. I glanced over at Sal who had been trying to keep Q calm. Sal saw what the Albino was doing, but he didn't say anything. I took one last look over at Nemesis' section. Albino was still looking my way, this time punching into his palm as he mouthed the words *I'm gonna fuck you up*.

"King!" Sal yelled out. I turned to him and he waved me to come on.

CHAPTER 52

Home Bound

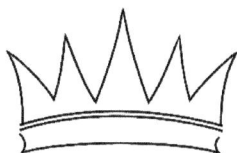

So far, the tour had been going great, but I couldn't wait for our next and final stop, which would be none other than my very own NYC.

Everybody settled into their claimed spots on the bus, including my seat, that Vanessa didn't allow anyone to sit in, not even Quenepa.

As we were about to pull off, we heard a bang on the side of the bus. Sal slammed on the breaks, sending a couple of the dancers tumbling over one another. He pulled open the door with a bit of an attitude, but no sooner than he did, I noticed a sudden change to his attitude.

"Is there a problem, Officer?"

"Mind if we come up?" I heard a voice reply light and distant. Sal gave it a second, and then nodded, waving the two officers on board. Ascending the steps with their badges held up, the two detectives stood at the front of the bus, their eyes giving each of us a virtual pat down. I couldn't possibly imagine what they might've wanted, so along with everyone else, we waited.

"How's everyone doing, this morning?" He asked, more so to break the silence. It was way too early for small talk, so all they got back was some mumbling.

"Has anyone seen this man?" One of them said, holding up a photo of the albino. They watched closely for any unusual reactions, but we were all in shock, and therefore, no one moved.

"His name is Calvin Curtis," said the second officer. "But some of you might know him as, Albino."

"For obvious reasons," said the cop holding up the photo.

My dancers all started talking among themselves, as the cop with the photo stepped closer, holding it up to my face.

"What about you?" he asked, "have you seen this guy?"

"The last time I saw him was over at the club, but he was still there when we left."

"We?" The officer asked.

"Yeah, me and the dancers."

"Where'd you go?" The other cop asked.

"Back to the hotel."

"How'd you get there?" The other cop asked.

"Sal," I said, gesturing toward the front. The cops turned and looked at him. "Did you make any stops?"

"Well, yeah. We were hungry, so we found a diner."

"Was... What's his name? Sal? Was he with you the whole time?"

"Yeah." I replied, sort of hesitating. The detective noticed and stood their string at me. "You sure?"

"Yeah… Hey, should I get an attorney?" I asked.

"Do you think you need one?"

"Just answer the questions, King. We have to go." Sal yelled out from the front of the bus. The officer looked back at Sal, and gave him a tight smile. Sal didn't respond.

"So, after the diner, where'd you go?"

"To the hotel."

"And then what?" The detective asked. I looked at him strangely, and then answered. "We went to our rooms."

"Was that the last time you saw your driver?"

"Well seeing that we don't share a room… Yeah."

"So you have no idea whether Sal went straight to his room or not?"

"I'm not sure if *anyone* went straight to their room or not!" Everyone looked at me. "And no one knows whether or not I went straight to *mine*. Besides why are you asking me about Sal when he's sitting right there?"

The detective looked again at Sal, then back at me.

"Because Sal's a pro, I wouldn't be able to see through him. You on the other hand, shit, you're a piece of glass."

The detective handed me a business card.

"If you hear anything, or, maybe just wanna call, and say hi."

I took his card, and watched as the two officers turned around. The first one exited the bus, but the one that was asking the questions stopped and looked at Sal.

"Drive carefully." The cop told Sal. "I hear the roads can be quite bumpy."

"Been driving them for years," Sal replied.

The detective laughed, and then stepped off the bus. Sal shut the door, and peeled off.

"Man, at first I thought them mother fuckers were coming for me!" Quenepa said as he stepped up beside me.

"Why would they be coming for you?"

"I took the mother fuckin' bathrobe!"

CHAPTER 53

Red Frames

I woke up to a loud applause, and watched as the huge buildings of New York City swooshed by. It's been an incredible tour, and now we finally get to do a show at home. Though I should've known better, I did question Mr. D's reasoning behind having us doing New York last, and now as we track down Broadway, I understand.

It seemed as if every city we did, added to the momentum of the tour, and now that we're finally home, the excitement was insane.

I started off as the opening act for Nemesis, but now, according to the dozens of billboards advertising us, this tour now belonged to the both of us, and other openers had been added.

Mr. D wanted to make sure we were all together before the show, and didn't allow us to go home. Instead, he put us up at The Palazzo Hotel.

It was good to be home, and even though we were only gone for a few weeks, the city seemed so strange, kind of small as a matter of fact. It didn't take long for me to grow accustomed to the trees, grass and cows during our tour, and now the constant view of bricks and concrete were sort of depressing.

We pulled up to a building that I had seen thousands of times, never realizing that it was in fact one of New York City's most prestigious hotels.

Sal pulled up in front and opened the door. We gathered all of our things and began exiting the bus. As I stepped off, I looked at Sal who stood just outside the door directing us into the building, noticing something that made my heart drop to the floor. Sal, as always, had on a pair of sunglasses, the only difference being… These frames were red!

"What do you need, King?" Sal asked me when I stopped in front of him and just stared.

I waited a second, and then shook my head. Sal patted me on the back along with a little nudge that kept me moving toward the entrance of the hotel.

As I entered the crowed lobby, I heard a bit of a ruckus and worked my way through the small crowd only to find out that it was Quenepa arguing with the hotel manager.

"What's going on?" I asked as I approached them.

"This mother fucker's trying to say I can't stay here."

"You are not allowed on these premises and you know that!" The manager said, his fat white face now a tomato red, and the few white strands of hair bounced around as he shouted. "Sonia, call the police right now!" He yelled out to the young Puerto Rican clerk behind the counter.

"Look, sir, we're performing tonight at the Garden, and by tomorrow we'll all be out of here." I tried to reason.

"You guys are not the problem, he is! For years, he's been a menace to this establishment, not to mention a disrespectful little shit!" and at that very moment, Quenepa jumped forwarded and smacked the manager so hard, that he spun around and then collapsed to the floor.

"Yo, what the fuck did you do? I yelled at Q, standing over the manager prepared to smack him again if he tried to get up.

Mr. Strudel remained on the floor, holding his neck and back, yelling for help. I pushed Quenepa out the way, and tried to help up the manager back up on his feet, but when I touched him he screamed like a little bitch, and pretended to go into convulsions.

"I will sue each and every one of you!" He yelled out, throwing his body into this comical fit, with one leg shaking violently, going as far as spitting up on himself.

While a couple of the dancers seemed concerned, everyone else was laughing hysterically.

I saw Quenepa step forward as if he was about to kick the manager in the head, and just as I was about to block the kick, Sal came up from behind and pulled him back by his collar.

"What the fucks going on?" Sal asked as he stood over me and Mr. Strudel.

"You have to help me!" Mr. Strudel cried, not realizing that Sal was with us." These…" He looked at us… "Savages, came in here and just started beating on me! Please help me!"

"Sir, no one was beating on you, let's get you up…"

"Ow!" The manager cried out when Sal tried to help him up.

"I can't feel my legs!"

"What happened?" Sal asked me in a whisper.

"Q slapped him." I replied.

"With what?"

"His hand," I replied

Sal looked at all of us and then exhaled, trying to figure out what to do. He walked over to the clerk and said something to her, she said something back, and then nodded and came out from behind the counter and locked the door.

"What are you doing? Don't lock it the Police are on their way!" Sonia ignored him and made her way back behind the counter.

"Everyone, get your keys and get to your rooms, we'll call you when it's time for sound check."

Nobody said anything, they just walked over to the counter as Sonia handed everyone their keys.

"You too!" Sal added, looking at both Quenepa and I. Quenepa rushed over to the counter.

"Don't give him a key!" The manager yelled at Sonia. She ignored him.

I looked at Sal, the red framed sun glasses, he wore, sort of haunting me.

"Get your key, and get upstairs." He commanded. I looked down at the Hotel Manager who laid there just staring up at the ceiling, and then went over to the counter.

"You called the cops?" I asked the clerk. She looked over at her boss, then back at me… She shook her head, then slid my key across the counter.

"Room 412"

"Thank you." I told her, before grabbing my key and heading over to the elevator.

Once inside I pressed the fourth floor and then turned, only to catch Sal and the manager both watching as the doors closed.

"Now get your fuckin' ass up." Sal's voice echoed up the elevator shaft.

As I opened my door, I heard the door across from me open. It was Q.

"Sup King?"

"So what was that all about?" I asked, both of us standing in our doorways.

"Man, I use to deliverer coke here." Q was kind of loud so I threw my finger up to my lips.

"Deliver?" I asked in a whisper.

"Yeah, just 'cause the mother fuckers who stay here are rich, don't mean they didn't get high. Shit, they got high more than anyone else I knew. They just had the luxury of doing their shit indoors.

"So that's why he doesn't want you in the building?"

"Well, I didn't use to deliver straight to the guest."

"What do you mean?"

"I use to drop it off with the old man, and he use to bring it to them, for a markup of course."

"So he was in on it too?"

"In on it? He was the one who use to set everything up."

"So what happened?"

"Well I needed a little extra cash so I cut the shit up a bit more than usual."

"He couldn't tell?"

"Didn't matter, was just an eight ball, them rich mother fuckers sniff that shit in one blow.

"So what happened?"

"He got busted, word got around, and people ain't wanna fuck with him no more."

CHAPTER 54

The Garden

We had dinner at the venue after sound check, and got some rest back at the hotel. Now it was show time!

The butterflies in my stomach were going crazy as I stepped into the van that would transport us back over to the venue.

Approaching the Garden this time, was nothing like it was for Sound check. In just a few hours, the entire scenery had changed, and I was in awe of the tremendous amount of people who were now lined up for the concert.

The marquee above the building exploded in lights as Nemesis' name took on a hundred different shapes, sizes and colors. I waited excitedly, hoping at the very least that my name would also be up there, and out of nowhere, there it was! And not only that, the effects they used were exactly the same as what they used for Nemesis. My eyes became so watery that I dared not look at anyone. Though, everyone was looking at me.

We pulled up to a gate where two security guards pulled them apart allowing the van to enter. We drove down a small hill to what looked like a garage entrance, and when the driver honked his horn, the door in front of us rolled up, and into the building we went.

A woman holding a clipboard, and a walkie talkie attached to her shoulder greeted us. "Yes, they're in the building." She said into her radio, and then waved us over to one of the two golf carts parked to the side. We piled into each of them and off we went, speeding through the tunnels of The Garden.

We got to our dressing room and I noticed on the door was a sheet of paper that was obviously torn out of a spiral notebook as it was missing the top corner. They didn't even bother to use scotch tape, but rather a strip of duct tape stretched across the entire sheet a bit slanted. It simply said king, all small letters, and in pencil.

"What kind of bullshit is this?" Quenepa said. I wanted to agree, but when I turned to Sal he subtly shook his head, so I stayed quiet.

Sal led the way into the room, Quenepa and I followed behind. Our dancers were there already, spread out on the floor, stretching. Princess came out from the bathroom and smiled at us.

"Can you believe that sign on the door?" He asked, seeming so annoyed. Sal didn't say anything. He just walked over to the cooler and grabbed a Coke.

"I'm finished!" Skye announced as she walked up to me with a No Trespassing sign that she took from somewhere. In the back of it, she drew this spectacular piece that said, in huge fancy letters along the rim of a crown, THE KING. It was drawn with a black marker, and then shaded in pencil. This girl never ceases to amaze me, what an incredible talent she was.

"We don't need their stinking sign," she said as everyone gathered around, and complimented her piece.

We stepped out into the hall and looked at the crap hanging on the wall, and laughed, but just as Skye was about to rip it down, I stopped her.

"What?" She asked. I stood there, just looking at the raggedy sign, but something was telling me not to mess with it.

"Leave it!" I said, my eyes locked on it.

"You're kidding me, right? Skye asked, and again was about to rip it down.

"I'm serious!"

She let go of the edge and shrugged her shoulders in defeat.

"One day, this will actually mean something."

"Rip that shit down, Rey!" Vanessa yelled out as she stood at the mirror touching up her makeup, everyone agreed.

"I'd like to keep this, if you don't mind?" I asked her, taking the sign from her hand.

"But I don't want to remove this one." I said, pushing down on the corner of the tape.

The production assistant lady who escorted us to the room walked up on me.

"I'll be back in thirty to take you to the stage," she said.

I never liked being apart from my crew so I always asked for a dressing room close to theirs, and still spent most of my time with them in theirs. This time, I was fortunate enough to have my dressing room inside of theirs, which I kept the door open anyway.

Getting ready for a show was sometimes even more fun than the show itself. The energy we shared was electrifying. I'd gotten pretty close to all of them, and it made the job just that much more enjoyable. Everyone stood around and watched as the finishing touches were placed on me. I was always the last to see what I looked like so most of the time I spent trying to read everyone else's face, and once all was done, and still before I got to see the end result I always received a round of applause. Sometimes I thought that even that was fixed, so that I wouldn't pay mind to the reality of my crazy-ass look.

The door opened and there was the production assistant ready to take us to the stage. My butterflies had now turned into bats, as we all piled back on to the golf carts and headed to the stage.

"Yo, check this shit out." One of Nemesis's buddies said from the doorway of his dressing room. Nemesis stepped to the doorway and watched as we drove pass. I looked at him with a slight smile and nod, hoping that I would get at least a good luck from him. But I didn't. Instead I got a sarcastic smirk.

"Looks like a fuckin' Circus." I heard one of them say. Nemesis spotted Sal on the cart beside me, rolled his eyes, and then pushed his way back into the room.

When we got backstage, we got into a huddle. Sal and Princess would never be a part of this huddle, because this was reserved only for those who would take stage.

"I love you, Vee." I said to my dear friend. "I love you too, King." She replied.

I repeated the gesture to each of my dancers, they too replied likewise. I then looked over at Quenepa, and smiled, he smiled back.

"You too, Q!"

"Always gotta get all gay and shit!" He said, as he always did. But it was the way we always ended our huddles, laughing hysterically. Mind you, Q had never once said he loved any of us.

Suddenly we heard our introduction and watched as the huge curtain slowly rose.

CHAPTER 55

Instant Fame

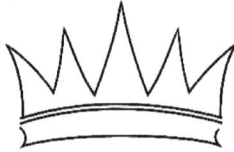

Laughter coming from the kitchen, every morning was for me a pleasant way a waking up. Grams and Rosie got along great, and Grams had someone new to tell her war stories to.

It was 8:00 a.m. and though I felt like I could stay in bed for a week, all I could do is just stare up at the ceiling fan, thinking about this incredible tour I was just on, especially last night!

Finally, I got up and jumped into the shower, which was conveniently located in my very own private bathroom.

"Good morning." I said as I stepped out into the kitchen area, dressed and ready to get my day started. And yes, I was right. Grams and Rosie were in the kitchen chatting it up, like they've been doing since they first met. I noticed a deeper growth in their relationship since I've been gone, and I was thrilled. For years, I was Gram's only companion.

"Hey, there he is!" I heard someone say, only to find Sal sitting at the counter reading the paper and drinking his

Bustelo.

"Good morning, Papi." Grams said as I stepped over and kissed her on the cheek. "Good morning." Rosie said, as she put my eggs on.

"So how you feeling?" Sal asked.

"I'm still wired from last night, not to mention a slight headache."

"So, I heard it was a great show." Grams said as she placed a coffee cup in front of me and filled it.

"Incredible! I mean, the place was sold out! I gotta stop hating on that Nemesis dude, really, he's got it going on."

"I don't know about all that." Sal said as he slid his newspaper across the table for me to read. The first thing I noticed was the headline. It read; OPENING ACT STEALS THE SHOW! I looked at Sal, and he smiled, so did Grams, but I was confused, even though I could clearly read the headline, it just wasn't processing.

"Go to page six," Sal said with a cool gesture.

"NEW RAP SENSATION, KING, SLAYS THE DRAGON, AND INVADES THE HEARTS OF ITS VILLAGERS...

I couldn't believe what I was reading. They couldn't have possibly been talking about me, and if they were, it had to be a set up, and knowing Sal and Mr. D, well... I wouldn't put it pass either of them.

After reading the article I looked up at Sal, who was just sitting there with a sort of smirk on his face. My eyes then dashed over to Grams, who sat there smiling. And then there was Rosie, who while serving my breakfast, was also smiling.

"This makes no sense, you know that!" I said to Sal.

"Why wouldn't it? You worked hard."

"Real hard!" Grams added.

I performed one song. Nemesis performed six. He's got radio play, and four videos. This is not supposed to happen like this." I stood up and began pacing in disbelief.

"Sal please, don't mess with me, man. You gotta swear to me that Mr. D had nothing to do with this!"

"Oh he had *everything* to do with it!"

"I'm talking about this article."

"It's real, King. In fact, Mr. D spotted it first and called *me*."

"Between the incident at the hospital, the video, and the four major cities you just toured, you've gained yourself a decent following."

I continued pacing back and forth, still trying to make sense of it all. It was like I just went from zero to a hundred in a split second.

"So now what?"

"Well, that's why I'm here on a Sunday morning. Mr. D wants you over at his office."

"For what?"

"I don't know, but he told me not to wake you, but that when you got up, to bring you right over."

Suddenly, we heard the elevator ring, and looked in its direction. There's no way for anyone to get on that elevator without first being announced.

"Are you expecting someone?" I asked Sal who got up and gesture us all to move behind the wall. I watched as he reached under his jacket and before he could pull out his gun. I guided Grams and Rosie into a room. I peeked out, and watched as he stood in front of the door with his gun pointed out in front of him.

The door seemed to take forever to finally open, and once it did, I heard someone yell out.

"No, don't shoot!"

Sal grabbed the little man with the thick mustache by the tie and pulled him into the apartment, slamming his face against the wall.

"Who the fuck are you?" Sal demanded to know as pressed his gun against the back of the man's head while frisking him.

'I'm sorry." The man replied with a stutter. "My name is Joe, and I'm with The Post."

"The Post?" Sal asked.

"Yeah. Here's my…" But the moment the man tried to move for his ID, Sal, pressed his body harder against the wall.

I told the women to stay put and rushed over to the scene.

"Go back in the room!" Sal ordered.

"I don't think he's here to hurt anyone."

Sal looked at me, a bit annoyed, but then eased off the guy.

"Thank you." The man said, as he straightened himself out, including his toupee.

"How'd you get up here?" I asked.

"I just got in the elevator and came up." The man said, Sal and I looked at each other.

"I just wanted to ask you a few questions, about last night's concert."

Sal pressed the intercom on the wall beside the elevator.

"This is Jonathan, how can I help you?" The doorman replied.

"Yeah Jonathan, this is Sal. We have a gentleman here from The News. Said he just walked through the front door, and got on the elevator. How the fuck is that possible?"

"I don't know Mr. Sal. I've been here all morning.

" Sal turned and looked at the reporter.

"Somebody's lying." Sal said in a sort of eerie tone.

"How else would I get up here? I mean, other than through the front door, this place is like Fort Knox."

Sal reached over and pressed the elevator button which immediately opened the door.

"Get in." He ordered the man." But before he can take a step, Sal pushed him in.

"But what about the questions?" he asked.

"I don't have a problem answering them." I told Sal. But he paid me no mind, and I watched as the elevator door closed.

I assumed Sal was just gonna escort him out onto the curb, but then I noticed, the elevator go up!

CHAPTER 56

The Big News

Looking off the balcony, Rosie noticed the entire front of the building lined with News vans. I would've never in a million years had thought that they were there for me, but Ciré had called us and confirmed. He gave Sal specific instructions on how to deal with the press, and ordered me not speak to anyone without him there.

We took the elevator all the way down into the private garage where Sal had parked. Upon exiting, I was surprised to see the Police out front, directing reporters away from the driveway.

Sal took his time driving through the City to the Funky Junky, and though we drove in the regular Sedan, it still set off its own aura. You can tell this car was special. Its mysterious blackness and deep smoked windows, made people turn and look. Even the sound of its engine was like no other on the road.

We pulled into the Funky Junky's own underground garage and then headed for the elevator. These things that I thought were mere vanities of the rich and famous, I came to learn were in fact necessities.

Reporter's entire livelihoods depended on interviews and candid photos, with the big bucks going to the exclusive and those that garner the most shock appeal, propelling them to do whatever it took to get up close.

On our way up the elevator, Sal looked at me. "You okay?"

I nodded, and then turned my attention back to the digital numbers over the door.

"I'm gonna grab myself some coffee." Sal said as we entered the office. I nodded and continued down the corridor toward Mr. D's.

"Good morning King," said one of the staff members sticking her head out her office. "Good morning." I replied, surprised to see anyone else here.

More smiling heads popped out to greet me, and now shit was weird. It's a Sunday, and the Funky Junky seemed to be operating as though it was a regular weekday.

I needed to know what was going on, and just as I was about to speed up, out from around the corner came Roller Girl. We scared each other, and I quickly grabbed hold of her as she tried to stay up.

"You're here too?" I asked.

"Yes, and Mr. D is wondering what's taking you so long?" Roller Girl grabbed on to my arm and we continued toward his office.

"So what's going on?" I asked.

"You'll see." She said, her smile, confirming at least that I wasn't in any trouble.

As we approached the office, Roller Girl let go and skated off down the adjacent hall.

"Come in!" Mr. D called out, quicker than he normally does when I knocked.

"King, my man!" Mr. D said as he came over and shook my hand, while escorting me back toward his desk.

. "Sit down buddy." He said gesturing to that dreadful big black bean bag.

"Mind if I stand?"

"No problem," he said taking a seat on the edge of his desk.

"So…" he began, "seems like you made a pretty big impact on this tour."

"Thank you," I replied.

"You're welcome, however, it wasn't meant to be a compliment."

"Um… I don't understand!"

"It's an observation."

"An observation?"

"Yes, and what we got from is it that you're ready for the next move."

"But I was just the opening act, I mean, we didn't even do the entire tour."

"Twenty percent of that tour, helped generate over eighty percent of your record sales so far."

I stood there and just looked at Mr. D, waiting for the punch line, or rather this next move he was talking about.

He picked up a stack of papers and held it out toward me.

"Recording contract?" Mr. D nodded and smiled.

"Solar Records, the Major's Major, doesn't get any bigger than that."

"I'm sorry man, I don't get it. I thought I was signed to the Funky Junky?"

"You are, for productions, but now we're talking major dough here, Keep Reading." I looked back down at the paperwork, but it was blurred, and the zeros kept overlapping. I shook my head and then glanced up at Mr. D.

He gestured for me to continue, when finally, it all began to straighten out, and once it did... I nearly fell out!

"It says Twenty-Eight Million Dollars." Mr. D, nodded. "They're giving me twenty-eight million dollars?"

"Actually, they're giving *me*, twenty-eight million dollars, and for that money, they want three albums, with at least four videos each. We are also responsible for putting together a promotional tour, that will hit at least thirteen major cities.

This all seemed incredibly overwhelming. As much as I've studied this business, nothing at this point made sense, and I couldn't sort through the craziness going on in my head.

"So out of this twenty-eight," Mr. D said, seeing that I was a bit off. "After everyone is paid, your take should be just over three million dollars."

Suddenly I felt faint. I walked over to the bean bag and plopped down in it. I placed my hands over my eyes, and could feel myself shaking. Mr. D poured me a glass of cold water.

It took a minute before I could even speak, but Mr. D waited patiently.

"So where do we start?" I asked him.

"We start tonight at 7:00 p.m. over at the Solar Office, where we sign. Antonio has a custom suit waiting for you back at the apartment, and Rosie went to pick up a dress for your grandmother."

"She's going?"

"Of course," Mr. D said. I really appreciated how he was with my grandmother, he knew that was the way to my heart.

"Now once you sign, a living expense will be placed on your card. It's enough to live comfortably. The rest will be placed in an escrow account until all obligations are fulfilled."

"How long will that take?"

"Well, if we bust our ass, No more than two years. At that time, we will transfer your advance. This is just a precaution, in case something were to go wrong."

"Go wrong?"

"Let me be straight with you, King. There's a long history of artists blowing their money on nonsense like drugs and woman, and then are unable to finish the project. At that point we're responsible, so until that is all done, we won't forward the full amount, just enough for you and your grandmother to live on."

Mr. D helped me up from the bean bag. I notice him glance over my shoulder, and when I turned around, the entire Funky Junky staff had snuck in, and scared the shit out of me with a roaring applause.

CHAPTER 57

Trip to Solar

I was pretty quiet on the way to the signing. I just listened as Grams and Mr. D talked up a storm as they sat toward the front of the limo facing backwards. Roller Girl, and Vanessa talked typical girl talk, and Quenepa was telling Porky one of his imaginary gangster stories. I sat at the back facing forward as we both claimed motion sickness if we were to ride backwards.

"You okay, King?" Vanessa asked, and so I snapped out of my daze.

"Every time I start to get use to one situation another seems to creep up."

"But these situations are good." Roller Girl replied.

"Trust me, I'm not complaining."

"You're scared Rey?" Porky asked. I looked at him for a moment, and then gave a subtle nod.

"A little bit."

"Don't worry, everything's going be okay." He assured

me. I just smiled.

"It's natural. Vanessa added. You're doing big things. Big people and big money being placed behind

You, being scared is therefore appropriate."

"It doesn't even feel like I'm doing anything." I said. "What do you mean?" Quenepa asked.

"I don't know. I sometimes feel like I'm on some sort of assembly line, being put together as I move forward. I can't explain it."Mr. D, though talking to Grams glanced my way, as if he had been listening to me all along.

Grams and Mr. D suddenly busted out laughing. I had never seen Mr. D like this. So relaxed and just chilling. I was trying to figure out what they were laughing about.

"What's so funny?" I asked.

"I was just telling Don, how when you were little and you were first learning to use the toilet."

"Are you really talking about that?" I asked embarrassed.

"That's some funny shit, King, literally."

"I wanna hear the story." Roller Girl said to Grams.

"Me too!" Porky yelled.

"No you don't." I told them. I could see Grams about to tell the story, so I tried to interrupt.

"Grams, please don't."

"Ah let her King, It's funny," Mr. D. Added.

"Yeah, I want to hear a Baby King story," Vanessa jumped in.

"It's disgusting, believe me,"

"You were just a little baby." Grams said.

"Please tell us Ms. Rosario." Roller Girl begged, as everyone else cheered her on. Except, Quenepa, he wasn't trying to hear it either. I just sat back and placed my hands over my face.

"He was about two years old." She began as I sunk even deeper into my seat. "And he had just learned to caca in the toilet."

"Caca?" Mr. D asked.

"Shit!" Grams translated. I glanced at Porky and he was already hysterical.

"Anyhow, he became so good at it… "

I just sat back and slid my hands from my face to my ears. I looked across at Mr. D and he was laughing hysterically. Roller Girl and Vanessa looked at me, and they too were cracking up. I didn't know what part of the story she was up to, but it was obviously the funny part as everyone was hysterical, even Sal as I can see him through the review mirror, laughing.

Quenepa had a smile on his face as he just shook his head while looking at me.

Though Grams had a way of embarrassing me most the time, I was still glad that she was the way she was. People naturally liked her, and once they got to know her, they loved her. I looked at these people that I was in the car with, and a sense of joy took over. I wasn't born into a big family, and I didn't have many friends. Grams dedicated her life to taking care of me, and the older I got, the more I understood what a sacrifice she had made.

At this very moment, I realized that *these* were my people, my family and friends. And I was okay with that. In fact, I felt very lucky, very blessed.

I glanced back over to Quenepa and noticed him trying desperately not to laugh, but he wasn't doing such a good job. Porky was lying back on the seat holding his fat belly, laughing so loud that he was the one making everyone else laughing. As I looked at him, I couldn't imagine any parent not being proud to have this great kid as their son. Despite all he's already been through, he was the nicest, kindest soul I had ever known.

"We're here!" Sal called out as he pulled to the curb in front of a huge building on Avenue of Americas. He got out and opened the door for us. We were definitely a sight, as we each stepped out of the limo. People couldn't figure us out right away and just stared as they walked by us.

"Well Kid. Congratulations." Sal said as we all stood around. "What do you mean?" I asked him.

"I mean congratulations on your deal." "But you gotta come up too, Sal."

"I can't kid, where am I going to park this thing?" He asked. I looked around and spotted a lot across the street.

"Right there!" I pointed. Sal looked at Mr. D, and he just shrugged his shoulders. "We'll wait for you inside, Sal." Mr. D said.

Sal looked at me, and squeezed my shoulder, before getting back into the limo and heading toward the lot.

Grams grabbed my arm and we all walked into the building. The lobby alone was huge, and decorated with million dollar paintings, and sculptures scattered throughout. It was like a museum, and was very entertaining as we waited for Sal who finally came rushing in.

Mr. D walked up to the security desk and gave them his name. The approval came back and we were each asked to sign our name in a book, some sort of visitor log before being walked to one of the many elevators, except this was the only one that went to the Penthouse which was where Solar Records resided.

The security guard held open the door as we all stepped inside. He then stepped halfway in, and with the use of a key, pressed the penthouse button, and then stepped back out. Fifty-Two stories later… we arrived.

CHAPTER 58

Signing to Solar

Silence took over as we rode up on the elevator. My butterflies grew as we rang passed each floor, until that final bell parted the doors. Those butterflies suddenly froze, then dropped to the pit of my stomach.

A succession of camera flashes greeted us. Two photographers and another holding what looked like a movie camera weren't there by coincidence, evidence in the form of my Publicist, Ciré who stood quietly in the background.

An assistant introduced herself, and then waved us to follow. I looked back to make sure Grams and Porky were with us, when I caught the two of them striking poses for one of the cameras. I tried to get their attention without grabbing anyone else's. Roller Girl picked up on it and helped me out.

We walked through the office which resembled The Funky Junky, except this one was a bit more mature. No crazy colors and weird conversational pieces lying around. The people worked in cubicles, paid us no mind as we made our way to the conference room. It was obvious, this was just a typical day for them, and I, no different than any other artist who's made their way through.

Solar handled many of the current Superstars, including Nemesis, a conflict of interest that made no sense.

The assistant opened the huge mahogany door, and guided us inside with a nod. Mr. D led the way, followed by myself, Vanessa, Grams, Pork, Roller Girl, and Sal.

I watched as Mr. D, and another gentleman around the same age, greeted one another. It was obvious they'd known each other for some time however I wasn't sure if they'd ever actually done business.

"Mr. Goldman, this here is Reynaldo aka King."

Mr. Goldman and I shook hands, his was firm and confident. He was groomed to perfection, with short black curly hair and green eyes. His mustache and goatee looked as if they were trimmed by Michelangelo himself. He wore a huge diamond stud in his left ear, and the hand that shook mine was decorated in gold and diamonds. He made wearing a suit look cool as hell, while mine was typical clownish, thanks of course to Antonio.

"So you're the one giving me the run for my money?" Mr. Goldman asked, his mouth and eyes sort of contradicting one another.

"Excuse me?" I asked.

"In just four shows, you managed to dim my Star into a light bulb."

I Looked at Mr. D and he just smiled. Mr. Goldman stepped back behind his desk and invited me and Mr. D to sit in the two seats placed in front of him. The photographers continued to snap photos and the cameraman kept filming. Ciré stood off to the side, taking notes, while giving small directions.

"Donald here had promised me a year ago that he was going to bring me my next Superstar." Mr. Goldman began to explain. "I told him he better hurry because I already had my eye on another." I glanced at Mr. D and he was just sitting there, listening. "He told me that I might want to hold off from signing anyone else, because *his* guy was going to suck up all the interest."

"This was before I even met you." Mr. D said to me.

"Well, I didn't listen to him." Mr. Goldman continued. "Instead I signed who I felt was that perfect artist and we preceded with his presentation.

Was I right? Yeah, I was. He blew up and in a very short time, made us a nice profit, and had it not been for you, he'd probably still have a career."

"What do you mean would *still* have a career?" I asked.

"I'm not in this business to take second place." He replied. I shook my head, because I couldn't make out this mother fucker's parables.

"What I am trying to tell you, King, is in order for me to sign *you*, I have to drop *him*!" I heard everyone behind me gasp, as did I. I laughed a bit, and shook my head.

"You don't have to do it like that, now." I started to say when Mr. D interrupted. "What are you talking about, King?"

"I mean to drop Nemesis just to sign me, I don't know if

that's a good idea."

"Are you out your mind?" Mr. D said, a bit upset. "We've put a lot into you for this very reason. I know how Mr. Goldman operates. He'll put into us, what *we* put into us. Nemesis was simply in the right place at the right time, other than that, he's nothing special. You're special King, and we're presenting you on a silver platter, not a paper plate."

"But we're talking about someone losing their deal because of me."

"But it isn't because of you." Mr. Goldman assured. "It's because of me. You're not making me do anything, and if you turn down this deal and someone else walks in, believe me, they're not going to be thinking about Nemesis either. It's called business. And the best man always wins!"

I turned and looked at my people. Grams realized I was in a tight spot. I would never want to hurt someone like that. Roller Girl and Vanessa showed no expression, while Sal and Q weren't even paying attention. However, Porky seemed all into it. His eyes were big, as if they were trying to speak to me.

Mr. D pulled the contract out from the folder he brought with him. His attorney had already looked it over, and it got an approval. He slid the contract over to me, and then placed a blue ink pen on top of it. My eyes met with Mr. D, and then with Mr. Goldman. I reached over and picked up the pen. Half of me was excited, the other half, uneasy. I knew everyone was waiting on me, but I had to give this a quick thought. I tried to convince myself that even if I didn't sign, Nemesis could still as easily lose his deal to someone else.

"Sign it, Rey!" Porky yelled out in his innocent little boy voice. Mr. Goldman looked at him and winked.

"So, is there anyway of me signing and Nemesis still staying on?"

"What are you doing?" Mr. D, asked, obviously annoyed.

"I'm sorry, but it doesn't seem right. Besides, it's music. We need other acts out there.

I don't need the whole world to love me, half will do!" I looked at Mr. Goldman, and noticed his eyes had softened. "I know it's hard to understand Mr. Goldman, and I truly apologize, but…" Mr. Goldman held up his hand and stopped me.

"You have a deal." He said with a smile.

"Huh?" Mr. D said as he looked up.

"Would you like that added to your contract?" Mr. Goldman asked. I looked at him, and his eyes put me as ease.

"Your word is good enough." I replied, and at that moment, Mr. Goldman reached across the desk and we shook hands. I then grabbed the pen and signed to Solar Records.

The cameras flashed like machine guns as we all stood, congratulating one another.

Porky smiled and grabbed me around the waist and I took Grams into my arms. "You did a good thing, Mijo." She whispered.

CHAPTER 59

After The Signing

While wondering when I would finally wake from this wonderful dream, its reality dug itself deeper and deeper into my world. My single "I Am King," became the hit of the summer as well as the anthem of practically every guy in the country. It felt as though the world thought only of me, and did nothing else except anticipate my next move.

Mr. D was able to not only maintain my momentum with just that one song, one video, and that short tour, he was even more impressively able to escalate it. While everyone looked at me as the star, I couldn't help but look that way at Mr. D, for I would be kidding myself if ever I thought I would've been able to pull this off on my own.

I was up each day by 5:00 a.m. and by six, Sal and I would be on our way to The Funky Junky. By 7:30 I was in the dance studio rehearsing and working on new routines, and after that, I shot directly across the hall to the gym where I would put in at least two hours of training.

My downtime consisted of eating lunch in the Writer's

Room where I would sit for a couple of hours listening, and picking from the many ideas that would be presented by the half dozen song writers on staff.

The songs that we all agreed upon I would demo over a basic drumbeat so that Red could work on the music. Other production companies had their own demo artists, who would lay down reference tracks. Mr. D didn't do it that way. Instead he had me lay down my own demos, so as to give us all a better idea of whether or not it was a song that would work, saving us all time, and of course, money!

In just about a month's time I had demoed at least eighty songs, for an album that would only feature twelve, including "I Am King." And every day I wondered which twelve would make the cut.

Grams and I had become sort of Porky's illegitimate guardians. We did consult with a caseworker, who told us that it could be a lengthy process, and that his parents would most likely contest it.

However, for a few hundred dollars a month, and a 3:00 a.m. visit from Sal, we somehow managed to convince Porky's parents to let him stay with us.

Though I took care of him as if he was my son, I treated him more like a little brother.

He got his own room, and of course I hooked it up with everything a kid his age might want.

After the horrible hand life had already dealt him, I had no hesitations when it came to spoiling him. But Porky was a very unique child, always happy, and excited about everything. They loved him over at the Funky Junky, especially the women. They thought he was adorable, and I teased him about it all the time.

I would catch him pulling Roller Girl through the corridors on her skates, helping another staff member rearrange her office, or sometimes just sitting in someone's office eating Pizza.

Even Mr. D loved him, and every so often, he would bring Porky some weird-ass toy.

In the beginning he would come by with Sal, hang out for a few hours and then Sal would drop him off home. Now it's gotten to where Porky would get up with me in the morning and hang out at The Funky Junky all day long. He loved every minute of it, and knew the place better than most.

One of Porky's favorite new discoveries within the Funky Junky, was the Gym. I tried to warn him about Jacq, how he could sometimes be a real dick. I worried about Porky getting on his nerves with the hundred and one questions, and Jacq in return yelling, or saying something cruel. Porky got enough of that with his parents. Until one day, after rehearsal I took a peek into the gym, only to find Porky laying on the bench pressing about one hundred pounds. But what surprised me even more was Jacq, who stood behind him, spotting his lift, yelling out encouragements with every successful pump of the iron.

Most of the staff clocked out at 6:00 p.m., and would then go down to the cafeteria where a dinner buffet would be laid out. The Funky Junky wasn't the kind of place where employees rushed to leave. On the contrary, it was a pleasant place to work, and most took advantage of the free dinner.

However, there was a slight catch. You see, it was during this time that Mr. D would play some of the new material that was being worked on.

The system was quite brilliant, as he didn't want the room quiet. He wanted everyone to relax, enjoy themselves, socialize, whatever. Because he felt that's exactly how people listen to radio. If a song is that good, then it will stand out, and most would have no choice, but to listen. Those were the songs he was interested in.

Many dinners went on, where none of the new material was even noticed. But then there were those that did, and those were the ones he went after.

If enough attention was attracted by a particular song, Mr. D would stop the music and ask our opinions.

Everyone was invited to participate, from our producers and musicians, writers, our video director, stylist and publicist, even the dancers and all of the administrators and assistants. Porky became a regular, as did Frank, the Janitor, but were pretty honest, and made some really valid points.

Before starting, Mr. D would always go over the importance of being truthful. He reminded us of how important the honesty would be to the success of our company, and how important the success was to our livelihoods, or to be a little more precise… Our jobs!

Arguments weren't only common, they were encouraged. Mr. D saw a level of passion that he found invaluable, and he would stand quietly and listen intently to both sides. Sometimes, these arguments would get a bit out of hand, and even become physical.

One of the writers got shoved against the wall by Quenepa when he stated that he thought the Court Jester idea was ridiculous. It took most of us to pull Quenepa off him. The writer's opinion however was out voted as we all felt that the Court Jester idea was brilliant and added something new to the whole rap thing.

Trust me, many times my very own delivery was smashed to smithereens, and the majority would rule in favor. A few of those times, that smash came from Porky. His honesty was uncanny, and he would keep apologizing to me while in the midst of tearing me apart. He made everyone laugh and applaud. I could never be mad at him, he did as he was told and he was extremely honest, and actually had a good ear.

By the time we chose half the album, another twenty songs were demoed, and some of the newer one's ended up bumping the ones already voted in. It seemed like an unending task, but one thing for sure. We were compiling an album that was sure to birth many hits.

The songs that were chosen were brought back into the studio, this time with a full production behind it. By then I'd be familiar with the song, and all of its flaws would be corrected.

CHAPTER 60

1st Day of Middle

Sal pulled up in front of the School and then looked back at us.

"Do I really have to start today?" Porky asked as he looked through the window at the kids and their parents entering the school.

"Of course you have to start today." Grams replied.

"Man, this looks like a great school. I wish I'd gone here." I added.

"How do I look, Grams?" Porky asked

"Absolutely adorable!" she said pinching his pink pudgy cheeks. Porky looked at me and exhaled.

"Nah Pork," I said. "You look cool, man, everybody's going to wanna be your friend, You watch." And finally we got a smile out of him.

"Ready to go?" I asked, and after giving it a moment, he nodded. I opened the door before Sal could even get to it, and immediately stepped out. Parents recognized right away, and whispered who knows what to their kids.

As Sal was helping Grams out the car, Porky turned and asked me in a low voice.

"Does she have to come?" He didn't mean anything bad by it, he loved Grams and she loved him, but she does have a way of embarrassing you at times.

"I'll watch her." I promised, and so he was okay with it.

Grams stepped out, and together we headed for the entrance.

"Have a good day, Pork!" Sal called out, then leaned against the car to read his paper.

Parents dropping off their kids, stopped and stared as we headed into the building.

In the main office, Grams and I stood at the counter while Porky took a seat and waited for us to find out his class.

"How can I help you?" One of the ladies asked looking at me with a huge smile. "By the way, I'm a huge fan" she then added, I returned the smile and thanked her.

"Victor Santiago," I began pointing to Porky sitting on one of the chairs against the wall. We registered him last week, and they said to bring him in today."

"I followed his story," she said. "I cried for days."

"Very sad, Grams added."

"Let me go pull his file, I'll be right back."

As the woman made her way over to the file cabinet, we noticed she said something to the other woman sitting at her typewriter that made her look our way. That woman then got up and whispered to her co-worker, who also looked our way.

"Why don't you sit down?" I told Grams, since it seemed like we were gonna be a while.

Grams went over and sat with Porky. I turned away quickly when she licked her thumb and then wiped his face with it. I used to hate when she did that to me.

While looking away, I noticed a rather large crowd gathering right outside the office door, mostly adults, but when I smiled at them, they pulled back.

A tall gentleman stepped out from a back office and walked over to me.

"Hey, how's it going?" He said with a huge white smile that lit up his dark complexion. He had to be at least six four, and his hand practically swallowed mine when we shook.

"I'm Mr. Brooks, the Principal, welcome to MS 126"

I introduced myself, followed by some friendly chit chat, after which I gestured toward Porky.

"So are we enrolling both these kids? Mr. Brooks joked, scoring major points with my grandmother..

"No, just him," she replied, playing right along. Mr. Brooks extended his hand toward Porky, his long fingers reaching hallway up his arm.

"And what's your name young man?"

"Porky," he answered. Mr. Brooks laughed, and looked over at Grams and I. We gave him a bit of an embarrassed smiled.

"Porky, hmm, okay, but let me ask you this. What does your family call you?" Porky looked at Grams and I, and said it again,

"Porky!" God, I wish we would've prepped him.

Mr. Brooks took a look at Porky's transfer papers.

"Victor Santiago?" He asked, and though hesitant, Porky nodded.

"Wow, This is a great name, sounds like a Football player. You like sports, Victor?" Porky nodded.

"What's your favorite sport?" Porky placed his finger on his chin and squinted up into the air.

"Um… Dodgeball!"

"Dodgeball? Wow, that's tougher than Football." Porky agreed.

"Yeah, I use to play that with my dad."

"You did?"

"Uh huh, but he always won."

Grams turned and looked up at me with the saddest eyes.

"Well, guess what Porky? We play Dodgeball here too. In fact, we just got in a shipment of brand new Dodgeballs."

"Basketballs?" Pork asked.

"No no, Dodgeballs." He corrected, looking over at us again.

Anyway, at the end of the year, we give out awards, and on those awards we put your name. Now, would you want your award to say Victor Santiago, or Porky?"

Porky placed his finger back on his chin and looked up

toward the ceiling giving it some serious thought.

"I'd like it to say Victor Santiago!" he finally blurted out, as both Grams and I exhaled.

"And I agree with you one hundred percent!" Mr. Brooks said. "So what we have to do, is make sure everyone knows that your name is Victor Santiago, so how about this. Let's introduce you in the school as Victor Santiago, and let's keep Porky for just close friends and family, how's that?"

Porky gave Mr. Brooks a thumbs up… And so did I.

"So you sit here, and I'm going to have a little talk with your parents, oaky?" Porky nodded.

Mr. Brooks waved us to follow him into his office, but Grams didn't want to leave Porky alone so stayed with him.

Principal Brooks invited me to sit when we entered his office. He took his seat behind his desk.

"You know Mr. Brooks. My grandmother and I, we're Porky's… I mean, Victor's Guardians."

"No relations?" He asked.

"No sir, he was a good kid in a very bad situation. We just wanted to help him out."

"Well, he's very lucky, like many, this school also has it's share of sad stories. By the way, it's a real honor meeting you… Should I call you Mr. King?" "No please, Rey is fine." I replied with a slight laugh.

I personally haven't really been keeping up with your career, but my daughter has, so I'm familiar with all the big things that have gone on, in fact, you know, she's never going to believe this."

I didn't know what to say, not to mention I was here to settle Porky into school, not talk about his daughter being a big fan, though I did feel he knew more about me than he was willing to admit.

"Yes, I was told to just bring Victor in so he can start school."

"We got time, classes haven't even started yet, would you do me a huge favor, please?" Mr. Brooks asked. I hated agreeing to favors before I knew what they were, but I really needed this guy on my side.

"Sure," I replied.

Mr. Brooks put on the biggest smile and then picked up the phone and began to dial.

"Hi Pumpkin" he said in sweet and soft tone.

"Hi daddy," I heard her reply.

"How you are you feeling?" he asked and then covered the phone to explain that she's home with the flu.

"Mama's trying to make me eat soup, Daddy I hate soup!"

"Well, your mother just wants you to get better. Look, sweetie, I have a bit of a surprise, that might actually make you feel better."

"A puppy?" she asked. Mr. Brooks looked at me and smiled.

"No sweetie, something better than a puppy!"

How I wish he hadn't said that, because now it was me against a puppy.

"What is it?" she asked, sounding super excited.

"Remember the other day, you were singing that song for us?"

"Uh huh!"

"Well, the guy who sings that song."

"You mean, King?"

"Yes King, he's here with me right now, in my office."

"No fucking way!" The little girl yelled out. Mr. Brooks looked up at me, hoping I didn't hear that, I acted like I didn't.

"Yes sweetie, he's sitting right across from me."

And at that very moment I heard the loudest scream over the phone. So loud in fact, that Mr. Brooks had to move the phone away from his ear.

"Here sweetie, why don't you say hi." I didn't expect to be handed the phone, and was a bit hesitant at first, She was still screaming.

"What's her name?" I asked Mr. Brooks.

"Angela," he replied.

I tried interrupting her, but it was no use, so I just waited. And when finally, she simmered down, I spoke.

"Um, Hi Angela," I said, nervously.

"Yes. Who's this?"

"Hi Angela, this is King," and again, she started screaming, in fact she practically screamed throughout our conversation.

After taking care of everything we had to do in the office,

we headed for his new class.

"Wait!" Porky said before entering the classroom. He stepped ahead and peeked through the narrow window on the door, then he turned to me and asked,

"Can we just do this tomorrow?" Grams was ready to oblige, but I jumped in.

"Tomorrow isn't going to be any different than today, Pork, you might as well get it over with." Mr. Brooks, who had personally escorted us to the class, nodded in agreement.

I heard something behind me, and so I turned around, and when I did, a couple of girls that were peeking out from the classroom across the hall, quickly pulled back.

"Ready to go in?" Mr. Brooks asked,

"yeah, but would you guys mind not coming in?" he said to me and Grams. I understood, Grams didn't.

"No problem, kid, you go in, and have a great day okay?" Grams went to hug Porky, and he quickly pulled away. She looked at me, no idea what was going on. I just shook my head, and told her,

"I'll explain later,"

We stepped out the way as Mr. Brooks opened the door and guided Porky by the shoulder. Grams and I watched through the window as Porky got the dreaded classroom introduction. He looked so nervous, his rosy cheeks rosier than ever. I could hear the class being asked to say Hi, and at that very moment, exactly as it was when *I* went to school, the entire class, in one thunderous roar greeted, *Hi Victor!*

He must've felt us watching, and when he turned to look

our way, Grams and I quickly ducked!

They placed Porky at the front of the class, which I thought was good, at least for now.

"He's good," I said to Grams, kind of nudging her to lets go. But she was having trouble leaving. You would think she gave birth to this kid, or at the very least, raised him, but that was just her nature.

"He'll be home in a few hours!" I assured her, and finally, she broke away from the door, and as the two of us walked through the hall I turned to Grams whose eyes were so watery.

"What's wrong?" I asked, as she sucked in the tears and shook her head.

I could see she was trying to say something so I just waited, until finally she spoke.

"It seems like just yesterday that I was enrolling you into school.

"Well, it wasn't just yesterday."

"You think he's going to be okay?"

"He's going to be fine." I assured her as we pushed through the double doors exiting the building.

CHAPTER 61

All Hail

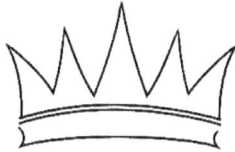

My album, ALL HAIL had become a multi-platinum seller, and seven out of the twelve cuts made it to number one on the Pop Charts. My videos were everywhere, and I practically lived on tour, the difference this time? I was the headliner!

My stage production was topnotch, and why wouldn't it be? Touring has been generating millions of dollars in record sales for Solar, the Funky Junky, and yes, even me.

Just half way through the tour, and after covering all expenses, I had accumulated over twenty million dollars, with a percentage going directly into Gram's account so that she could take care of herself, home, and Porky.

This money definitely didn't come easy, In fact, I bust my ass to get it. There weren't enough hours in the day for me to work through the extensive To-Do's everyone expected from me. Interviews, in-stores, appearances, recording, rehearsal, fittings, writing sessions, the list goes on. Oh, and don't forget, I also have a family!

I didn't do many one offs anymore, only tours, but when I did do them, they were usually private events for celebrities, politicians, and sometimes, even gangsters, and to be honest, the gangsters were some of my best customers.

King merchandise could be found literally everywhere, from bodegas to Bloomingdales, toy stores to gum ball machines, and of course my concerts, where the merch usually sold out way before the show even began.

Mr. D not only operated my productions, he also handled my management, which consisted of a full staff of Booking Agents, Road Managers, Bodyguards, and a shit load of Production Assistants. I realized later on, that the true purpose behind Mr. D taking on management was simply his way of always keeping one hand in my pocket, and the other controlling shit.

Touring was where I made most of *my* money, and made it the quickest. Everything else, I made a mere percentage, and the payouts were quarterly.

Mr. D took credit for the King brand, so of course we shared in those profits. He was fair when it came to these things, and even promised that the day I chose not to do this anymore, that he would retire the name altogether.

Every once in a while I'd be in a city where Nemesis might be playing one of the local clubs. I've thought about dropping in at times, just to say what's up, but my good intentions would've definitely been taken wrong, so I stayed away.

Solar kept Nemesis, in contract as they had promised me. But now I'm realizing what a bad move that was, because they stopped releasing any new material on him, so his career now was based solely off of his past hits. He was a simple track act now, and performed mostly in small clubs, and lounges, with a production that consisted only of a DAT tape, and if the budget allowed, maybe a road manager.

CHAPTER 62

Smoke a Joint

This was my first time in Miami, and man, was I having a great time! Everything about this city was incredible. The weather, the people, the food, the scene, and damn… the girls! It was too bad though, we were out first thing in the morning.

I stepped out onto the balcony of my hotel room and leaned over the banister taking in the cool coastal air. The starry sky made the ocean glisten and the small breaking waves made me wanna camp out here all night.

I heard the glass door of the balcony beside me slide open. A wall separated us, and I couldn't see Q until he too leaned over his banister. Though I came out for some fresh air, he came out to smoke a joint.

"Sup King?" He said before shooting a stream of smoke out into the air. "Just taking in the night?"

"Yeah, this is the life, yo, too fuckin' bad we have to leave so early tomorrow." I said.

"For real, shit, I could go for a couple of those Cubanita Mamacitas right about now." Q replied. I couldn't help but laugh.

"Hey Q, let me ask you." I began. "What do you think about this whole situation?" Quenepa took another pull and held it in.

"What do you mean?" He asked, his voice, choppy as he spoke, while still holding in the smoke.

"I mean, people usually only see the glamorous part of this whole thing. The limos, tour buses, lights, autograph sessions, you know? But they don't really get to see this part of it."

"You mean the part where you chill on the fourteenth floor balcony of a luxury suite, overlooking the ocean while you smoke weed?" He said and then took another toke of his joint.

"I don't know, it gets kind of lonely, don't you think?"

"It's lonely because you want it to be. King, you got bitches who would line up just to eat your ass, nigga!"

It never fails, Q always has to say some crazy-ass shit.

"I'm not talking about girls, I'm talking like family and friends. You know, people who really love us. I'm starting to wonder if this time away from them is even worth it.

"Man… Take a hit of this shit, you starting to depress me." Q said, stretching his arm around the wall and over to my side.

"Nah, I'm good!" I said, waving off his offer.

"Obviously, you're not, or else you wouldn't be talking all this sad shit." Q, holds up the joint and continues. "You see this here? It's like a crystal ball, it allows you to see the world as it truly is, so that you can make the right choices in life."

"But you can also get hooked?" I replied.

"Hooked?" Quenepa laughed. "This ain't no fucking Heroin. It's weed. You can't get hooked on this shit! You smoke it, and it clears your mind, lets you see shit. Then you laugh a little, eat a bunch of junk, then go your ass to sleep. That's it!

"I don't know man. It's not right."

"What do you mean it's not right? This shit was created by God. All natural!

I gave what Q was telling me some thought, and though it wasn't often, this time I think he might've been right, and so I reached over to his side of the balcony. Q looked at me with a smile, and then passed me the joint.

"Don't drop it!" He warned me. I took it between my two fingers and sort of stared at it for a moment.

"Come on man, you letting that shit burn out... Smoke mother fucker!"

I snapped out of my silly little trance and did as he said. The smoke went down so smooth that I could barely tell if I was even getting anything, so I pulled on it even harder, watching as the orange glow turned red, and raced toward my fingers.

"Easy nigga, now hold it in!" Q, instructed, and then reached over to get back his joint.

"Damn man!" He said inspecting what was left. I busted out laughing. Q joined in. "For a nigga who don't smoke you damn near smoked my whole shit!"

After a few minutes of silliness, we stopped laughing, and I just stared out into the darkness of the ocean, listening to the waves that were now beginning to sound like crowds of people.

"You feeling that shit!" He said with his sinister smile. I looked at him, and then started laughing some more.

"Ah shit, you one of them dudes, huh?" Q asked, his laugh making mine even harder.

"So what's supposed to happen? I don't feel shit!"

"Yeah right," Q replied. You're fucking stoned!" He continued, pointing at me and laughing.

I turned back toward the ocean. Q's voice turned echoey and distant, and I concentrated some more on the ocean. It was as if all my senses were being turned up. I could smell the salt from the ocean, feel its mist on my face, and the sound it made had become sort of musical.

For the first time ever, I felt like I belonged. As if the ocean and I knew each other our entire lives.

I turned and looked over at Quenepa. He looked at me and smiled. I smiled back. This was absolutely incredible. I took a deep breath and it felt like I was inhaling the stars. I was beginning to understand how people felt when they thought they could fly. I looked over the banister and imagined myself jumping off, and gliding across the shore. But I was stoned, not stupid. I shook the image from my head and then turned to Q, who was now standing on his balcony with two girls. One he was kissing, the other he was feeling up.

"Where the fuck they come from?" I asked.

Q pulled away and started laughing.

"You ladies know who that is right?" Q asked, flicking his chin in my direction.

"Hi King." One of the girls said, as the other waved. Their thick Spanish accents, made them even sexier.

"Open your door King, we're coming over." Q said, as they exited his balcony.

"What?" I asked.

"Open your door, nigga!" He ordered in a loud whisper.

I became nervous and immediately turned to go back in when I crashed into the glass door not realizing that it was closed. I was lucky my head didn't break it.

I rushed into my room, throwing underwear behind the couch as I made my way to the door, of which Q was already banging on.

"'Bout fucking time!" he said as he stood there with a girl on each arm. They both had on tiny tight jean shorts, and bikini tops. Those high ass heels they wore like pros, made their smooth and tanned legs look like works of art.

"Fuck happened to you?" Q asked as he entered, the two girls staring and giggling at my forehead. I turned to the mirror and couldn't believe the size of the knot that glass door left behind.

CHAPTER 63

Morning After

The banging on the door got me quickly up on my feet. I was disoriented, and had forgotten that I was still in the hotel. I realized that I was completely naked, and grabbed my boxers off the floor. I put them on as I clumsily made my way to the door and opened it.

Without saying a word, Sal stepped inside. I watched as his eyes began to scan the mess that I was trying hard to figure out, as the empty bottles of champagne and pack of rolling papers on the dresser, told me more than I could actually remember.

It seemed as though he wasn't surprised. Disappointed, maybe? But not surprised.

He looked over at the bed.

"Who's that?" He asked, gesturing toward the mound of covers. I had no idea, and was kind of scared to find out. Sal walked over and grabbed the corner of the blanket as I held my breath.

A hard yank of the covers revealed a girl, laying there

completely naked. Sal looked over at me, and could tell, I didn't know who the fuck that was. I leaned over to the side a bit for a better look of her face, when I realized, it was one of the girls from last night.

"Do you know her?" He asked.

"Well." I began, still confused. "We hung out a bit last night, but I thought she left."

Sal made his way over to her purse, where he pulled out her ID, and inspected it carefully, before putting it back.

"What happened to your head?" He asked, just as he was about to leave.

"I ran into the sliding door." I replied, embarrassed. Sal shook his head.

"Get your shit together, and come down. We're out of here in twenty."

As soon as the door closed, Quenepa scared the shit out of me, when he popped out of my bathroom in just his underwear.

"What the fuck!"

Q looked at me and placed his finger up against his lips.

"Come on nigga, you weren't that fucked up!" He said. "Just don't say nothing to Sal about me being here."

"Why not?"

"Because right away I get blamed for everything."

"I mean, it is sort of your fault."

"Come on man, don't bitch out on me right now!"

"I'm not bitching out, but this shit isn't in my nature, and

Sal knows that."

"Man, you're a mother fuckin' superstar right now, and so is your nature, so all this shit right here is very much possible. Now help me get that dumb bitch out the tub."

"What?" I said following Q back into the bathroom, and sure enough, there she was.

"What's wrong with her?"

"How you gonna ask me some shit like that, after last night."

"But what you give her?"

"Stop fuckin' around, you know what we gave them."

"Them?" I asked before turning to the other one all sprawled out on my bed.

"They're prostitutes, Q, we didn't have to drug'em!"

"Don't flip on me, man, that shit was your idea!"

"*My* idea?"

"Yeah, you wanted to fuck her in the ass, and she wasn't down with that shit, until I told you I had something that would make her be down to do whatever the fuck you want her to do."

"But I was just joking, oh, my God!" I said, throwing my hands over my face in disbelief that any of this was happening.

"And that's all you kept saying last night, *oh my god*! Now let's get this bitch out the tub and into the bed, let their asses wake up together, so they could think they were fucking each other."

I walked into the bathroom, and grabbed the girl's arms while Quenepa grabbed her legs.

We lifted her, and immediately the blood from her ass broke free and made its way down the drain, I nearly passed out.

We got her out and because Quenepa was pretty short, we pretty much dragged her from the bathroom, across the room and onto the bed, leaving behind a long bloody streak in the carpet.

We got her as far in on the bed as we could, leaving one leg on the floor, suddenly, we heard a loud bang coming from the corridor. We froze, and listened closely, trying to figure out what it was, until we heard.

"Q, wake up, time to go!" Sal yelled from out in the hall.

"Fuck!" Quenepa said in a panic.

"Sal's cool you, let's just tell him what happened and..."

"...are you nuts? After that last incident, he warned me, one more thing and I'm out. Trust me, Sal don't say shit unless he means it.

I watched as Q looked around trying to figure out what to do. Sal wasn't gonna stop until he answered his door.

"I'll tell him, I'll tell him it was all my fault."

"He won't believe that shit," Q replied.

"But there's nothing else we could do."

And at that very moment, Q rushed toward the balcony.

"What you doing?" I asked, following him outside.

By the time I got out there, Q had dragged one of the

balcony chairs over to the banister.

"Yo, what are doing?" I said as I grabbed hold of his arm.

"King, please man, just help me."

I looked over the banister and just that alone made me dizzy as we were on the fourteenth floor, and directly below us was the hotel swimming pool with at least a hundred people hanging out. Most of them children!

"That's crazy bro, you're gonna kill yourself."

"I gotta do it, King. If I don't keep this gig, them streets are gonna kill me anyway.

Now get the fuck off me!" Q yanked his arm from my grasp so hard that he lost his balance and toppled over the banister.

"Q!" I yelled out, grabbing hold of him again.

By one arm I held him as he dangled his feet in the air, his body slowly starting to turn.

"Keep still!" I yelled out. It was a good thing Q was a little guy, because a few more pounds and I wouldn't have been able to hold him.

"Don't let me go!" He cried out, terrified like I'd never seen him before.

"Hurry up man, feels like I'm slipping!"

"I got'chu Q, you're not slipping!" I lied, as my sweaty hands felt like they were about to give. I looked down, and wanted so bad to warn everyone to move, but that would've freaked him out, and for sure he would've fell.

I reached down, and Q was able to take my other hand,

but it wasn't a good grip, and that hot Miami sun wasn't helping. Then I heard a loud pop, and felt the banister give a bit, as one of the old corroded bolts snapped.

Q yelled, and everyone below us heard. In a matter of seconds, the pool area cleared out, and a huge crowd gathered on the beach to watch.

After a moment of trying to lift him back over, Q looked up at me, and said.

"I'm good now, King. You can let go now." His voice was sort of calm and eerie.

"I'm not gonna do it, Q, stay with me, man."

I could feel the banister leaning some more.

"This whole shits gonna go, and you're gonna go with it," he said, But I didn't care, I wasn't letting go.

"Think of your grandmother, King, you can't do this to her, and what about Porky?

Q was right, and this banister felt like it was about to give at any moment. I looked down at him, my crying eyes seeing nothing but a blur.

I closed my eyes, and was about to let go, when suddenly all the weight lifted, and when I opened my eyes Sal was pulling Q up over the banister, letting him crash down on the hard balcony floor.

We were looking at Q when we heard another snap, and watched in horror as the entire banister gave out and fell, dangling now from just one bolt.

Sal looked at the two of us, furious.

"What a fuckin' mess!"

CHAPTER 64

A Million Things to Say

We've spent more time on the bus than we did in the hotel rooms. Each city I visited I made a promise to myself to one day come back, because the only experience I had of some of this country's greatest cities, was through the window of my tour bus.

It seemed like it would never end. Each single released from the album became a hit. My concerts were sold out to the point that promoters were starting to book doubles, which extended my tour for another month, performing sometimes, seven days a week.

Money continued to pour into my bank account, yet I had no way of even spending it while on tour.

Though I was really missing Grams and Porky, I have to admit, I was having a ball! I called home whenever I got to a new hotel, and made sure they knew how to contact me in an emergency. I spent at least an hour talking with both Grams and Porky, as they each picked up one of the two phone lines we had in the apartment.

Grams had Porky on a pretty good sleep schedule, just as she did me growing up. She always had great reasons why I should be getting to bed early. From, Santa Claus is watching, to you won't grow, to the most effective, I'm gonna beat your ass! I don't remember Grams ever laying a hand on me, but for some reason, I never wanted to test her.

When Grams and I spoke on the phone, I did most of the talking as her days were pretty repetitive, but when I spoke to Porky, he always had a million things to say. He was a kid full of dreams, as each time he spoke of something new he had discovered, and found extremely interesting.

He seemed so much like me, like, he could've been my son, or at the very least, my little brother.

The only thing that bugged me a bit was when I would ask about school. It was then that his attitude would change.

This was pretty odd, as Porky really loved school, and now it seemed like something he just wanted to get over with. I spoke to Grams, and she acted as if she never noticed which I also found weird, Grams was the most observant person I'd ever known. She'd observe the strangest things and then mention them to me later. Like one day she told me. "That guy sitting at the table beside us at the restaurant was a cop!"

"How you know?" I'd ask.

"I noticed a bulge on his hip." She'd reply.

"Maybe it was a hernia or something?" I'll suggest.

"Definitely not a hernia, because when he left, I didn't notice any limp."

This was very typical of Grams, so for her to not notice

anything wrong with Porky didn't make sense.

"Maybe he's just home sick, Mijo. I mean, his parents sent him to live with complete strangers." This was true, and so we made it a point to always try and speak good of his parents when around him. We tried to set up visitations or at least phone calls, but his parents were pieces of shit, and showed no interest whatsoever.

Porky's parents gave us custody after we agreed to a monthly payment. Little did they know, there really wasn't anything I wouldn't pay to have this little guy with us, he was the best investment I ever made.

I was fortunate to have had my grandmother, who adored me, and took care of me like I was her very own. Porky unfortunately never had that, or anything like it, and the fact that not only was he still able to smile, his smile was infectious, which proved what a special kid he really was.

Hanging with Porky for a day was the best prescription for a heavy heart. He lit up rooms when he entered them, everyone seemed to love this kid, and loved being around him.

Mr. D even offered to have a tutor come to the Funk Junky, there an empty room in the building that he would've gladly converted into a classroom.

Though I appreciated it, I explained how important I felt it was for Porky to have a normal education, and be around other kids his age, especially when his parents could legally take him back anytime they wanted.

Grams assured me that he still held good grades, but did notice a lack of enthusiasm waking up for school in the mornings. Usually he would be up and dressed before everyone else. That was no longer the case.

We had only a couple of cities more to go before this tour was over. I was having the time of my life, but damn was I exhausted. Quenepa and I had become very close. He was really a good guy. Just a bit confused, but good.

CHAPTER 65

Doing Doubles

The show we did at the Atlanta Convention Center was one of the best we'd done so far on this tour. When I heard we were coming here, I wasn't too excited. I imagined a whole other scene, but damn they fooled me.

It was after midnight and I was exhausted, but I wanted to pack because we were out first thing in the morning.

This is one city I wouldn't mind visiting again someday. A couple of more days here would've been cool, but we were on a schedule.

I was about jump in the shower when I heard a knock on the door. I went over and looked through the peephole. It was Quenepa.

"What's up?" I asked through the closed door.

"Open up nigga, I wanna show you something."

"Man, show me in the morning. I'm done for the night."

"Bro, two seconds!" he insisted, and though I knew it would be a bad Idea, my dumb-ass opened up anyway.

"What?" I asked, and before saying anything, Q pulled in front of him, the finest fucking girl I had ever seen in my life! I was silent.

"I thought so." He said, before pushing his way in. "King this here is Linda, Linda, that there's King!"

"It's Lydia," she corrected, taking my hand seductively into hers "Nice to meet you." She said, staring deep into my eyes.

Q stepped the rest of the way in and locked the door behind him.

"Man, we gotta get up early," I told Q, as Lydia walked over and sat on my bed. Q plopped down into the recliner that nearly swallowed him whole, and pulled a blunt from his hoodie.

"Man, Linda's a huge fan, and I promised her we could hang for a few minutes.

"It's Lydia." She again corrected. "I saw your show tonight, it was incredible.

"Thank you," I replied. "Lydia, I don't want to be rude, but…"

"Chill out King, fuck! We ain't trying to move in and shit, we just stopped by to smoke this joint, then we out!"

Q lit the blunt and took a long slow drag. As he held it in, he gestured for me to sit down on the bed next to Lydia. At first hesitant, I finally did just to hurry things along.

"So how you like Atlanta?" she asked as Q handed her the blunt.

"I love it, the people are great."

"Must be real cool, being on the road, performing in different cities." she said.

"It is." I replied. "But it does get exhausting. You don't really get any rest, or even a decent meal. We practically eat garbage the whole time."

"Still sounds great to me," she said as she held the blunt out toward me. I considered taking a toke, but declined.

"Really?" she replied, looking over at Q as if it was a part of some sort of deal.

"King, come on bro, that shit is rude. Girl just wants to smoke with you, make her day, yo!"

"I ain't trying to be all fucked up on this ride."

"A couple of tokes ain't gonna do nothing to you." He said waving me off as he sat back in the chair. I took a deep breath and then exhaled before taking the blunt from Lydia.

"Oh my God, I'm getting high with King!" She said excitedly as she bounced her fine ass on my bed and clapped her hands. A slight laugh slipped from my lips as there was something cute about her. I got up and passed the blunt back to Quenepa.

"Do you guys ever bring, you know, fans with you?" She asked.

"On the road?" she nodded her head really fast and smiled. "Nah, we already travel with too many people." Q and I laughed.

"But if you could, would you?" She asked staring at me, her smile even wider as she awaited my answer.

"Well, I guess."

"I would do anything to go on the road with you." She said, her big brown eyes widened with a touch of innocence that didn't match the rest of her.

"Would you suck his dick?" Quenepa asked as he licked his finger and then wiped it on the blunt in an attempt to control the burn.

"Damn, Q, always gotta say some shit!" I said, embarrassed.

"Who wouldn't?" Lydia surprisingly blurted out. I turned and looked at her, and again, she smiled, her white skin turning blush.

"You see, that's what I've been trying to tell him. Bitches would do all kinds of shit just to be around him." Q added. He took another toke, and then held it out toward Lydia, who got up from the bed and walked over to get it.

This scene felt like a setup, because I finally got to see the incredible ass this girl was carrying around. That combined with the weed, had my shit ready to bust out of my pants.

Lydia stood directly in front of me, as she worked the blunt, her tight jeans exposing every nook and cranny. I could feel sweat beading across my hairline, and the hardness that formed in my pants was literally starting to hurt.

Lydia dropped down on her knees between my legs and placed the burning end of the blunt in her mouth to give me a shot gun, which of course I accepted. She then handed me the blunt so I can smoke some more. With her hand on my chest, she guided me back.

As I lay there, blowing smoke up toward the ceiling, I

could feel as she began to unfasten my pants. She reached in struggling to pull me out, as it had wedged itself hard against my leg.

I looked down at her in disbelief of what I knew was about to happen, and then glanced over at Q, who was sitting there waiting for the show to begin.

Lydia took my dick in her hand and without even a warm up, she placed her lips over it, wiggled her head down until she gagged.

"Yo, she ain't playing!" Q cheered, before getting up and taking the blunt from my hand.

"Don't wanna start no fire," he said, then plopped back down into the chair.

Yeah it was weird that Q was just sitting there watching us, but this girl was so good, she made you not care who the fuck was there.

"You see man, you have to come to terms with your success." Quenepa began to lecture, though all I wanted him to do, was shut the fuck up so I can concentrate.

"You are literally one of the biggest artist on the planet, and with that comes benefits that you must indulge in. Cash flow, fresh clothes, fast cars, and of course the finest bitches the world has to offer."

I was trying desperately to tune this mother fucker out, 'cause if not, this girl's gonna end up with a cramped neck.

"Bitches that at the very least, wanna suck your dick!" Q continued. "In fact, niggas is gonna wanna suck your dick too, even straight ones."

I turned my head toward Q, hoping that he could read my eyes, which were crying for him to shut the fuck up.

I placed my hands behind me and lifted myself up. I was hoping that by watching her, it'll drown out all the bullshit coming out of Q's mouth.

I couldn't believe the skill this girl had, and though I didn't have many to compare her with, something told me, I will never again experience anything like this.

Suddenly, Quenepa got up and walked over to where we were, and dropped down onto his knees behind Lydia. I was trying to shoo him away, without having her break her stride.

I watched as he reached around her and unbuttoned her pants and pull them down to her knees. She had me completely paralyzed, so I just fell back and closed my eyes.

Lydia was sucking a mile a minute and I could feel every nerve in my body pulsate as her mouth took it from the tippity tip, to the base and back up.

I tilted my head to the left and through the slits of my eyes watched as Q, looking like a goddamn Chihuahua pumped her from behind, when it suddenly hit me, we were fuckin' doing doubles!

This shit was getting' weird and I wanted to get it over with, and so I lifted myself back onto my elbows to put my focus on Lydia, because the Court Jester was messing me up.

Lydia opened her watery eyes and stared at me, anticipating the eruption that was about to happen.

My torso dropped back down, and my chest began to heave, as if I was going into cardiac arrest. My body tensed, and my toes were expanding inside of my shoes. I couldn't help but notice Q also was at the edge.

The room filled with moans from all three of us, and I could feel my juices, working their way form the back of my neck, down my spine, across my ass to my balls, and then finally… My door is kicked open!

CHAPTER 66

Barbie Perfume

"What the fuck!" Sal said, as he pushed his way into the room. I immediately pushed Lydia's head off my dick and stood up, fastening my pants. Quenepa did the same, and Lydia? Well, all she could do was pull up her pants, and wipe her mouth.

"Damn, Sal, why you gotta bust in like that, yo?" Q said.

I on the other hand was way too embarrassed to say anything.

"You two sonofabitch's sounded like you were being cut in half. He replied. I watched as he looked at Lydia, staring hard into her eyes. She looked around not knowing why Sal was looking at her that way. She dropped her head and looked at the floor. Sal took her by the chin and raised her head and looked deeper into her eyes.

"How old you?" He asked. I watched as a knot seemed to get lodged in her throat. "Nineteen." She replied. She then grabbed her bag, and attempted to leave, but Sal grabbed her by the arm.

"Sal, she's cool man."

"How old are you?" He asked again. This time, his voice was stern. I watched as another knot lodged in her throat. She looked around, and I noticed her eyes starting to tear up.

"Sixteen!"

Q didn't say anything, but he did smile.

Me? I felt dizzy as hell. I dropped back down onto the bed, and just sat there in shock.

I looked up at Sal who was just looking at me, watching my reaction to this mess that I was now a part of. I looked over at Lydia, and that's when I saw it. The hair, the makeup, her body, the texture of her skin, shit! Was she even sixteen?

What the fuck was I thinking? What was I seeing?

"I had no idea." I said, looking up at Sal. Lydia didn't say shit. In fact she kind of just sat there, like some dumb fuckin' kid! Damn, I was sick!

I rushed over to my wallet and started flipping through the bills, when I decided to just grab it all and give it to her. She took it without hesitation, as there had to be at least a thousand dollars.

"I'll have the front desk call you a cab." I said, as I made my way over to the phone. But Sal stopped me.

"Don't do that." He said. I turned and looked at him. "We don't need to attract any attention." He then turned to Lydia and asked her.

"Where do you live, sweetheart?"

"Over by Edge Hill," she replied.

"How far is that from here?"

"It's pretty far." She said.

"Okay, you two bozo's pack your shit and get some sleep, we're out of here first thing. He waved Lydia to follow him out.

"Hey, let me get your number!" Q asked Lydia as she and Sal headed for the door. Sal stopped and looked at Q with the most vicious look, making him back up quick.

"I'm really sorry." I said again, and each time Lydia looked at me, she seemed younger and younger.

"I'm sorry!" I called out for the final time just as the door closed behind them. I couldn't believe what just happened. How could I have not been able to tell she was so young?

Everything about her yelled minor, jail bait! I swear, I think she was even wearing Barbie perfume.

All I could say was, thank God for Sal.

"I stepped out onto the balcony for some fresh air, to try and unwind when I spotted Sal and Lydia walking over to his car. He opened the passenger side and let her in.

Was she even aware of how lucky she was that it was us and not a bunch of crazies? We could've been anyone, and done anything to her. All I kept thinking was, she's someone's daughter, someone's little girl.

I hoped he wouldn't say anything to Mr. D. That would be so damn embarrassing, beside, I would never want him to ever look at me that way.

The next morning we all piled back onto the busses, and took our regular places. "Last night was fucking crazy." Q said out loud.

"What was crazy?" Vanessa asked as everyone else turned and looked at us. "Nothing." I quickly replied, giving Q a fuckin' evil eye.

"Don't give me that shit!" Vee insisted. "What happened?" Sal stepped up onto the bus and looked at us. Okay you fucking misfits, settle down while we blow this joint.

Everyone got into their seats as Sal pulled closed the door, and then pulled out of the hotel parking lot.

"Come on, man, what happened?" Vee asked again, this time keeping it down. I looked at her and if I would tell anyone, it would be her. But this was way too low for me to admit to anyone, ever! I needed to come up with a lie, just to end her curiosity.

"I had an argument with the hotel manager," was the lie I started to tell, when Sal came and broke it up, ordering me to say no more."

Sal had the radio on up front when a bulletin came on. It was about a young girl who was found murdered this morning. A sixteen year old girl by the name of Lydia Young was found about five minutes from her home in Edge Hill. She had been killed by a single bullet to the head, and placed on the side of the road.

My heart sank, and my eyes immediately shot up towards Sal who was looking at me through the review mirror. I turned toward Quenepa, and he wasn't even paying it any mind. Instead he was clowning around with the girls.

At our first rest stop, I waited until everyone had gotten off the bus and went into the store. I sat down in the passenger seat across from Sal and waited until he was done looking over his map. He took down a few notes, and then placed the map on his lap and turned to me.

"Please tell me you had nothing to do with this?" I begged. Sal looked at me for a moment, before saying a word. Then he asked.

"You have a job, right?"

"Yeah," I replied.

"Well, so do I."

Sal then turned to the road, and began to drive off, and never again was this situation addressed.

CHAPTER 67

Turned On

I thanked the doorman for bringing up my bags and handed him a twenty. Suddenly, I heard.

"Rey!"

Porky nearly knocked me over, wrapping his arms around my waist pressing his head against my chest. He didn't even give Grams a chance to greet me first, but that was fine, she just stood back and watched with a smile.

I held my hands up, a bit too uncomfortable to return the affection, but it didn't matter.

Porky still held on.

"I missed you so much, Rey." He said still holding tight. I looked at Grams and she gestured for me to hold him back. At first hesitant, I finally did. I looked back at Grams and she smiled as if I had just done the greatest thing ever.

"I thought you weren't coming back, Rey."

"Why would you think that buddy?"

"I don't know." I looked at Grams and her smile

vanished.

"I'll always be back, buddy. You never have to worry about that."

"You promise?" He asked. But was that something I could really promise? I looked back at my Grandmother and she nodded.

"I promise. Now can I go say hi to my Grandmother?" Porky let go, and laughed.

"Okay."

Grams came right up and hugged me, similar to the way Porky had just done. It was the first time I realized that they were both around the same size.

"Hello Mijo." Grams greeted me with a huge hug and kiss. How was your trip back?"

"It was Good, glad to be home." She let me go and took both my hands and looked me in the eyes.

"You've been a good boy, I hope," jabbing me straight through the heart, and though I've been far from that good boy she had hoped, I found no point in ever telling her the truth.

"Welcome home Mr. King," said Rosie, stepping out from the kitchen.

"Thank you, great to be home" I replied, sniffing the air with closed eyes, "Oh, my God, how I missed that."

"Rice and beans, with fried chicken wings and Tostones," she announced.

"Your favorite!" Grams added. I handed my knapsack

over to Porky to place in my room, and was about to go straight into the kitchen when suddenly I heard both women yell out.

"Go wash your hands!" I stopped and laughed my way to the bathroom.

I sat at the table with Porky while Grams and Rosie set the table.

"So how you been?" I asked him.

"I've been good." He replied as Grams served him his food.

"He just needs to pay a little more attention." She said without looking at either of us.

Porky looked at Grams, and then at me.

"What's going on?" I asked him, while Grams then served me, and Rosie placed the Tostones and Fried chicken on the table.

"I pay attention." He replied.

"Victor!" Grams said with a stern look, a look I remember all too well. I turned back to him.

"Just sometimes the class is too boring, Rey."

"It's not supposed to be exciting." Grams went to cut in, but I looked at her and shook my head. I was home now, and I needed to handle this.

"Talk to me, Pork." I asked. He looked down at his plate and scooped up a little white rice and placed it into his mouth. Grams took her seat across from Porky.

"Rey, I don't see why I need to go to school at all. I mean

the stuff they teach us, it makes no sense and I can't see how I will ever use any of it, especially History. The past is the past, why do we need to learn that stuff? I think it's a big waste of time.

"You see!" Grams said, looking down at her plate.

"You know what Porky. People are not going to like what I have to say… But I agree with you!

"Reynaldo!" Grams blurted out as Rosie did an about-face back into the kitchen.

"You do?" Porky asked.

"Yep! and I feel the same way about science. Like why do we need to know how to build a volcano? Like, that's really stupid!"

"You see!" Porky said to Grams, who then gave *me* the look of death.

"But you see, when I got older, I understood what was happening."

"What do you mean?"

"America wants to be known as the greatest country in the world, am I right?"

"Uh huh."

"We have the world's greatest actors, right?"

"Uh huh."

"The world's fastest runners, right?"

"Yeah."

"The most beautiful women,"

"I guess."

"And of course, the world's heavyweight champion."

"Uh huh."

"But unless they have the world's smartest kids, then none of that other stuff matters, you see what I'm saying?"

"I think so!"

Grams turned and looked at Rosie, who acted as though she was minding her business.

"Do you think, kids in other countries know how to build volcanos?"

"No!"

We all stayed quiet for a moment, allowing what I just said to sink in.

"I never thought of it that way, Rey."

"But now you do! And you know what? There's nothing wrong with knowing all this extra stuff. And even though you might not ever need it, and if ever you do, guess what?

"I'll already know it!"

"Boom!" I responded, my hands simulating an explosion.

I glanced over at Grams who looked at me a bit impressed. I was proud of how I had handled it, and thought I had gotten through to Porky, until he asked.

"Okay, that makes sense for Science and other things, but what about History? Like, why do we have to know that stuff?

I looked across the table at Grams who quickly looked back down at her plate, and continued eating. I could see the smirk on her face as I looked to her for some help, but got none. I always sucked in History, and now I had to try and make sense out of the same question I had my whole life.

"History is a very important subject." Rosie said from way over in the kitchen.

"We can't see where we need to go, unless we know where we've already been." She continued making her way back into the dining room to clear the table.

Porky looked at her and squinted. Something he usually did when trying to process information.

You see, life actually repeats itself, Victor. But each time around, things should get better... easier. What the past does is allows us to learn from the mistakes of other people, so that we don't have to waste time learning those same mistakes ourselves. We can learn from new mistakes, which would then move us forward."

Rosie caught herself, and immediately apologized and went back into the kitchen.

I looked over at Grams who was smiling, 'cause while I was on the road, she got to know Rosie, and realized how smart she was. She thought I'd be impressed, but she was wrong... ... I was turned on!

CHAPTER 68

Tongues Tangoed

I thought everyone was asleep when I stepped out into the kitchen for a glass of water, until I noticed Rosie out on the balcony, sitting with a glass of wine. She looked incredible from where I stood. A little white tee with super short cut jeans and bare feet. She looked like she just wanted a little alone time, but I couldn't help myself, and decided to go say what's up.

I scared her when I slid open the balcony door.

"Oh, I'm sorry, Mr. King, I just came out for a little air before I went to bed." She said, gathering her things to leave.

"No, please. I didn't mean to disturb you, stay."

"Thank you, Mr. King, but I do have to get up early and…"

"First of all, please, stop calling me Mr. King."

"But…"

"No buts, please, when I'm home, I don't even like hearing that name.

"I'm sorry."

"Just call me Rey"

"Okay."

I walked over to the banister and looked out at my beautifully lit city.

"It seems so perfect from here, doesn't it?" I asked. Rosie looked at me and then out at what I was looking at. She walked over to the banister, and took a sip of her wine.

"So what's your story, Rosie?" I asked, still staring out.

"My story?" she asked, turning to me.

"Yeah, your story"

Rosie turned back to the view. "I don't really have one."

"Of course you do. Everyone does."

Rosie remained silent, and I could tell she was giving it some thought, so I waited.

"Papi was a doctor in Cuba."

"Really?" I asked, turning to her. Rosie nodded.

Very distinguished, very successful! He helped a lot of people during the revolution. Things were getting pretty bad though, and so he made plans to come to the states, but then found out that Mommy was pregnant and postponed the trip.

They waited till I was three years old before scheduling another trip, and during that time, Mommy enrolled in Medical school, specializing in Pediatrics, while Papi continued serving the people." Oh, and teaching me how to swim." She smiled, and shrugged her shoulders.

I was young, but remember how excited I was to go to the

states. That's all anyone ever talked about. My parents never told me about the possible dangers, and when I got older, the swimming lessons finally made sense.

"The week that we were supposed to leave, Papi was executed by the police. My mother was devastated. I could still remember that like it was yesterday.

I truly believe that had I not been born, she would've ended her own life.

Mommy got in touch with the people who were going to help us get to the states, and told them that she wanted to proceed with the plan. My father had already given them half the money, with the remainder due the day of the trip. But they never honored my father's deposit, and Mommy had to pay the whole thing.

I remember hiding in bushes with my mother and a bunch of other people, waiting for the boat to come get us, but it never did. Come to find out, it had flipped over, due to a storm.

Mommy had sold everything we had to pay for that trip, and the people that ran it disappeared. We had to go live with cousins now because we didn't have anything, But then something happened, Cuba and the U.S. made some sort of an agreement that would allow Cubans to fly to the states. My parents helped a lot of people over the years, and now Mommy had to try and cash in a few of those favors.

She never told me how she did it, but somehow, we ended up being among the first passengers to fly off the island.

We ended up moving in with my aunt and uncle in the

Bronx. At first they were very excited to have us. They remembered how we lived back in Cuba, but when they saw us arrive with just the clothes on our backs, that welcoming mat was quickly pulled.

Mommy's education wasn't recognized here, and her credentials as a doctor were worthless. She would have to start all over, and at this point, that was impossible. Instead, she started working for Senor Duck, got us a room in someone's rat infested basement, and saved as much as she could toward my education.

"Is that...?"

"Yes it is. Mr. D's father."

"So, you went to college?"

"I'm still in, this is my last year!"

"So you're going to be a doctor?"

"Yes, a Pediatrician, like Mommy"

"So, how much longer?"

"Once I'm done with school, I'll still need a three year residency to complete before I can actually carry the title."

"That's amazing."

"Thank you,"

"And intimidating."

"Intimidating?" Why do you say that?" she laughed.

"I mean, you have to be pretty smart to make it through medical school. I barely made it through High School. " Rosie laughed and then turned back to the city.

"*Pretty* smart wouldn't have cut it," she said before taking another sip of her wine. "You have to know your shit!" She continued.

"So why work here?"

"I lost Mommy during my first year. She was sick, but she didn't tell me. She knew it would've messed me up. Instead she instilled in me everything she thought I needed to know to survive.

"So I guess that's my story!"

I looked at Rosie, my eyes working their way up her gorgeous legs, body and face. There was no doubt, this girl was beautiful, but the way the moon was hitting her, made my heart suddenly shift into second gear.

She felt me staring at her from the side, and so she turned toward me and stared back just as hard, when finally, I stepped forward and kissed her, and though it was only a quick tap, we both still closed our eyes.

With our lips now just a few inches apart, we remained, allowing what just happened to sink in, and when it did, and we realized what exactly was happening, we did it again.

I had never experienced anything like this in my life. Everything seemed perfect, and in sync with the universe. A cool breeze draped us in its arms. Rosie's thick succulent lips made it impossible for me to stop.

I pulled her in closer, and she gladly accepted. My hands were low on her hips, and I wanted so bad to touch her ass.

I could feel myself stiffening, pushing up against the front of my pajama pants. A part of me embarrassed that I was unable to control it, but my other half, wanted her to know.

Again, I pressed up against her, and this time, she pressed back. I felt her hands move down my back and onto the top of my ass, so I gladly followed her lead. Our tongues tangoed, as if they'd known each other all their lives.

I knew I was moving way too fast, and I prayed I wouldn't screw this up, but I just couldn't help myself, and finally allowed my hands to glide gently over her ass.

I waited for her to push me away, and maybe even smack the shit out of me. But that never happened. Instead she let out a soft moan that clearly told me, she liked it, and wanted more.

I pulled my lips from hers and kissed her neck, careful not to leave any marks. Grams hated hickeys, and would spot it immediately. Rosie let her head drop back as she took mine in her hands, and guided my every kiss.

Her moans were getting louder, and sexier.

I felt like I was about to explode, and I could tell that the front of my pajamas were soaked.

By now I was able to get a couple of fingers up under her shorts, caressing the crease just below her perfect ass.

Rosie managed to turn around while I kissed her neck, giving me now the back and sides, which I accepted graciously.

She placed both her hands on the banister, manicured in sexy red, with gold rings and a bracelet that stood out against her smooth olive complexion.

I placed my hands now on her hips and I felt her push her ass up against me. I knew she could feel how bad I wanted her, and I would've already taken her to my room, but I didn't want to break the magic that we were performing right here on this balcony.

Rosie leaned forward, arching her back. Her ass opened like a flower and of course, I couldn't resist grinding on it. At first, soft and subtle, but that wasn't working for her, and quickly I was learned what she liked and didn't!

By now I was practically fucking her through her shorts. She lifted her ass and arched in a way that her pussy, already warm and wet, was now aligned perfectly with my dick.

The spectacular view, with its full moon, and cool night air, was like something out of a romance novel.

I wanted to close my eyes and just lose myself, but I couldn't take them off this sexiness in front of me. Her tee shirt rode up a bit from the back, and exposed some of her ass, when suddenly, her shorts dropped to her ankles.

She had on no panties, and the front of my pants now looked like a tent. It didn't take long to find the escape hatch to my pajamas, and immediately piercing my target.

The two of us were drenched, leaving no friction between us. And though my thrust should've been distributed in small increments, I found that to be impossible, and therefore went the extreme to both ends.

Rosie gave off a moan that seemed to echo about the city. I pulled back, keeping my timing and rhythm, intact.

The breeze that traveled across the balcony would cool the space between us, only until it closed when I pushed back inside her.

Rosie rested more of her body on the banister, as she was now finding it difficult to stand. I kept pulling out, and reentering over and over. It was as if my hips had become double jointed, as I was moving in ways I had never thought possible.

I could feel myself ready to explode, and the shaking of her legs told me that, so was she.

I just couldn't stop, and pulled out, only to dive right back in. My dick seeming to have tripled in size, she trapped me within her internal walls, and held me there until she was done. She then pulled away and quickly spun around dropping to her knees she guided me down her throat, graciously allowing me to finish our race.

She sucked in sync with each pump she felt make its way through my shaft. And finally, when I opened my eyes, and wiped the tears that had gathered. Not only was I out of breath… I was out of words!

Rosie stood up, and gave me a wink. She then pulled up her shorts, grabbed her glass of wine, and turned back to the city, exactly as she had left off.

We didn't say anything to each other. I turned and went back into the apartment and back over to the refrigerator for a drink, when I heard this strange beeping sound. I listened closely, as the unusual tone changed with each beep, which is when I spotted Porky sitting on the chair, playing his electronic Football game.

I turned to the balcony and realized that from where he sat, had he turned around, he would've seen everything.

"Hey Rey," he said to me, his eyes glued to his game."

"Hey buddy. How long you been out here?" I asked.

"Just a little while," he replied. I stared at him, yet his eyes never once looked up from his game.

CHAPTER 69

Got Something For You

After taking my shower and getting dressed I walked out into the kitchen and sure enough, there was Sal, sitting at the counter, drinking coffee and reading The News.

Grams was getting ready to take Porky to school. She loved to walk, and this was a nice one, not to mention safe, so we let her. Rosie looked amazing this morning, in jeans, and a tee shirt, her long brown hair pulled tight into a pony tail.

"Good morning everyone, I said as I sat at the counter across from Sal. Rosie placed a glass of orange juice in front of me, I smiled, and she returned it. Sal noticed immediately. He notices everything! He placed his paper down on the counter and looked at Rosie, then back at me and squinted, but he never said a thing.

Grams stood by the door while Porky came over and gave me a hug, then Rosie, and finally, Sal.

"Come on lover boy, you're going to be late for school." Grams called out. Porky turned and rushed out the door.

"See you later." Grams said before exiting." Rosie came

up to me with a frying pan full of scrambled eggs and pushed some onto my plate.

"How you doing?" I asked her, a bit awkwardly.

"Good," she replied while pushing eggs onto Sal's.

Bacon, eggs, toast, pancakes, and juice, became a regular breakfast these days, not that Rosie couldn't make anything else, but because it reminded us of the very few times we could afford IHop.

Sal on the other hand usually had something to say.

"Oh look. Bacon and eggs... Again!" He would joke, though we all knew he was serious.

"You do know that once in a while you can have like, steak for breakfast. Maybe some potatoes, hash browns, or even a Belgian Waffle, you ever had one of those? I shook my head.

You know how to make Belgian waffles, don't you Rosie?

"Yes Mr. Sal." She said with an exhale.

"You see!" he said, pointing at Rosie and backhanding my arm.

"Sounds great, just that right now, I kind of like what I'm eating!" And at that very moment, as if the whole scene was planned, Rosie bent over to grab a napkin that fell on the floor.

My face must've done some weird shit, because right away, Sal gave me this strange-ass look before asking.

"What's going on?"

I immediately snapped out of my love trance and looked

at him as I took a sip of my OJ.

"What are you talking about?" I asked. Sal looked at me with suspicion, and then at Rosie who was paying neither one of us any mind. I wanted so bad to tell him, so bad to tell everyone, but for now this had to be our little secret.

The phone rang and Rosie answered it.

"Rosario residence," she said. "Oh hi, how are you? Yes, he's right here, one moment please." Rosie stretched the cord over to where I sat. I looked at her as if to ask, *who is it?*.

"That Quenepa boy," she replied, and I could've sworn she rolled her eyes. Sal looked at his watch, wondering why he's calling here so early.

"What's up, Q?" I answered.

"King! I got something for you, brother!" He replied, overly excited.

"What is it?" I asked.

"Man, it's a surprise, but you gotta get over here like now! Is Sal with you?"

"Yeah, we're eating."

"Fuck that, take this address."

I made a writing gesture to Rosie, and so she rushed over with a pad and pencil.

I wrote down the address, while I threaten him not to be wasting my time. He promised he wasn't, then hung up.

"What is it?" Sal asked.

"It was Q, he said he has a surprise for me.

"A surprise? what, he grew another inch?"

"He said to meet him here." I handed Sal the address.

"And you wanna go?" Sal asked.

"Well, yeah. I'm curious."

"How much you wanna make a bet that it's something really stupid!" Sal said, shaking his head and gobbling down his food and coffee.

CHAPTER 70

It's Not A Song

As we pulled onto the block, we both looked at the addresses on the entrances of the string of tenements that lined both sides of the street.

"There it is!" I said, pointing to my right. Sal immediately pulled over and parked in front of a fire hydrant.

"We can't park here." I said, but he just waved me off and headed for the building. I raced after him looking to see what the apartment number was.

"6E." I said as his finger found it among the hundred or so buttons on the directory beside the door.

"Who is it?" asked the crackly voice through the intercom that I recognized as Q.

"It's us asshole. Open the fucking door!" Sal commanded, and immediately a buzz let us in.

'I swear to God." Sal began, as he removed his gun from under his arm and shoved it in his waistband. "If this mother fucker called us here for some bullshit, he ain't ever leaving this fucking building." Sal's threat had me praying the entire way up.

We found the apartment right away, and just as I was about to knock, Q opened the door, and had on his face, this big stupid ass smile. Damn, if he only knew.

"If this is some dumb-ass shit, you better tell me before I cross this threshold, because once I do, there's no turning back." Sal warned before entering.

"Come come come!" Q said, hurrying us in and then quickly locking the door behind us.

He placed his eye to the peek hole, to make sure no one was watching.

"What's going on?" I asked, but he didn't answer. Instead he placed his finger up as if to silence me. I noticed Sal reach behind his back, but I held his arm and quickly shook my head.

We followed Q down the apartment's long narrow hallway, and stopped at a doorway where a blanket of colorful beads separated us from the living room.

Q looked at us with this crazy-ass grin, and then stepped through the beads, holding them to the side so we can enter.

"What the fuck!" I gasped, when I spotted some old guy sitting on a chair. His hands and feet, tied together from behind, with several rounds of duct tape wrapped around his torso, and a piece placed over his mouth.

The old guy's face was beaten so bad that his nose was broken, eyes closed shut, and one of his ears looked like a potato.

His white tee shirt soaked through in blood that ran down to his boxers, continuing into a puddle that settled on a table cloth placed underneath to obviously control the mess.

I glanced down at Q's hands and just as I expected, his fist were swollen and covered in blood.

"What the fuck did you do?" Sal asked as he went over for a closer look, trying to see if he recognized him.

"You're the guy from the restaurant." Sal said. I recognized him too and stepped closer. We turned and looked at Q who stood there with his chest out, as if he had just captured Bigfoot.

"I don't get it." I told Q, who then turned and pressed the play button on a reel to reel deck that sat on a shelf. I nearly fell over, when I heard Yes Yes Y'all. Yup, the same exact one that's been taunting me for over a year now.

I just stood there, my mouth stuck on open.

"I don't believe it."

"Will someone tell me what the fuck is going on?" Sal demanded to know.

"This is the song I told you about." I began. "The one I told you someone stole and recorded." I went over to the old dude and looked into his one good but teary eye. He was terrified, and his nerves had him farting up a storm.

In one swift motion, I ripped the tape from his mouth, taking with it, what looked like a piece of his lip. The pain sent the man howling, until Q stepped up and punched him in the side of the head.

I watched as his eyes rolled up into his skull, and his head fell to his chest.

"Q! Chill bro!" I said, stopping him just as he was about to throw a second.

The blood coming from old dude's nose and mouth seemed to be running a bit too fast. I tried lifting his head back, hoping to at least slow down the leak.

I had no idea what the fuck to do and looked to Sal for some guidance. He had found himself a spot on the couch and was sitting there reading a magazine.

"What do we do?" I yelled.

"It's your fuckin' mess. You tell me!" He said, his eyes not once leaving the mag.

I then turned to Q, who at that very moment handed me a hammer.

"What the fuck am I supposed to do with this?" I asked, But Q just stood there, looking like a mad scientist, his fingers wiggling uncontrollably against his chest.

With the hammer in my hand, I glanced over at the man, who looked like he was about to go into cardiac arrest. I dropped the hammer and watched as he began to simmer down.

"What are you doing with my song?" I asked the man in a low and calm tone.

"Who cares?" Q jumped in. "We got'em, now take that mother fucker out!"

The old guy suddenly busted out in tears, pleading for his life, and even though I had no intention of taking it, he didn't know that.

"I'm sorry, I didn't know whose it was." He finally said, his accent, thick and raspy. One of the flags on his wall confirmed his Cuban decent, the other, that he was gay!

"How did you get it?" I asked him.

"It was left in the locker room where I use to work." He replied.

"So you just take shit that you see laying around, and that isn't yours?"

'No, it was there for about a week. I put it inside my locker in case someone came looking for it. Somebody else would've just thrown it away."

"But why did you go and record my shit?" I asked. The man, remained silent, trying to figure out what to say when suddenly, Q appeared beside him and whacked him on the side of his face with a telephone book!

"Yo!" I yelled, jumping back as the man, still bonded to the chair toppled over.

"Fuck you doing?" I yelled at Q, pushing him back. "Bitch took too long!" He replied.

"He could barely speak English, give him a minute."

I looked down at the old guy, hoping to God he wasn't dead. Q went to lift him back up.

"Don't touch him!" I ordered, and then rushed to the kitchen and soaked a dish towel in cold water to put on his head.

He started to come to, and I could tell he didn't remember that he was tied and started panicking.

"You're a real asshole, Q." Sal said as he got up and pulled out his knife to cut the man loose.

"Fuck you doing?" Q asked Sal as he was bent over cutting the rope and duct tape.

"This guy didn't do anything." Sal said. "And you're gonna give him a fucking heart attack."

"Who cares? We're gonna kill him anyway, right?"

"Kill him? for what?" I asked.

"What?" Q begins, "I go out my way to get this mother fucker for you, after you been crying like a little bitch about someone taking your dumb ass song, and now you wanna flip on me? Fuck you, King!"

"Look man." I said, trying to stay calm. "I'm sorry. I appreciate this, but this isn't what I wanted."

"The mother fucker stole your shit, yo!"

"But I didn't steal it. I swear." The Cuban said as he was being freed.

"Shut the fuck up, faggot!" Q yelled, and immediately the Cuban did as he was told. "Look." Sal began. There's a bit of a mess here. We need to figure out how to handle this. But in the meantime, we gotta keep it down."

"I'm just gonna take the reels and go," I told him.

"Yeah, and tomorrow you'll be on the front page of the Daily News, you dumb fuck!" Q said. I looked over at Sal, and his eyes seemed to agree. I looked back at the old guy as he stood up rubbing his wrist. His eye dripping a mixture of blood and tears, and his hanging lip swung as it quivered.

"So what do we do?" I asked Sal.

"What do you think? You gotta take him out," Q jumped in again.

"Mira, I swear to God. I will not say anything." The Cuban begged. I looked over at Sal, and he was totally expressionless. I then looked over at Q, and his face told me we had to kill this guy.

"He could tell you whatever it is you want to hear, but trust me, the minute you walk out that door, that mother fucker's gonna be on the phone with the cops, and it ain't gonna be hard to find you.

"Stop saying that you sonofabitch!" The Cuban yelled out angrily at Quenepa, who quickly picked up a microphone stand and was about to whack him across the face, when I jumped in between them and yanked it from his hands.

"What is wrong with you?" I asked, but before Q could even answer there was a knock on the door. We all got quite and looked toward the door. Sal pulled out his gun and put it to the Cuban's head, holding his finger to his lips for everyone to stay quiet.

They knocked again.

"Cuba, it's Blanca, is everything okay in there?" Asked the old shakey voice on the other side of the door.

"Who's that?" Sal asked in a whisper.

"Just my neighbor, she lives downstairs." Sal stood there for a moment, trying to figure out what to do.

"If I don't answer she *will* call the police." The Cuban assured us. Sal looked at us, and then back at the Cuban, and gestured for him to answer, but b careful with what he says.

"Everything's okay, Mija, I just knocked over a chair." He called out, and then looked at Sal for approval, which he got.

"Well can you open the door, I just want to make sure you're okay." She replied. The Cuban looked back at Sal, who, after looking over the Cuban's busted up face, shook his head.

"I have an idea, but I'll need some help," the Cuban told Sal. "You try anything slick, and I'll put a bullet in *your* head, *and* hers." "She's use to me having company, if you know what I mean."

"I hear voices in there." The nosey neighbor called out."

"I think we should kill her too!" Q suggested. I looked at him and gestured that he go sit down.

"Cuba, if you don't open this door this instant, I am going back downstairs and calling the police!"

"I need you to make believe you're my company!" The Cuban said.

"Me?" Sal asked. And the Cuban nodded. "Fuck out of here. I rather just kill that bitch."

"She'll go away. I promise."

Sal looked over at Q.

"You got us into this shit. You're getting us out!"

"What?" Q asked.

"May I?" The Cuban asked Sal. "I know what to do."

"Try something stupid, and I swear…"

"I promise." He said and then called out to his neighbor.

"Blanca, un momento Mija!" the Cuban called out

toward the door.

He then rushed into his bedroom and came out carrying a few items. He went over to Quenepa and plopped a long curly wig on his head.

"Fuck you doing?" Q said yanking the wig off and throwing it on the floor. The Cuban looked at Sal.

"I know what I'm doing." He assured us. Sal then took the gun from the Cuban's head and aimed it now at Q's.

"Are you fuckin' serious?" Q asked. Sal's eyes confirmed.

Q, frustrated as a fuck, picked up the wig and put it on. A short burst of laughter escaped my mouth and everyone looked at me.

"You go hide in the bathroom." The Cuban said, and I did as I was told, keeping the door open just enough for me to see what was happening.

"Now put these things on." The Cuban told Q, handing him a pair of studded pink framed glasses, and a pink sequin robe.

"I'm not doing this shit!" Q angrily whispered.

"What's going on in there?" The lady asked knocking some more.

"I'm gonna shoot this stupid bitch in two second." Sal said, getting really annoyed. "Put the shit on already!" Sal ordered Q. Who huffed and puffed himself into costume.

The Cuban then turned down the lights, then went and laid on the couch, pulling a blanket up to his eyes.

"Now go answer the door." He whispered. Q just stood

there in disbelief.

"Answer the fucking door!" Sal said, pushing him toward it with the barrel at the back of his head.

Q began to stomp his way to the door when the Cuban called out to him. Q turned around and looked at the Cuban, who then, with his arms gracefully flowing in front of him, instructed.

"Be gay! He said. I myself nearly lost it and needed both hands to hold in my laughter. "You heard him... Be gay mother fucker!" Sal commanded as he stood behind the door and nodded for Q to open.

Though this was a serious situation, I felt like I was going to burst out in laughter as I watched Q walk to the door like some deformed woman. He opened it and there stood a short chubby woman still in her robe and slippers.

"Ay Dios!" She gasped upon seeing Quenepa. "Hello, she began, trying hard to put up a smile. I'm Blanca, I live down stairs." Q just looked at her but said nothing.

"Hi Mija!" The Cuban called out from the couch. Q moved to the side so that Blanca could see him there.

"You got me worried for a second there."

"Oh, I'm sorry, we were busy." The Cuban replied. "That's my new friend, um... Raton!"

"Raton?" she asked, "Nice meet you. Q just stared at her, making her very uncomfortable.

"We met at the laundromat, and I just had to take him home, isn't he adorable?" Blanca looked at Q, but then totally ignored the question.

"Well, I just wanted to make sure you were okay, I heard so much banging."

"And you'll probably hear some more. But now you know!" The Cuban replied. Blanca's face distorted.

"It was nice to meet you." She said to Q, who simply closed the door and locked it. I was coming out of the bathroom just as Q walked over to the Cuban and punched him dead in the eye. Sal grabbed him and threw him to the floor.

"Fuck, Q, that's it already!" I said.

I looked at the Cuban, sitting on the couch holding his eye. We all looked at each other, not exactly knowing what to do.

'Yall some dumb asses, for real, ! I'm telling you, the minute we step up outta here, that mother fuckers dialing nine one one!"

"I've been getting my ass beat all my life, and believe me, never have I called the police. Besides, this wasn't shit!" The Cuban said in a way that made me believe it.

"What?" Q said about to swing on him again, when Sal and I stopped him.

"One more time!" Sal told Q, looking him straight in the eyes. "And I swear, I'm putting a bullet in your stomach."

"This is some bullshit!" Q said before turning and leaving the apartment.

"I'm gonna need the tape though." I said to him, and immediately the Cuban got up, removed the reel from the machine and handed it to me.

"Anything else?" I asked. The Cuban at first hesitant went over to his piano and picked a boom box up from the floor, and ejected a cassette and handed it to me.

"That's it." He said. I looked at the cassette, and written on it was *The Yes Song*. I shook my head and then stuffed it into my pocket.

"Are we clear?"

"Very clear," the Cuban replied. "And thank you."

As Sal and I made our way to the elevator, the Cuban stuck his head out.

"Can I say one thing, please?" He asked. We stopped and looked at him.

"That's a great song." He said. I looked at him for a long moment, before replying.

"It's not a song… It's a Rap!"

The Story Continues with Book 3

An Excerpt From Book 3

As soon as he started smashing the plaques that covered the wall behind his desk, I dashed for the door. My plan to escape had failed, when I realized that it had been locked, strangely though, from the outside. I shook the knob violently in a desperate attempt to get out, but it was no use.

I turned around and saw Mr. D now walking toward me, his bat held low, dangling beside his thigh. With nothing to protect myself with, I instead got into the best boxer's stance I knew and awaited the onslaught.

"Come on, Mr. D, chill out man!" I pleaded, when suddenly he tossed me the bat. I caught it and immediately placed it on my shoulder. I didn't understand why he would do that until he raised his hand, and in it, I noticed a gun, and it pointed straight at me... Pow!

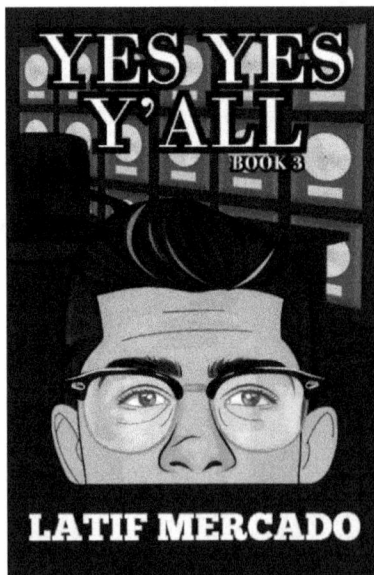

Dear Reader

I just wanted to take a moment to personally thank you for reading Book 2 of Yes Yes Y'all, and though the dream of many authors is to one day have a Best Seller, and move a million copies, mine on the other hand is simply to move you!

Whether my stories make you laugh, cry, scream, or just allow you to share with my characters, their incredible journeys, I pray that you could find in them, something just for you. It could be the answering of a long grueling question, making you think about something you've never before giving thought, or just remind you to tell that special someone, that you love them.

Though none of the books so far are autobiographical, they do however run a parallel dimension to my own life, and therefore knowing them is in fact, knowing me!

I intend on writing until life's last page, when God finally says, The End! But until then, it would mean so much to me, if we could stay connected.

By logging on to Latifmercado.com, and subscribing to my mailing list,- you'll receive my Newsletter, alerts of anything new coming out of the La' Camp, Freestyle events headed your way, and of course exclusive gifts and offers just for you!

Thank you again, and I'll see you soon

Your friend

Latif

About The Author

Latif Mercado has been a part of the Freestyle Music scene for well over 25 years, and though his role in the beginning was minimal, the role he's been playing ever since, has been massive, and a major force behind the genre's continued success.

As a Booking Agent with a who's who roster of Freestyle Legends, as well as his managerial involvement with such industry icons as Lil' Suzy and The Cover Girls, rarely would you find a Freestyle event happening without Latif somewhere in the mix.

In an attempt to make people aware of the fact that

Freestyle isn't just a music, but rather a culture, La' began writing books, in hopes of reaching fans through a medium they would never expect, and in 2011, his debut novel, FREESTYLE FOR LIFE, did just that!

Since then, Latif has released several books that, not only feature Freestyle as part of its overall theme, but also its main characters of Latin decent.

Though born and raised in New York, Latif currently resides in North Carolina with his wife, two grown children, four grandkids and a dog named Coco.

Latif loves hearing from his readers, answering questions, and sharing whatever advice he possibly can, whether it be on writing, or maybe something Freestyle related, so be sure to reach out, even if it's just to say hi.

For more information on Latif, or to connect with him on the various platforms, please go to LatifMercado.com

Books By LA'

FREESTYLE FOR LIFE

FEASTYLE

FREESTYLE PROMOTIONS
And the 7 Simple Steps To Getting Started

HOW TO BOOK A FREESTYLE ARTIST
IN 5 EASY STEPS

YES YES Y'ALL Book 1

YES YES Y'ALL Book 2

YES YES Y'ALL Book 3

www.ingramcontent.com/pod-product-compliance
Lightning Source LLC
LaVergne TN
LVHW051448080426
835509LV00017B/1705